Runaway

Runaway

Wild Child, Working Girl, Survivor

EMILY MACKENZIE

and

Clifford Thurlow

SIMON &
SCHUSTER

London · New York · Sydney · Toronto · New Delhi

A CBS COMPANY

First published in Great Britain by Simon & Schuster UK Ltd, 2013
A CBS Company

1 3 5 7 9 10 8 6 4 2

Simon & Schuster UK Ltd
1st Floor
222 Gray's Inn Road
London WC1X 8HB

www.simonandschuster.co.uk

Simon & Schuster Australia,
Sydney

Simon & Schuster India, New Delhi

A CIP catalogue record for this book is available
from the British Library.

This book is a faithful account of the author's experiences. However, some names
and details have been changed to protect the privacy of certain individuals.

ISBN PB: 978-1-47111-525-7
ISBN Ebook: 978-1-47111-526-4

Typeset by Hewer Text UK Ltd, Edinburgh
Printed and bound by CPI Group (UK) Ltd, Croydon CRO 4YY

For Jon
An inspiration
Loved and missed by all who knew him

Contents

Acknowledgements

I would like to pay tribute to J, my partner, who has been there for me throughout the ordeal of reliving my most painful memories to write this book.

Special thanks to my co-writer Clifford Thurlow, who has patiently and sensitively helped to shepherd and record my thoughts to tell my story in the way it deserves to be told. To Andrew Lownie, the perfect agent, and Kerri Sharp and her team at Simon & Schuster, for their advice and unwavering support.

Foreword by Emily MacKenzie

I was placed in voluntary care by my spiteful mother at the age of twelve. I was gang-raped, made pregnant and had an abortion at thirteen. In council care, secure units and remand homes I was sexually assaulted, neglected and subjected to dangerous drug regimes. I ran away many times. The last time, when I was fifteen, I became a prostitute in Soho and the plaything of men addicted to sex with underage girls: rich, powerful, sometimes famous men who knew they could get away with it. I feel lucky to have survived at all.

My tears have flowed many times telling my story in these pages. The language is at times uncompromising and blunt. It is the only way that truth can be told and I make no apologies for it. If my book reaches one social worker or policeman or teacher who, as a result, recognises the signs of abuse and saves one child from its terrors, then dredging up my memories will have been worthwhile.

Some of the names and places in this book have been changed to protect the innocent. My one regret is that it protects the guilty, too.

Prologue

The moment I wake up I smell his semen on my face. My eyes are swollen. My bottom hurts. My ribs are bruised. I've got a horrible taste in my mouth and he's taken my clothes.

I stand on the bed to open the curtains before trying the door. It's locked, and I remember there's a bolt on the outside. I can tell by the light it's still early. I snuggle back under the covers and look around the small room. The wallpaper is pink with damp stains and a poster of two kittens. A mobile hangs from the ceiling and a doll's house stands on a chest of drawers.

It's a little girl's room and I wonder for a moment if I am a replacement. But I'm not a little girl. I'm sixteen and wish my dad would come and find me.

I get up again and try to open the window but it's painted shut. Not that it would help much up here on the fourth floor. I'm trembling. The covers slip from my shoulders. It's not cold,

I

it's stuffy if anything, but it's scarier being locked up without your clothes. I remain at the window for a long time with the vague idea that someone might see me standing here naked and send for help. Stay calm, I tell myself. I say it out loud. You have to do everything he wants. He'll kill you if you don't.

Tears roll down my cheeks. I knew I was taking a chance when I got in his car. But I needed the money. You always need money. Anyway, it was a good time to get off the street. My best mate, Donna, had run away. Flash, her pimp, was looking for her. If he'd found me, he'd have given me a wallop just for the hell of it.

I don't have a pimp and don't want one. This is good and bad at the same time. People don't hit you when you've got a pimp. Pimps want you to look the biz. They get you a room, buy you clothes, perfume, make-up. And use your money to pay for it. Donna is eighteen and fed up with having ten or twelve blokes coming to her room every day. She's a real blonde with blue eyes and always makes me laugh. 'I've had more pricks in me than a second-hand dartboard,' she said once. I'll never forget that. She had £20 in her pocket and she's cleared off, back to Manchester, probably, where she comes from.

We all come from somewhere and we all find our way to Soho like it's a magnet drawing in the nutters and runaways. I escaped from reform school and slept rough at first behind the rubbish bins in Jermyn Street. I've been kicked and pissed on by strangers, and at times I have been so desperate that the feel of that warm piss on cold nights was almost a comfort.

It's 1972. All you hear on the radio is 'All the Young Dudes' by Mott the Hoople. Soho is a dump full of seedy clubs run by

Maltese gangsters, but it's a big improvement on living with the brutes and psychopaths in children's homes. It's a funny word, 'home'. If you're a girl growing up in a children's home in England, nine chances out of ten you will be bullied, beaten and raped. You get used to it.

Once I got to London, I learned how to get free food from the Sally Army and wash at the public baths. But you start to feel like a bag of rubbish sleeping out on the pavement every night. Turning tricks pays for a place in a hostel – bunk beds, sixty to a room, the smell of fear and dirty clothes, a sense of belonging in a way.

All the girls are on the game and that makes it seem normal. Most of them have been abused by fathers and stepfathers. Getting paid for it makes sense, and it isn't always terrible. Sometimes, the johns are kind and I wrap that kindness around me like a blanket.

The girls have a sense of community – us against the world. They've been teaching me the tricks of the trade and it was dead easy to start pulling. I wasn't aware of it at first, but I'm a valuable commodity. The punters want fresh meat. That's what they call you. The younger the better. I'm thin with dark hair cut short – they did that in the home – and dark eyes below arched eyebrows, boyish in girlie clothes.

So what happened yesterday, and how did I find myself in this mess? It was almost seven o'clock and the punters were coming into the West End. Another girl, Debs, warned me that Flash was going crazy searching for Donna and I'd be in real trouble if he saw me, seeing as I was wearing her clothes – a leather miniskirt with a fringe, a halter-top and white plastic knee-boots. Flash had bought the gear for Donna, and I knew when she gave them to me she was going to do a runner.

I clip-clopped down to the arcade and it wasn't long before a john appeared. It's like a jungle, that place. Runaways have a certain smell. And the johns know how to sniff you out. I was leaning over one of the machines.

'Want a go?' he said.

'Don't mind,' I replied, and he dropped 10p in the slot.

He rolled a fag while I flippered the silver balls around the pin-table.

'Blimey, you're useless,' he said. He lit up. I noticed he had stained teeth and a gravelly voice. 'So, what you up to?'

'Just minding my own business.'

He grinned. They like it when you're a bit mouthy, like you need taming. He looked me up and down. He knew what I was. I knew what he was, and I knew what he was thinking: yeah, fresh meat, I wouldn't mind giving her one.

'There's nothing much happening here,' he said. 'Want to go somewhere else?'

'If you like.'

There was a pause. There always is. He was wondering if I was underage. Worried he might get caught. But he couldn't stop himself. This made him feel ashamed and, later, he'd blame me for that. I was a temptress. A slag. I needed to be taught a lesson. I've been beaten by my stepdad since I was ten. I know what might happen but you always hope it won't.

It was my turn to look him up and down. He was wearing a denim shirt, denim flares and a silver cross on a leather thong.

4

He had a moustache that curved down from his lips and long hair over his collar. He was trying to look young but he was forty or something. His moment of conscience had passed.

'What's your name, then?' he asked.

'Emily.' It's my real name. I'd thought about inventing a new one, like Donna, but hadn't got round to it.

'Wanna come back to my place?' he asked.

I knew this wasn't a good idea. I could get a room for £5 an hour around the corner in Berwick Street. I could charge a tenner and make five quid in an hour. Five minutes sometimes. Staff at the children's home are on thirty quid a week. One punter a day and I'm doing better than they are.

'We can get a room?' I told him, but he shook his head.

'Nah, let's go back to my place. It's not far.'

'Ten quid,' I said; it's always best to get paid first so you can leave them in all their glory without having to ask for your money.

'A bargain at twice the price,' he replied, and grinned. 'I'll give it you in the car.'

So I took a chance and followed him down Brewer Street to the car park. He'd got an old Ford Cortina, a green one covered in rust and smelling of roll-ups. He gave me the £10 and I pushed it into the bottom of my white plastic bag. He drove with one hand on the wheel, the other fiddling with the wooden knob on the gear stick. He skidded round Piccadilly Circus and headed towards the river.

'Big Ben,' he said, pointing.

I looked back and smiled. I didn't feel anything. The sun went down as we crossed Westminster Bridge and the river turned orange. The houses became smaller as we wound our way into run-down London and arrived at a council estate. He lived on the fourth floor in a block of concrete flats with the smell of piss in the stairwells, long balconies with red doors and clutter. He rolled a ciggie as he walked.

'You want one?'

'Nah, I'm all right.'

'Good for you . . . what's your name?' he asked again.

'Emily.'

'Bill,' he said, as if he'd thought about it first, and I knew it wasn't his real name.

My underarms were damp. It's what happens when I'm nervous. You get to know when they are going to be all right and when they are going to go crazy. I was tempted to turn and run off, but I had his ten quid in my bag and he'd only catch me. Men can always run faster and hit harder. Be nice. Act normal. Do everything he says.

The flat inside was a mess but I could tell that he probably had a wife. I watched him turn the key on the inside of the lock, locking us in, and slip the key in his pocket. He stubbed out his fag and turned to look me up and down.

'Tell me something, how old are you?'

'Sixteen.'

'You don't look it.'

'Well, I am.' I shrug. 'Last month, if you must know.'

'Sixteen. Look at yourself . . .'

Then I heard this hard slap, flesh against flesh. I've been hit a million times but it's always like the first time. Stars danced around in front of my eyes and my cheek burned like it'd been pushed into boiling water. He hit me again across the other cheek. I was instantly dizzy and started to wobble in my plastic boots.

He held me up with one arm and dragged off my halter-top. I smelled the fag smoke on his breath. He unzipped the leather skirt and pulled it down over my boots. I slumped forward across his shoulder like a rag doll as he ripped my knickers off. He slapped my bum, really hard, one slap after the other, and I remembered my stepfather hitting me with a whip and saying 'you're bad, you're evil, you're wicked'.

It was a relief when I slipped down to the floor. He was panting for breath like a dog after a run. He took off his shoes and jeans and Y-fronts. I was sure he was going to piss on me. They often do that, but this one didn't. He looked down at me with my bruised cheeks and probably felt like he was the king of the jungle. I concentrated really hard to stop myself crying.

I smiled up at him. I spread my legs as he lowered himself and I arched my back to make it easier. I sighed with pleasure as he pushed into me. They like that. They want to think you're doing it because you fancy them. They are so amazingly attractive. This is your dream come true. They are doing this because what you need is a good seeing to and he's the man to do it.

He grunted and dribbled over my neck. It was quick. He pulled out and ejaculated over my face. He shoved his prick in my mouth and I sucked away as if my life depended on it. He groaned, finally, and rolled off me. We both lay there on the dirty carpet, staring at the ceiling.

'That was great,' I told him.

He leaned up on one elbow and looked down at me. It was dark now except for the light from outside and I could barely see his expression.

'I'd better get going,' I said, but he didn't reply.

He jumped up, turned on the TV and dropped into a white leatherette couch with red cushions and wooden arms. He slapped the place next to him.

'Get over here.'

It was like I was his pet. I dragged myself up. My knees shook and my heart pounded in my chest. He pointed at the place next to him. The cushion was split down the middle and I thought, that's me, I've been split apart like that cushion. He pulled me down so I could rest my head in his lap. I sucked him again till he got hard.

'Make it good and wet, girl.'

I knew what was coming next. They call it a 'trip around the world'. They fuck you, they come in your mouth, then they roll you over and arse-rape you. 'You haven't had a woman until you've had her up the arse.' That's what some bloke said to Donna once. I balanced over the arm of the couch and my ribs were crushed as he rammed into me like a dog. It hurt. It really, really hurt. Tears pressed into my eyes. I couldn't control it, but I didn't cry out loud. I let the air catch in my throat and gasped with pleasure.

When it was over, he wasn't sure what to do. I glanced back over my shoulder at him and he had this glazed, lost, bitter look like he'd been cheated.

'I need to use the toilet,' I said.

He thought about this for a second, like it might be a trick. Then he strode across the room, opened the door, and pointed down the narrow hall.

8

'In there,' he said. 'And don't lock it.'

I hurried into the bathroom. There was a yellow bath, sink and toilet, the smell of damp towels, a tube of Colgate. I looked in the mirror. The girl in the reflection didn't look like me because I wasn't sure how I was supposed to look. My face was swollen, my eyes half closed. For a moment, I saw myself when I was a little girl, when Mummy loved me and Daddy was there to protect me. Then Mum left Dad. She went to live with Alan and Alan beat me with a rhino-whip.

Now I'm sixteen with a wide mouth and strong teeth I've sunk into more than one male nurse as he pinned me against the cracked white tiles in some institution and raped me. Give a man power over a young girl and he will abuse her. He can't help himself.

As I sat to pee, the door opened. He watched me. I wasn't even embarrassed. Wardens at the homes like to watch girls going to the toilet. I went to get up and he came towards me.

'Stay there,' he said. I sat back down and he pulled off my boots. 'Don't want you wearing out my carpets, do I now.'

'But I ought to get going,' I said, and he laughed.

'You're not going anywhere.'

The door across the hall had a bolt on the outside that looked new in the light from the bathroom. He opened the door and we entered a room with pink wallpaper. There was a bed, a lamp with a pink shade that he turned on, a mobile spinning aimlessly above our heads. He closed the curtains. 'This is your room. Don't make a sound and upset my neighbours.' He raised his hand. 'You know what'll happen.'

He turned off the light and bolted the door behind him. I crawled under the blankets and it felt like I was in a black hole. My bottom's burning like it's on fire, my ribs hurt, but the tears that come to my eyes are not for the pain. It's what I deserve. I forget sometimes, but I am a bad person. I am being punished for killing my baby. When I was thirteen, one night I sneaked out of the children's home and went to a pub. A boy I knew from school took me back to a flat he shared with his brother and five men passed me around like a bag of sweets. I got pregnant. I had an abortion and bled for weeks.

I rolled up into a foetal position and thought about the foetus that was plucked out of me. This is my life. Beaten the first time aged seven by Mum. Taken away from my father in a custody battle at ten. Moved to a children's home at twelve. Gang-raped at thirteen. Not loved, no. But sent away for psychiatric assessments and the isolation ward in a Victorian asylum.

The only person who visited me was my dad. But my dad isn't my real dad. My mum isn't my real mum. And my sister, Amy, isn't my real sister. I'd been adopted at birth. I didn't belong to anybody. Nobody knew where I was. I was a prisoner in a strange man's flat. I could disappear and no one would ever know.

CHAPTER I

The First Beating

I have an old black and white photograph of me sitting up in a shiny black pram in the front garden of the house in Lancashire where I grew up. I was born in June 1956, a summer baby, always smiling, and no one thought it odd when neighbours stepped through the gate to tickle me under the chin. I thrived on the attention and, so the legend goes, always had an eye for the men.

The street was orderly, solid and conventional, words that could describe my father who, as people put it at the time, had a bob or two. He was a countryman in Harris tweed, polished brogues and a trilby hat made by Dunn & Co. He spoke slowly in a soft voice and never lost his temper, even when the time came when he should have done. He always stood with a small nod of the head when a woman entered the room and, believing in fair play and honesty himself, was blind to the absence of that quality in others.

With his wholesale fruit and vegetable business, three vans and twelve staff, he was a true-blue Tory with a military moustache and views endorsed by the *Daily Telegraph*, which he read in the light of the French windows, elbows resting on the arms of a leather wing chair, his pipe between his lips, heavy-framed glasses putting a barrier between him and the rest of the world.

Having been wounded on two separate occasions during the war – the second time a bullet burrowed so deep into his leg the surgeons were unable to get it out – he had a slight limp that was worse in cold weather. He was twenty years older than my mother but, in the lean years of post-war ration cards and reconstruction, she probably considered him a good catch.

Mum came from a family that had once had money and then maintained their sense of superiority after they lost it. She was taller than Dad, vivacious, a fast talker and walker with wide-set blue eyes, wide shoulders and a slender waist she was proud of. She loved hats that perched on the side of her head and kept a drawer full of gloves that matched her handbags and the shoes that stood marshalled on shelves in her bedroom, and which I was forbidden to touch. She was determined, more than ambitious, and Dad always let her get her own way.

In another photograph I have, protected by a sheet of tissue, my mother poses with her head turned to one side and her hands supporting her chin. A smile flicks up the corners of her lips, but I see irritation in her eyes, a look of frustration that I know now was as much sexual as anything else. The war had robbed her of her father, her childhood and the sparkling future she must have imagined. When the photo was taken, Mum had already grown bored with her marriage and blamed Dad that she was unable to conceive, although why that was, exactly, she never went to the doctor to find out.

My job was to give Mum a sense of purpose.

I had been adopted at birth, something I knew as soon as I was old enough to understand, and took great pleasure in the story of how my parents had gone to a special building where the largest room was lined from floor to ceiling with babies in Moses baskets waiting for new families. I was chosen, precious, bonny with big brown eyes and instantly adored by my parents and extended family.

As soon as I was able to walk, I started dance classes. Mum styled my hair to match her own, dressed me in silk and velvet, and I soon had my own collection of dancing shoes on their own special shelf. Talent competitions were all the rage and, most weekends, we'd pack our overnight bags and set off, Dad at the wheel of his new Humber that smelled of polish and leather, an AA badge on the shiny grille. The car was being 'run in', which meant Dad drove so slowly Mum was always anxious that we were going to be late, although we were always early.

My routine consisted of a tap dance followed by a song, 'Run Rabbit Run', 'Barnacle Bill the Sailor' or, my favourite, 'On the Good Ship Lollipop'. People said I was the next Shirley Temple, who I imagined was a little girl like me being taken by her mummy and daddy through the sprawls of bombed-out buildings being rebuilt in Manchester, Leeds, Liverpool, Chester, Derby and Blackpool with its tower and big grey sea.

After the shows we would stay the night in the best hotel. A little bed would be wheeled into my parents' room for me, and what I remember most are those hotel breakfasts served by waitresses in black and white uniforms, silver toast racks and gleaming cutlery on starched linen tablecloths, a place for everything and everything in its place, as Mum liked to say. Her obsession that I become a performer became my own. After all the anxiety and haste, I felt at home on the stage, accepted the applause as my due and cried my eyes out when I didn't win a prize.

When I was three, my life was complete. Mum and Dad went back to that special place with the shelves full of babies and came home with Amy, my new sister. She was fair, like Mum, not dark, like me, but we grew to look similar and I have never been sure whether this is nurture or coincidence. Amy was a calm child, delicate with white skin and innocent, pale-blue eyes. I abandoned my assortment of dolls to care for my little sister as if I knew intuitively that, one day, no one would be there to protect her except me.

Just after my fourth birthday, Mum and Dad took me to the school shop, where I was fitted out with two uniforms, one for winter, one for summer, a blazer, tartan skirt and straw hat with a blue ribbon. George, a driver who worked for Dad, and whom Mum grandly called the chauffeur, would come every morning and drive me to the little prep-school at The Priory, an old mansion surrounded by stone walls in the country.

I lived the life of the storybooks I was learning to read and were popular at the time. We were like the families in those books with a kitten named Tuppence; Mrs Flowers, the daily, who came in to help Mum and tidy my room; Dad tamping down the tobacco before lighting his pipe; the long garden and nice neighbours with their nice children to play with. I was bright, popular, a show-off and wept bitter tears the first time my mother hit me.

It was the summer I turned seven. Amy was four and big enough to join me on my adventures. About a mile away, across the fields behind the back garden, stood an abandoned cottage that reminded me of the house in *Little Red Riding Hood*. I didn't want to share what I thought of as *my* secret with the other children, and one day took Amy with me to explore because I was afraid to go on my own.

We went through the back gate, ran across the field and my heart was thumping when we reached the cottage. I half expected a wolf in a bonnet to come out and growl and chase us away. We stood there for a long time, holding hands, waiting. But the door remained closed and it was quiet except for the insects buzzing in the air. We made our way around the building. At the back, I found a sash window that was open an inch. The frame was dry from the warm weather and it wasn't difficult to pull the window down and climb over the top. I opened the door for Amy and we chased through the rooms searching for treasure like the children in Enid Blyton's *The Secret Seven*.

We came to a stop at the big fireplace.

'That's where the treasure's hidden,' I said, pointing up the chimney, and Amy's eyes lit up.

'Really?'

I nodded. 'It must be,' I said.

It's what happens in children's books and I wanted it to be true. Having made Amy excited, she didn't need much encouragement to climb up the chimney to look for the treasure. The mantel was as high as she was. She poked her head beneath and I cupped my hands to lift her up. In seconds, she had gone, vanished around the curve.

'Amy,' I called, and her voice was muffled.

'I can't find it,' she answered.

'Come down, then.'

She kicked her legs; soot filled the air.

'I'm stuck . . .'

I reached up the chimney, but I was unable to get her out no matter how much I pulled and prodded.

'I'm stuck. I'm stuck.'

'It's OK, it's OK. I'll go and get help.'

'No, don't go. Don't leave me, Emily.'

'I won't be long.'

I left her crying and ran home as fast as I could. Luckily, Dad was in the garden. I told him what had happened and we rushed back in his car, he couldn't run on his bad leg. He got Amy out in no time. She was covered in soot like a little chimney sweep and her eyes were brilliantly white staring down at me from Dad's arms.

Mum was waiting in the hall when we got home. Amy was sobbing still. Mum took her from Dad.

'Go to your room, Emily,' she said calmly, and I did as I was told.

Mum put Amy in the bath, came into my room, closed the door and paced across the carpet in two long strides. She slapped me across the legs, once, twice, really hard, like I'd seen people slap ponies. The air vanished from my body. I was too stunned to cry. I just stood there, shaking, and she hit me again, over and over, smack, smack, smack, smack, smack. It was like something had snapped, like she was suddenly a different person.

'Mummy, Mummy, Mummy . . .'

She couldn't hear me. Her eyes were glazed. She said I was selfish, a bad girl. I was spoiled rotten. She was screaming, punctuating her words with each slap.

'Don't . . . You . . . Ever . . . Do . . . That . . . Again. Don't . . . You . . . Ever . . . Do . . . That . . . Again. Not . . . Ever . . . Ever . . . Ever.'

Now I cried. I thought my life was over. 'I'm sorry, Mummy. I'm sorry, I'm sorry, I'm sorry,' I sobbed.

She was breathless, shaking, red-faced. She stood back, stared down at me and her hair, always pinned in place, was hanging over her eyes. She closed the door behind her as she left the room, closing one chapter of my life and opening another. We had lost something that day, the bond of trust replaced by the bond that ties the weak to the strong, the beaten to the beater. My mother had enjoyed hitting me. I had seen it in her eyes, and she started to look for any excuse to hit me again.

Children become what parents make them. Mum had got it into her mind that I was selfish and inconsiderate. From then on, everything I did, everything I was, would appear to conform to her expectations. It was like Pandora's box had been opened. All the evils had been let out and would never go away. In a heartbeat, my entire life had changed. I had gone from being a cherished child to an abused child. I was marked. The stamp of her hand on my bottom and thighs was a message that would be read by other beaters and abusers in the future.

While Mum had been taking me to talent shows, what she enjoyed most was the dressing up, the buzz backstage while Dad sat in the auditorium. The judges were usually men. If one of them praised me, normal with little girls, Mum read this, perhaps correctly, as flattery of her in her flared skirts with cinched waists and a bra that showed her figure. I had been a projection of her dreams in the 1950s. It was now 1963. Television and pop music had killed off talent shows and what talent I may have had at three was a fading memory by the time I was seven.

Amy survived her chimney ordeal but life was never the same again. I was more wary, more aware of the subtleties and nuances of adults. Mum now only had to draw breath and glare at me across the table if I was 'playing with my food', and I would have to decide whether to 'be a good girl' and eat it all, even if I didn't want any more, or show I 'didn't care about the starving children in Africa', an accusation that would end inevitably with Mum running me upstairs, slapping the backs of my legs as we went.

I noticed the looks that passed between my parents; his disapproval when he thought she was being too strict, her annoyance if he dared to tell her how to bring up her own children. When I was born, Dad was forty-two, Mum twenty-two. Now I was seven, he was nearly fifty. He looked old and weary. Mum was still in her twenties. The Beatles were on the radio. Skirts were getting shorter. Only a handful of family photographs have survived the years; it is astonishing that any have survived at all, and the most up-to-date one of my mother was taken on the seafront in Morecambe that same summer. She is wearing shorts and a tight top, her hair blowing free. Amy and I are standing at her side looking up as if at a statue. Mum is staring into the camera lens, vibrant, beautiful, aching for life.

Mum now started to look for any excuse to give me a slap. She would remove the hot spoon from stirring her tea and press it on my arm. She stabbed my hand with a sewing needle. I would come home from school and she would lead me straight to my bedroom and point at all the dolls and toys on the floor. She'd scream as I tried to explain . . .

'Mummy, I didn't do it . . .'

'You're a lazy, lying little bitch.'

'But, Mummy—'

'Don't you but me. How dare you . . .'

Smack. Slap. Push. She had taken to hitting the side of my head, knocking me sideways but leaving no red marks on my face.

It never occurred to me that these attacks were more likely to happen when Dad wasn't home and I didn't dare tell him in case he took Mum's side and started hitting me as well. I didn't know why things had changed and didn't have the words to ask. As a child, you live in the present. Things are as they are and you quickly forget how they had been. I tried to please my mother and make her love me again. I tidied my room – a place for everything, everything in its place – and couldn't work out whether I had left it so untidy or someone else had made the mess. But who: Amy, the daily, Dad? It couldn't have been Mum.

I had always been good at my schoolwork. That, too, began to suffer. When you are contented, your head is clear, learning is fun and you absorb knowledge like a sponge. When you are anxious or frightened or hungry or feel unloved, when you go to school with a smack not a kiss, your mind wanders, you lose concentration, you misbehave to get attention. I couldn't protect myself from Mum, so I pretended it wasn't happening and, after each slapping, made myself believe that it was my own fault. You carry contradictory thoughts in your head. You live in a state of fear and the uncertainty of life as an abused child creates mental health issues that never go away.

One day I was playing in the garden with an old set of golf clubs belonging to Dad. I hadn't noticed Amy coming up the path behind me. I whipped the club back and hit her in the face. There was blood everywhere. It was superficial, she didn't need stitches, but the blood made Mum see red and she came running down the garden towards us. There were canes Dad used to support plants. She grabbed one on the way and swiped the back of my legs. The blow was so hard, it knocked me to the ground. She hit me again, the cane hissing as it came down through the air. I buried my head in the dirt and she just kept hitting me until I heard Dad.

'Gwen. Gwen. Stop that for heaven's sake.'

I looked back as he snatched the cane from her hand and broke it over his knee.

Mum was standing there, shaking, that glazed look in her eyes.

'What the hell do you think you're doing?' Dad said. 'You don't do that to a child.'

'And you don't tell me what to do! Don't ever tell me what to do!' she screamed. She pointed at Amy without going to her. 'Have you seen what she's done this time?'

'Gwen, it was an accident.'

She looked back at me. 'Devil's child,' she spat and grasped Amy's hand before marching up the garden to the house.

Dad stood me on my feet and smoothed back my hair.

'I didn't do it on purpose, Daddy.'

'I know. I'm sorry, Poppet. She doesn't mean it.'

'I try to be good.'

'It's not you. It's me,' he said.

I didn't know what he meant and I was just happy he was there to look after me. He turned me round and lifted up my dress. Bright red weals had erupted across the tops of my legs, my bottom and back. I had been too stunned to cry while she was beating me, the shock numbs your senses, but it had worn off and I cried now, tears that poured from my eyes and soaked the front of my dress. The pain was like no pain I had ever felt before. I was soaking wet and on fire at the same time.

Dad took me to the bathroom, holding my hand. He found some Nivea cream and nervously smoothed it into the red marks. It was a time when fathers did not touch their little girls and I could sense his unease.

'I was practising my back swing,' I said. 'I didn't mean to do it.'

'I know.'

'Mummy hates me.'

'No, Emily, she loves you. She's having a hard time at the moment. We have to be patient with her.'

Dad helped me dress in clean clothes. I made sure the dirty ones were put in the laundry basket and we went downstairs. On the table, there were sandwiches, cakes and fizzy orange juice.

Dad didn't mention the beating. Nor did Mum. She had the ability to instantly forget what she didn't want to remember. Amy sat quietly in the corner staring at a book without turning the pages. To the outside world we were the perfect, happy little family, but we were becoming more and more dysfunctional.

CHAPTER 2

That Girl

Mum got into the habit of speaking to me with an impatience that often flared into anger, and spoke to Dad in a monotone without emotion. She needed an outlet for her energy. She had tried tennis and golf, but didn't have the hand and eye coordination required to shine, and put her energy into beating and disciplining me. Just as she had once believed I was going to be a famous stage performer, she now believed I was a 'bad seed', the cause of her own disillusion and lack of purpose.

She started calling me 'daddy's girl', although I can see in the photo of Mum in her shorts that day in Morecambe that this was exactly the part she had played in the early years of her marriage. I had taken her role. She was young, beautiful, bored. Dad wanted a quiet life, and I did what he had told me to do. I practised patience. I tried to be good, but whatever I did was never enough. If I was playing with Amy I was accused of 'bothering her' and if I wasn't playing with Amy she said I was 'ignoring her'. If I asked her what she wanted me to do, she'd tell me I was 'stupid' and to use my imagination.

I had finally worked out that when Dad was at work, if I didn't keep out of her way I'd get a bash on the side of the head, or a hot spoon on my arm, and the sneer she wore when she looked at me she kept on her face when she looked at him. Amy had always been quiet and became quieter. Mum had divided us into two sides and claimed Amy on her team. She praised her, spoiled her, she enjoyed dressing her up like a little doll as she had once enjoyed dressing me before I went on stage at those talent shows. That time belonged to the past and now on a Sunday we usually visited our grandparents, the two sides like different countries with different customs and attitudes.

At Dad's parents, it was safe and serene like stepping back into my Enid Blyton books. My paternal grandparents embodied those qualities once said to characterise the English: a belief in courtesy, loyalty, integrity. It was bad form to boast or embellish and, when I was with them, I was like them, polite, helping without having to be asked, waiting my turn to speak.

Grandpa MacKenzie wore a watch chain looped across his waistcoat. He was an older version of Dad with fine grey hair, the same slow way of talking, a moustache bronzed by tobacco smoke and the inevitable pipe, in fact he had several in a rack on the mantel. Grandma looked as if she had stepped out of Victorian times with her high-collared dresses and white apron. She wore her silver hair in a plait and had sparkly eyes that took in more than they revealed. Mother dwarfed her in her heels, but Grandma had a presence that made it appear that Mum was always looking up at her.

They lived in a big house with acres of lawns, flower beds and an orchard with apple, plum, peach and pear trees. Aunt Alice, Dad's unmarried sister, lived with her parents and, with help from a woman in the village, cooked exotic roasts, duck, goose and venison, with vegetables straight from the garden and pies made from fruit canned at home and stored in the cellar.

Before lunch, while the men were smoking their pipes, Grandma would take Amy and me on a walk through the garden. She taught us the names of the flowers and plants. She showed us how to press wildflowers and we wrote down what they were in our project books. Grandma showed interest in what we were doing. She didn't pretend to listen when we told her, she really listened. She played the piano, painted watercolours and there was always a book on the table beside her chair, the place marked with a red silk bookmark.

My father had lost his two brothers in the opening weeks of the Second World War. During his years in the infantry, Dad had served in India, Malta, Shanghai and North Africa. He said the worse experience of his life was the 'hellhole' in the bowels of a ship smelling of gangrene and blood that brought him home to England after being wounded the second time. Many died on the voyage and he felt lucky to have survived.

It could have been the war and the loss of his brothers that had made Dad kind, philosophical, accommodating. But his parents were the same and it is one of my many regrets that I never knew them better. They died within a few weeks of each other the following year, when I was eight, and their passing marked the beginning of the biggest change in my life.

★　　★　　★

My mother was like her mother. There had been money once, but it had gone and, like a lost limb, she felt the pain of not having it. Granny's major concern was what she imagined the neighbours thought of her and her family and she lived her life as if they were secretly filming us through the chinks in the net curtains. We had to be reserved, guarded and keep up certain undefined standards. She liked ironed white tablecloths, silver napkin rings, towels folded precisely in three, not doubled over; the letterbox shiny with Brasso, the house regimented with a strict military discipline that extended to Amy and me. She believed if you 'spare the rod you spoil the child'. I am certain she beat my mother and my mother's sister, Doreen. She maintained power over her daughters, even as adults, and my mother copied her in every way.

After visits to Granny Wheeler, Mum would return home resolved to turn me into the mirror image of her perfect self. Mrs Flowers kept the house clean, but I had to dust the shelves in my bedroom, line my clothes up evenly spaced so they weren't crushed in the wardrobe, big things like coats at the end, school clothes and blouses in the middle. Woe betide Emily MacKenzie if a damp towel was left on the bed or a toy wasn't put away. Mum trained me like she was training a dog to be obedient, silent, to come instantly she called, hands clean, clothes immaculate, hair in place. If I smiled she said, 'What are you grinning about?' And if I kept a straight face she'd say, 'Now what's wrong with you?'

My mother didn't eat very much; she adored being willowy and thin. She knew I didn't like vegetables, but made a point of heaping my plate at the evening meal. If I didn't eat every scrap, she would march me upstairs, my hair gripped in one hand while she slapped my legs with the other. Amy was 'just a child', she didn't require the same firm discipline, and Dad was forced into the unenviable choice of saying nothing or intervening and having another row, something becoming more and more frequent. I would see the pain on his face when Mum erupted in another burst of violence, but just as I was getting used to being hit, he was becoming accustomed to seeing me being hit. What was once abnormal becomes normal and pain becomes relative. If you have been beaten with a cane the sting lasts a long time; if the skin is broken, the razor-thin scars last forever. In contrast, if you just get hit around the head a couple of times you feel lucky.

After reading something in one of her magazines, we were plunged into a new obsession: our bowel movements. We were expected to use the toilet before school each morning. She would inspect the results, and fly into a rage if we were unsuccessful. If I didn't 'move my bowels', I would get a slap. If, on the other hand, I was successful and Amy failed, I would be called a show-off and still get a slap. If I cried, I'd get another slap for being a crybaby. If I didn't cry, she'd call me a tough little bitch. 'Don't think I can't break you because I will.'

'I'm sorry, Mummy.'

'Sorry, Mummy. Sorry, Mummy. You little . . . nothing. Just shut your lip.'

My shoulders would sag, meriting a slap. The tears that pricked behind my eyes I tried to control. I would sit in the car next to Amy while George drove us to school and hum 'On the Good Ship Lollipop' as if the song was a line back into the past when Mummy loved me. It was my fault. I never did win a big prize at those talent shows. That's what she wanted. I had let her down. *I had let myself down.* That's what she said. She had chosen me as a baby and I had failed to be the little girl she wanted me to be. I had watched Dad in the garden with seeds he was going to plant and wondered what it meant to be a bad seed. I tried to think of something I could do to make things better, but my head just went round in circles and I couldn't think of anything.

There was a nice teacher at school named Mrs Lloyd-Jones. She noticed that my work had gone downhill and one day, when I had a bruise over my left eye, she told me to stay behind after class. She asked me what had happened. Mum had been particularly angry about something the previous evening and pushed me into a door. I told Mrs Lloyd-Jones that I'd tripped over and knew by the way she looked back into my eyes she didn't believe me. She asked me if my father ever hit me, and that was typical; people get things wrong, they think of the obvious and, behind the closed doors of families, nothing is ever obvious. I shook my head.

'No, no. Never. He'd never do anything like that,' I said.

Mrs Lloyd-Jones made me promise that I would tell her if I ever felt troubled or if anything was 'wrong at home' but I thought what happened in my own family was a secret and I should never tell anyone.

One Saturday when I'd come in from the garden and left mud on the carpet in the living room, Mum sent me to my room and said I wasn't allowed to play outside for the rest of the weekend.

Later, she caught a glimpse of me watching Amy playing with the neighbours' children from my bedroom window. Two seconds later, the door swung open, she hit me across the back of the head and grabbed me by the hair. She pulled me up on my toes, marched me down to the hall and locked me in the cupboard under the stairs.

I rolled up under the shelf with the old pots of paint and turpentine. It was dark. I closed my eyes to stop being frightened and sat very still. I pretended there had been a landslide and I was dead. Mum hated me because I had let Amy get stuck up the chimney and everything I did to try to get back in her good books ended with a smack, being sent to my room, her teeth gritted, her face red with anger. If I told her I'd got a good mark for something at school, she just turned away, so I didn't tell her any more. If I went to help in the kitchen, she said I was 'in everybody's way'.

'I am trying to be good.'

'Good is what good does. Go and tidy your room.'

My tummy hurt. The turpentine fumes made my eyes sting, and I thought if I drank it and had to go to hospital perhaps she would be so upset and sad she would love me again. I was thinking about that when I realised I needed to go to the toilet. I banged and pleaded, but the door wouldn't open from the inside and nobody came to get me. 'Please, Mummy, please,' I cried. I slapped the door, my face streamed with tears and I wet my pants.

Dad was out. He was out more often lately, and it was night-time when he came and found me. He took me upstairs and ran a bath. I put my wet underwear in the laundry and Dad hugged me dry in a big towel. When he went downstairs, Mum screamed at him. On that rare occasion, he shouted back. She said he had ruined her life. He said he had given her everything. She said he was dull and stuck in the past. He said she was self-ish, thoughtless, inconsiderate, all the things she always said about me. It went on and on. Amy and I sat at the top of the stairs in our pyjamas and listened. They said more things, things I didn't understand, but I had a feeling that something terrible was about to happen.

What happened at first seemed a nice surprise. Mum packed bags for Amy and me and we went on holiday for two weeks with her mother and Auntie Doreen. We stayed at a hotel in Torremolinos, in Spain. It was the beginning of package deal holidays. We flew on a plane with families who had lots of kids who misbehaved and ran around during mealtimes when they should have been sitting at the table being good like Amy and me. Everything seemed alien, even the weather, which was hot every day. The men staying in the hotel talked loudly and drank lots of beer. The women wore hardly any clothes, even in the dining room, and every night in the bar they would throw themselves around doing The Twist.

When we got back to England, we didn't go home. We went to Granny Wheeler's house, where we remained for almost two years. The endless fights between my parents had spilled finally into the courts – a legal separation leading to divorce and a custody battle over me and Amy. Mum won, of course. At that time, the attitudes and wishes of children were not taken into consideration. Mothers were always favoured and, in our case,

Dad was older while Mum was young, energetic and a really good actress.

Dad was given visiting rights, but three times out of four, Mum would call and cancel. Amy has flu . . . Emily has been too naughty . . . We're going away this weekend . . . Dad got older and sadder. I grew furtive, hostile, silent. I was afraid of my mother and knew now from where she had got her short fuse and vicious temper. God only knows what it was that I kept doing wrong, because I can only remember that on a daily basis I was slapped and smacked. My mother had this horrible habit of hitting me on the side of the head, and her mother joined in, hitting the other side, my head going back and forth like a punchbag between them.

Dad wasn't there to protect me. I couldn't protect myself, so I stayed out of their way. I would hide in the garden. Mum would call, but I would stay hiding for as long as possible, hoping she'd forget she was looking for me. She grew tired of this game and started locking the doors. Then I'd have to return after dark with my tail between my legs, knock and know I was going to get a beating the moment the door opened.

Amy and I still attended the same little private school and George usually came to collect us. Occasionally Dad would be there at the end of classes and drive us home. He had sold our house – it was too big for one person – and gone to live with his sister in his parents' house, retreating back into the past. He had lost his hair. His moustache was white. I was coming up to ten. It was 1966. Flower power. Long hair. Love-ins. Sexual liberation. Dad was modest, fair, a man of his word. Like his parents, he personified a way of life and a way of treating others that had gone and would never return.

He always asked me if everything was all right and I always lied and said it was. I didn't want to make Dad unhappy and, by now, aged ten, there was something useful that I had learned: the more you are spanked, slapped, bashed and burned, the less it hurts, the more it becomes normal, the more you accept it. For a long time, I had wondered why Mum never hit Amy. Now, I didn't even think about it. I was the bad seed, the selfish little bitch who didn't care about the starving babies in Africa. I was bad-mannered, untidy, disrespectful and stupid, stupid, stupid.

'What are you?'

'I'm stupid, Mummy.'

'I can't hear you.'

'I'm stupid.'

'And you think because you're stupid that's an excuse?'

Finish your plate. Slap. No playing outside. Bed.

One time, Granny's favourite necklace went missing. I heard her shout at Mum and I heard them going through drawers and arguing. Then I heard the words 'that girl' and knew they were talking about me. The door burst open and Mum stood on the threshold with her hands on her hips.

'Where is it?'

'What, Mummy?'

'You know exactly what I'm talking about. Now where is it?'

'I don't know. I haven't done anything.'

'What have you done with Granny's necklace, you little thief.'

'I haven't touched it . . .'

She came across the room to hit me, but stopped herself. I thought for a moment she had seen sense. She knew I would never dare touch anything that belonged to Granny. But, no, she went to my wardrobe and took out the plimsolls I wore for PE at school. She tested one on her palm and stood over me.

'Well?' she said, glaring down, her eyes beginning to cloud over.

'I haven't touched it, honestly, Mummy.'

Honestly.

It was a word she hated. She pushed me down on the bed, dragged me over her knees and pulled down my pants. She then beat me with the plimsoll until my bottom felt like it was on fire, the same as when she'd hit me with the cane. It is hard to know how long beatings take. It seems like forever. But it may have only been a few minutes before I heard Granny at the door.

'Found it,' she called.

Mum paused. She hated being wrong. She wasn't happy that I had been honest and stood up with an angry look on her face. Now that she had stopped beating me, the pain started, flames streaking up my back into my hair. The front of my body was wet with perspiration.

'That will teach you, anyway, won't it?'

'I told you I didn't touch it.'

Her eyes flared. 'Are you talking back at me?'

'I hate you,' I replied, and I have no idea where the courage came from to say it.

She smiled. 'Do you now?'

'I want to go back to my real mother.'

She placed the plimsolls back in the cupboard, closed the door and looked back at me.

'She's dead,' she said. 'Dead. Dead. Dead.'

It would be a very long time before I learned the truth.

CHAPTER 3

Alan Briggs

Children are a blank sheet of paper. What parents write creates the story of who we become. It had never occurred to me to steal anything. I had everything I needed. More than I needed. But once my mother had called me a little thief, it was like a prophecy I was doomed to make come true.

It didn't happen straight away. In fact, after that last beating with the plimsoll, the beatings suddenly stopped. I still got the occasional slap, but saw that as a sign of affection. As an adult, you believe when you stand up for yourself people respect you more. As a child, you don't think that way. I just thought, Mummy used to love me, then she hated me, now she loves me again.

She had been spending more time out of the house, especially in the evening, and was always buying new clothes, short skirts, Indian tops, gladiator sandals, things she called 'mod' and nothing like the suits and court shoes she had always worn. She had added highlights to her hair and discarded the pins that held it rigidly in place. She now wore it straight to her shoulders and looked like she was trying to find her way as she peeked through her fringe.

Often she would try on her new things and call me into the bedroom where I would find her standing in front of the mirror.

'So, what do you think?'

'Beautiful, Mummy.'

She'd look over one shoulder like a model and pout at her reflection. Then she'd stand up straight and study her legs in her miniskirt.

'Not too short?'

I'd shake my head. 'It's perfect,' I'd tell her, and I meant it. She was tall and feminine and blonde with long legs. I wanted to be just like her.

One Saturday at the market she bought Amy and me white cheesecloth dresses with pink motifs on the front and white patent-leather boots. After breakfast on Sunday, she put us both in the bath and spent ages brushing our hair before tying it up in white ribbons. We dressed in our new clothes and were told to sit in the lounge and read. She leaned over me.

'I don't want any of your playing up today. Understand?'

'Yes, Mummy.'

'No answering back and don't you dare get yourself in a mess,' she said, and turned to Amy. 'Or you, Amy. Be good.'

Amy smiled. 'I will, Mummy,' she said.

She looked angelic with her blue eyes and blonde hair the same colour as Mum's. We went skipping downstairs to wait.

Granny was in the kitchen and came in, drying her hands on a tea towel.

'You'll do,' she said. 'Be good, now, this is an important day.'

'Yes, Granny,' we chorused.

Mum appeared in a yellow dress that was really short and yellow platforms that made her really tall. Her hair was glossy and she looked like a pony as she shook her head to part her fringe.

'Well?'

'You look lovely, Mummy,' I cooed.

Amy was nodding her head.

'Go on, scram, the lot of you,' Granny said, and looked proud as she followed us out to the drive.

We climbed in Mum's new Mini. The car was bright red with a white stripe over the roof and big white dots on the doors. I sat in the front and watched Mum's skirt ride up over her thighs as she pressed down on the pedals. She was a good driver, swerving round the bends and tooting if people were going too slow.

'If they're not going anywhere, why don't they stay at home?'

We laughed. Mum needed approval and we loved it when she was in a good mood. She had mentioned several times that she had a 'new friend' named Alan, and it suddenly dawned on me that's why Granny had said this was an important day.

'Are we going to see your new friend, Mum?' I asked her, and she wasn't angry. She smiled.

'Yes, he's dying to meet you.'

'Is he going to be our new dad?'

She shook her fringe as she looked back at me. 'Emily, what are you saying?' she replied.

It was the first time she had used my name in ages, which made me really happy. I looked back, grinning broadly, and noticed her cheeks were flushed. I thought everything was going to be all right now.

We were on the ring road and turned off into a part of town where I had never been before. We passed through rows of blackened buildings with tall chimneys, everything empty and quiet, being Sunday. The road dipped and I could see in the distance what looked like a toy town with houses that were packed tightly together in straight lines. Our old house that Dad had sold was like the houses in my storybooks with French windows opening out onto a lawn edged with sycamores and dotted with flower beds. Granny's house was smaller, but nice, with a nice garden. These houses were like boxes, and there were no trees.

Mum slowed and pulled to a stop beside an open gate where a tall man and three children were waiting in the tiny garden.

This was the first time I met Alan Briggs.

'Right on dot, that's what I like to see,' he said, glancing at his watch.

Mum looked coy as she gazed back at him in a way I recalled from those days when we went to talent competitions and the men backstage made a fuss over us. Alan was big and broad with dark eyes in a wide face that was lined and scarred like an old statue. He had brown hair turning grey and swept back in a quiff. I can see now in an old picture that he was like a leading man in a film, craggy like a cowboy, and what Mum considered handsome; in other words, nothing like Dad.

The two men were different in every way, although they were the same age and Alan had also been injured in the war. He called himself the Miracle Man, having survived blast trauma damage on the Russian convoys as a result of a German U-Boat attack on HMS *Lark* where he had served as a petty officer. Alan had been told that he would never walk again and set out to prove the doctors wrong. Not only did he learn to walk, he walked without a limp and maintained his fitness working at the brewery loading trucks with kegs and crates of beer.

Standing to one side were his three children: Billy, who was thirteen with a mean face, like someone had stolen his bike and he was out for revenge; Barbara, called Barbs, a hefty girl of nine with big arms and solid legs; and Anne, who they called Annie, who was six. Barbs was nine months younger than me but seemed older. Annie was a year younger than Amy but was like a baby still. She had snot congealed under her nose and mispronounced her words, so it was hard to know what she was saying, not that she said very much.

Finally, there was Patch, a white crossbreed Staffordshire terrier, the black patch over one eye providing his name. He was sitting on his haunches. He didn't bark, he just stared at us, his eyes glazed, his long pink tongue hanging out of his wide jaw.

'So, these are the girls, are they? Heard a lot about you,' Alan said. He was standing with his feet astride, hands on his hips. He stared down at me. 'Don't look much like your mum, do you?'

Mum laughed and he looked back at her with a broad smile. 'Better lock up, Gwen, they'll nick anything round here.'

She locked the new Mini. We trooped in file through a narrow hall into the living room and on into the kitchen. Everything was neat, but scratched and threadbare. All the doors, tables and cabinets had splits and dents. Even the walls had dents. Alan opened the back door to the garden.

'Right, you lot. Out. And don't come in until I tell you to come in.'

We marched out and stood looking at each other. Amy reached for my hand and I watched the curtains close on the back bedroom upstairs. I was ten. I knew what that meant: Mum and Alan Briggs were playing mummies and daddies.

The garden was about thirty yards long, ten yards wide, and marked by a fence that needed repairing. The bottom section was trimmed with barbed wire and looked out over a common. There were flower beds without flowers, old bikes and prams, a cracked water tank and an assortment of broken chairs.

'What happened to the chairs?' I asked Barbs, and she stared back as if she didn't understand what I'd said.

'What?'

I pointed at the chairs. 'They're all broken,' I repeated.

She continued to stare at me. 'What's your name, then?' she asked.

'Emily MacKenzie.'

She looked at Billy and imitated my voice, shaking her shoulders. 'Emily MacKenzie,' she repeated, and Billy copied her, exaggerating still more.

'Emily MacKenzie.'

Barbs glanced at Amy. 'What about her?'

'Amy,' I replied.

'You having dinner with us?'

'I don't know. I don't think so,' I said.

'That's all right then.'

She studied our clothes. Barbs wore a blouse with puffed sleeves and a brown corduroy pinafore that was too small for her. Billy was wearing the sort of grey shirt and shorts boys usually wore for school. Annie's pale-blue dress barely covered her knickers and was stained with spots of gravy and custard. They looked like the sort of children Mum had always told us not to play with.

'You wanna see our guinea pigs?' Barbs finally asked.

'Yes, please,' Amy and I both replied.

We chased down the cement path to the end of the garden where two forlorn guinea pigs lived in a hutch with smelly straw. Patch panted as he plodded along and the way he stared at the hutch with those glassy eyes made me think he was blind.

'Can your dog see all right?' I asked.

Barbs and Billy looked at each other.

'What's that?' Barbs said.

'I just wondered—'

'Nothing wrong with our dog. He's a killer,' Billy said. He bent down and put his arm protectively around Patch.

Annie and Amy were tickling the guinea pigs' noses. I glanced back at the house. Mum believed, like her mum, in a place for everything and everything in its place. Here, nothing had a place. Everything was broken and scruffy. In our white dresses and boots, Amy and I were dressed to impress, but I sensed that it had the opposite effect. We roamed around the garden getting our boots dirty. Barbs kept her eye on me at all times.

'You got a dad, have you?'

I nodded. 'He doesn't live with us. Mum got a divorce.'

Barbs took this in and then tapped the side of her head. 'My mum's got problems up here, in her head.'

'Is she in hospital?'

'No, she's in the nuthouse.'

We were silent for a moment.

'He likes your mum,' she then said, and I looked up at the bedroom. The curtains were still closed.

'Has she been here before?'

Barbs threw up her chin. 'Course. She's his girlfriend.'

I already knew that, but had been pretending to myself that it wasn't true. I had dreamed of Mum and Dad getting back together and all of us moving into the house that had belonged to my grandparents. All through my childhood I was looking back and wishing I could return to another time, when I was on stage, when Amy was a new baby, when I first started school, when Dad called us 'my three girls' and we went on holiday to the seaside.

The back door opened and they stood there looking happy. Alan had his arm around Mum's waist, holding her close. Her hair was untidy.

'So, you lot, still here then. No one dead yet,' Alan said, and we laughed.

'Is it time for dinner?' Barbs asked, and he shook his head.

'Always bloody hungry you,' he said, and glanced at Mum. 'Just like her.'

We trooped in from the garden and I noticed that hanging on the back of the kitchen door was a coiled whip like I'd seen at the stables when we had riding lessons. Alan Briggs was standing behind me and looked like a giant as I turned to look up at him. He leaned down and I stared into his dark eyes.

'That's my rhino-whip, toughest hide in the world,' he said. 'Taste that and you'll never forget it.'

CHAPTER 4

Night Terrors

It was past our lunchtime. Like Barbs, I had been feeling hungry, but there was a knot in my tummy while we were driving home and I didn't feel hungry any more. It started to rain. I watched the wipers go back and forth to the rhythm of the Beatles' song 'She Loves You' on the radio. Mum joined in, singing loudly, and turned the radio off when the record came to an end.

'So, what do you think?' she asked, and I wasn't sure what she meant.

'What, the song?'

She glanced at me through her blonde hair. 'No. Alan. Mr Briggs?'

'He's really tall,' I said.

'I know, I mean, as a person?'

'He seems nice.'

'What about you, Amy?'

'I like the guinea pigs.'

That made Mum giggle and I looked at her bronze legs dancing over the pedals. Her eyes were bright and all I could think about was the broken chairs in the garden and the rhino-whip hanging on the back of the door.

I had learned to only tell Mum what she wanted to hear. If I got a good mark in science or an art project, I didn't tell her because she'd call me a show-off. If I didn't feel well, Granny would say I was 'swinging the lead' to get a day off school, so I kept it to myself.

Sometimes when I was brushing my hair or cleaning my teeth, I'd look into the mirror and be surprised that I was no longer seven, Amy's age, but ten with lips pressed tightly together and dark rings under my eyes. At seven, before that time when Amy got stuck up the chimney, I was one of the brightest children in my age group at The Priory. Learning had been easy. Now, I found it hard to concentrate.

On several occasions, Mrs Lloyd-Jones had asked me a question in class and, even though she was looking at me, it seemed like she was speaking to someone else.

'Emily, are you daydreaming again?'

'No, Mrs Lloyd-Jones, I was, I was just thinking.'

'Well, do try and pay attention.'

I did try, but it was getting harder. At home, I often felt as if I was in the way. I had stopped hiding in the garden and stayed in my room listening at the closed door to see if Mum and Granny were talking about me. I felt anxious without knowing what was making me feel that way, and I felt guilty without having done anything to feel guilty about.

Ever since Mum had told me my real mother was dead, I'd been having dreams where I was running away from someone who was chasing me. No matter which way I turned, there was always a shadow close behind, reaching for me. In other dreams, I was falling down a long tunnel or a chimney. The dreams woke me up and I'd go through the next day longing to go to sleep and feeling afraid the moment I got into bed. I used to have my own bedroom, but at Granny's house I shared the room with Amy. I would lie there listening to her breath going in and out wondering if her real mum was dead, too.

Granny's house was close to St John's Church. The cemetery was at the top of the road and I had to pass it when I went to the corner shop for something that had been forgotten on the weekly trip to the supermarket. I had been doing this for the last two years, but when the nightmares started, I was suddenly afraid of all those cracked gravestones like rows of crooked teeth. I heard whispers and was sure it must be my real mum calling me from the spirit world. There was a tall statue of a knight with a raised sword that loomed over the other graves and made me think about the shadow chasing me in my dreams.

The only time I didn't feel anxious was with Dad. We saw him once every two weeks, sometimes less. He'd collect us from Granny's house and I'd listen from the top of the stairs while Mum hissed at him about money in that impatient voice she used with me. I'm not sure if I was getting taller or Dad was getting shorter, but when he sat in the driver's seat in his old Humber, he appeared to have shrunken and could barely see over the steering wheel. Dad was still in business supplying fruit and vegetables, but the small shops were closing down and the supermarkets used bigger suppliers with huge shiny trucks. Dad now only had one van, his driver, George, and two men working in the warehouse. The sale of the other two vans had paid for Mum's Mini.

We'd drive back to his house to have lunch with Aunt Alice. A lot of the rooms had been shut up and the dust sheets over the furniture made it look as if a family of ghosts had moved in upstairs, although downstairs when we arrived those Sunday mornings the smell of pies baking in the oven gave me at ten years of age a sense that something had been lost and would never be found again. The music of Bach or Beethoven or Mozart would be rising out of the record player and, just as Grandma had taught us how to remember the names of wild-flowers by writing them down in our project books, Aunt Alice taught us the names of the composers and what was meant by suites, overtures and symphonies.

Being in that big house with Dad and Aunt Alice was like stepping back into the age of nature trails and corner shops, of what Dad called 'playing cricket' and 'being aware of the right thing and doing it'. He read his *Telegraph* and went to the local Conservative Club. He always wore a suit with a tie, and I couldn't help comparing him with Alan Briggs with long side-burns and muscles bursting out of his T-shirt. Alan had a tattoo of crossed flags on his left arm in memory of the men who had died in the attack on HMS *Lark*. The war with its death and brutality was something Dad tried to forget. Alan Briggs believed he was keeping up with the times with his dolly-bird and bell-bottoms, but the war was still raging inside his head.

Dad knew Mum had a new 'friend' and asked us if we'd met him. All Amy could remember were the guinea pigs. I recalled the scruffy garden and Alan standing in the kitchen staring into my eyes.

'Is he a pleasant man?' Dad asked, and it's hard for children to know how to answer questions like that.

'He's got a rhino-whip hanging on the back of the door,' I told him.

'A what?'

'A rhino-whip. That's what he said. Does that mean it's for beating rhinoceroses?'

'Rhinoceroses,' Amy repeated. 'Does he beat rhinoceroses?'

Rhinoceroses is a funny word. It made us chuckle, but Dad just looked sad and old.

Aunt Alice came in.

'It's good to hear some laughter for a change,' she remarked.

'We're going to beat rhinoceroses,' Amy told her, and she smiled.

'Good for you. Are you hungry?'

'As a rhinoceros,' Dad said, and we all burst out laughing again.

He smoothed down his moustache and stood to go through to lunch. Dad had become his dad, and Aunt Alice was turning into her mother with her old-fashioned dresses and a red book-mark in her library book. Even Tuppence, the kitten, had changed. She was now a cat afraid to leave the house and spent her time wandering the upstairs landing sniffing at the closed doors.

I didn't see Alan Briggs again for several weeks, but the statue in the graveyard was a constant reminder of him. One night, when the statue was chasing me, I woke up screaming and it felt as if his stone hands were around my throat. Mum came running in.

'What's wrong? What is it?'

'He's trying to get me?'

'Who?'

'Alan.'

She turned on the light. Amy had woken up.

'What are you saying?'

'Alan. Mr Briggs. He's chasing me. He wants to get me.'

Her jaw tightened. Her eyes glazed. I knew that look. She didn't hit me. She grabbed me by the shoulders and shook me. She shook me so hard the back of my head smashed against the wall over and over, each bash punctuating her words.

'Don't you ever . . . ever . . . ever say . . . that . . . again.'

'Mummy, don't, please . . .'

'Not . . . Ever . . . Ever . . . Ever . . . Ever.'

Granny appeared at the door.

'For crying out loud, Gwen, I'm getting sick of this.'

Mum let me go and turned to face her. 'Go back to bed, Mum, you won't have to put up with it much longer.'

'Thank bloody God for that.'

Mum glared back at me. 'You just watch your step, you little bitch . . .'

'Mummy, it was a dream.'

She leaned in close so our faces were almost touching. She was wearing big blue hair curlers that made her face wide.

'This is my life. You are not going to ruin it.' She looked at Amy. 'Go back to sleep, darling. It's just your sister playing up again.'

She turned off the light and left the door ajar when she left the room.

I had been feeling anxious without knowing what I was anxious about. Now I knew. I had a bad feeling about Alan Briggs and had made the mistake of telling her. Mum didn't ask me to go and see her new clothes any more, but her skirts got shorter like her temper, and my name never again touched her lips. Mum was still out a lot, but when she was home, she watched me, waiting for me to put a foot wrong.

One day when we came home from school, I followed Amy into the kitchen while Mum was stirring a pot of tea. After kissing Amy, she bent towards me. I thought she was going to kiss me, too, but she didn't, she pressed the hot teaspoon against my cheek. She hadn't done that for a long time and I knew it gave her a little thrill when I jumped back in pain. Tears sprang into my eyes.

'Look at her. Attention seeking again, are we?'

'That hurt.'

'Come here – let me have a look.' I did, and she slapped me across the side of the head. 'Nothing wrong with you that can't be fixed, is there, girl?'

I went upstairs to the bedroom and remained behind the closed door until dinnertime when she heaped my plate with enough vegetables and meat pudding to feed a family of ten. The food on both Amy's plate and her own plate wasn't more than usual, but less.

'Why have you given me so much?'

'What did you say?'

'Look, there's too much. I can't eat all this. It's not fair.'

'Fair? Who do you think you are to tell me what's fair?'

Granny slammed down her cutlery. 'Always something, isn't it?' she said.

'See what you've done? We're guests in Granny's house—'

'I don't want to live here. I want to live with my dad.'

'What makes you think he wants you?' She leaned forward. 'Because I'll tell you something, girl, he doesn't. Now, clear your plate or clear off.'

'I'm not hungry,' I said.

She smiled. 'That's all right,' she replied, and took the plate back into the kitchen. She returned to the dining room and clicked her fingers. 'Off you go then. If you're not hungry, no point sitting at the table, is there?'

As I passed her, she lashed out with the back of her hand. The force of the blow knocked me against the door jamb. She gave me a shove from the back and closed the dining-room door.

I went to bed crying and ate all my breakfast before school next day.

That night, when we sat down to dinner, Mum brought out plates of home-made hamburgers and chips; it was our favourite. She served Amy and Granny, then placed in front of me the same plate of food that she had taken into the kitchen the previous night.

'We will not waste good food on you, girl. Now, get on with it.'

I sat there, gagging, until she took the plate away. It reappeared next night and every night until Friday, the food growing more foul and mouldy until, finally, the weekend came and she threw it in the bin. If I thought I'd scored a small victory, I was wrong. As a child, you can never beat an adult in any game. The weather was nice and I was made to stay in my room.

In her own way, Amy tried to shield me from Mum's moods and would remain indoors with me when I was grounded. Mum would then accuse me of making my sister stay in against her will, forcing Amy into the impossible position of having to, or appearing to, take sides. Mum had done the same with Dad. He always gave in to her. With Mum, there was no middle ground. You were either for her, or against her, and if you didn't support her a hundred per cent, she would fly off in a fury that was never forgotten.

Through this period the night terrors didn't let up. They got worse. Every night I was chased by shadows and I would wake up trembling with cold hands around my throat.

Dad knew there was something wrong. I'm sure he knew me better than I knew myself. He started to come more often to pick us up from school instead of George. He would pull up outside Granny's house, lean over to kiss my cheek and whisper, 'Is everything all right, Poppet?'

As a child you answer spontaneously from the way you feel at that moment. The deeper significance of the question 'Is everything all right?' is lost on children. If at that moment you feel happy, as I always was with my dad, you say, yes, everything is great, even if everything is about to fall to pieces.

We kept our coats and satchels in the cloakroom on the ground floor next to the entrance at school. One day, when I was dawdling, I noticed one of the bags had been left unbuckled.

Inside there was a pink furry toy called a Gonk and I had an overpowering urge to take it. I had never taken anything that belonged to someone else before, but the moment I put the toy in my blazer pocket, my anxiety vanished and I went through the rest of the day feeling relieved and happy.

I hid the Gonk in the back of my drawer in the bedroom. Next day, I took a purse with two half-crowns from another bag and felt the same thrill. I wasn't very good at arithmetic and English any more. I wasn't very good at anything. But this was something special and private, something that belonged to me. I took a bag of flying saucers one of the girls had bought at the little sweetshop near school, a ruler with a magnifying glass at one end, a Russian doll that came apart and contained more dolls getting smaller and smaller inside. It wasn't that I wanted these things . . . I just had an uncontrollable urge to take them.

The following week, I started out on Monday taking the new geometry set that belonged to my friend Linda Janner, who sat next to me in class. When she discovered it was missing, she must have guessed it was me.

That night, while I was in my bedroom looking at my treasures, Amy came in and told me to come downstairs because Mrs Lloyd-Jones was there. I knew why. I gathered up all the things I had taken and brought them down with me. Mrs Lloyd-Jones was in the lounge with Mum and Granny. I put the things on the couch next to where Mrs Lloyd-Jones was sitting.

Mum took a long breath through her teeth and trembled as she spoke. 'I'm so sorry,' she said. 'I really don't know what's wrong with the girl.'

'It's nothing to worry about. These things happen.' She smiled at me. 'You didn't even eat the flying saucers,' she added.

'I'm sorry. I, I, I . . .' I didn't know what to say. 'I don't know why I did it.'

'Because you're a little thief, that's why,' Mum said.

Mrs Lloyd-Jones looked back across the room, her eyes running over Mum's clothes, her legs, her hair, her dangling earrings.

'Mrs MacKenzie, these things happen sometimes. I don't believe for one minute Emily's a thief—'

'There's the evidence.'

'It's just a phase, that's all. Lots of children go through it. I will make sure these things are returned and no more need be said.'

There was a quiet moment, broken by Granny. 'Can I get you a cup of tea?' she asked, and Mrs Lloyd-Jones got to her feet.

She smiled and I was watching Mum as Mrs Lloyd-Jones brushed the back of my head.

'That's very kind, but I have to go. It's been a long day.'

We saw her to the door and the moment the lights on her car vanished down the road, Mum softly closed and bolted the door. She turned to me with that glazed look in her eyes. She was twitching, her jaw had tightened.

'No matter what I do for you, it's not enough, is it? It's never enough.'

'I'm sorry, Mummy, I don't know why I took those things.'

Amy had remained at my side. She knew what was coming, but there was nothing she could do to stop it.

'Go back into the lounge with Granny, Amy. Straight away now.'

Amy left the hall and Mum instantly grabbed the back of my hair and slapped me across the cheek, a forehand and a backhand, smash, smash.

'Because you've got the devil in you, that's why!' she screamed, and she went through her routine, spitting out her words between each strike with her palm . . . 'and the only way . . . to get the devil out . . . is knock it out . . . You hear me . . . knock it out.'

'Mummy, Mummy, Mummy, please stop. Please stop . . .'

She paused for breath and stared down at me. 'You're your own worst enemy, you know that.'

'I didn't mean to do it.'

'Always someone else's fault with you!' she shouted, and hit me again, one cheek then the other.

She kept hold of my hair as she ran me upstairs. She opened the bedroom door and pushed me so hard I fell on the floor. The door slammed behind her. My cheeks were stinging and I lay in the dark sobbing. I was grateful when Amy finally came and climbed into my bed.

'I'm sorry, Emmy,' she whispered.

'It's not your fault.'

'Why did you take those things?'

'I don't know. I knew I'd get caught.'

'Why did you do it then?'

'I don't know.'

'Don't do it any more.'

'I won't.'

'Promise.'

'I promise.'

The fact that I had stolen things from the other girls at school reflected badly on 'Mum's family' and she got it into her head that I had some inherent mental flaw which was nothing to do with her parenting – that I was the devil's seed, as she liked to say.

She made dozens of phone calls in the coming days, roped Dad in to pay the bills, and the following Wednesday I left school after lunch, took the bus on my own into town and made my first visit to the child psychologist.

CHAPTER 5

Chinese Water Torture

My appointment was with Dr Ruth Lewis at a place called the Children's Centre, which sounds like a friendly social services building, but turned out to be a Tudor manor house that looked to me like the lodge where Oliver Cromwell took refuge during his battles against the Cavaliers, a picture of which appeared in the history book we had at school. I entered through a big oak door that was leaning over so far I didn't know how it was standing up.

There was no reception desk, but a woman approached and asked me if I was lost.

'I don't think so,' I replied. 'I've come to see Dr Lewis.'

'Ah,' she said, and pointed. 'At the end there on the right there's a waiting room. Someone will come and collect you from there.'

The long wooden corridor seemed to sway as I walked and it reminded me of creeping through the haunted house at

Morecambe with Dad and Amy. The waiting room was half-panelled in wood with beams on the ceiling and the paintings of stern men and windy landscapes made it feel like a museum. It had just gone two. No one else was waiting, and it seemed strange that it was called the Children's Centre because I can't recall that I ever saw another child in the building.

At three, the same woman came and led me up some rickety stairs to the first floor. I entered an office where Ruth Lewis sat in a huge wing-back chair behind a gigantic desk, everything exaggerated like in a scene from *Alice in Wonderland*. Dr Lewis wore a white coat and glasses with frames that went up in points. She was probably in her thirties, but adults to children all appear to be about the same age.

'Sit,' she said, without looking at me.

Facing the desk, more or less in the middle of the room, was a straight-backed wooden chair, where I sat. I instantly had the sense that I was physically smaller than I really was, that I had shrunken like Alice when she fell down the rabbit hole. That physical feeling was also emotional, or psychological, in that I felt younger than my years, like I was seven still, and the last three years had been a dream. I swung my legs back and forth, which was comforting. Dr Lewis bent over a yellow notepad and never once made eye contact with me.

'Hello, Emily, how are you today?' she began.

'I'm OK, thank you.'

'How are you getting on at home?'

'OK, thank you.'

'And school?'

'OK, thank you.'

'Do you fight with your mother?'

'Not really. She shouts at me sometimes.'

'Why does she shout at you?'

'I don't know.'

'And your father?'

'No.' I shook my head. 'He never shouts at me.'

'Not even when you misbehave?'

'No, not really.'

'What does he do when you misbehave?'

'Nothing.'

'You are sure he doesn't do anything?'

'Yes.'

'How do you get on with your sister?'

'She's my best friend.'

'Are you jealous of your sister?'

'No. Why should I be?'

She didn't answer my question. She paused, then carried on scribbling.

'Now, is there anything else you want to tell me?'

I thought for a moment. 'No, I don't think so.'

'That's very good. Will you come and see me again next week, Emily?'

I shrugged my shoulders. I had expected the ordeal to be frightening, but it seemed . . . it seemed silly, like a game.

'Yes,' I then said.

Dr Lewis had been writing down my answers on the yellow pad. She stood, tore out the pages and dropped them in the basket next to the desk. She opened the door.

'Goodbye,' she said. 'See you next week.'

I went downstairs where I was met by the same woman I'd seen earlier.

'Would you like to follow me?' she asked.

She led me down to the basement. In a large room, like a gym, there was a punchbag suspended from the ceiling and a pair of boxing gloves on a bench.

'You are free to use these,' she said, handing me the boxing gloves. 'Your bus is not due for half an hour. When it is time for you to leave, I will come and get you.'

I took off my school blazer and put on the gloves, though I was unable to do up the laces. I had no idea what they expected to learn by sending me down to the basement to hit a punchbag, but that's what I did. I pretended I was a heavyweight champion and hit that bag the way Mum often hit me.

This routine was like the Chinese Water Torture and continued with little variation for the next three months. I enjoyed the ride on the bus and felt grown up going on my own.

Dr Lewis never looked at me, but I did look at Dr Lewis with her pointy glasses, a high-necked blouse below her white coat, her lips pressed tight in concentration. Her pen whizzed over the yellow notepad and, when I got bored watching her write down what I was saying, I looked at the light making stripes on the books as it passed through the venetian blinds. There were a lot of shelves but they were only half full, giving the office an impermanent feeling like a stage set.

The questions were basically the same, repeated over and over; this method, I assumed, was to try to catch me out, although sometimes Dr Lewis introduced a different theme.

Once she asked me where I saw myself in the family structure. I had no idea what this meant. Then we went back to the same old cycle.

'Do you know the definition of stealing, Emily?'

I shrugged. 'Taking things?'

'It is taking something which isn't given.' She paused. 'When you took those things, did you want to get caught?'

'I don't think so.'

'Was your mother upset?'

'Yes.'

'What about your father?'

'Not really. Mrs Lloyd–Jones, my teacher, said it was normal.'

She ignored that. 'Does your father discipline you?'

'No, he never touches me.'

'Never?'

'No,' I replied and then thought for a moment. 'He did put cream on my bottom.'

'He put cream on your bottom?'

'Yes, he rubbed it in.'

'Why did he do that, Emily?'

'Because I hurt myself in the garden.'

'You hurt yourself in the garden?'

'Yes.'

'And he rubbed cream on your bare bottom?'

'Yes.'

She looked up and looked away again just as our eyes were about to meet. I knew what she was getting at. She wanted to know if Dad touched me in places where he shouldn't or if he ever hit me. Mrs Lloyd-Jones had once assumed the same thing when I arrived bruised and battered at school. When teachers, social workers and psychologists deal with children, they have their own mental checklist that makes you conform to what they already believe. In reality, everyone is different and, however similar, no two sets of circumstances are ever exactly the same.

The questions went on and on. Once she had a theme, like a repeating pattern on fabric, she would come back to it, trying to catch me out.

'Did you like your father rubbing cream on your bottom?'

'Yes, it was nice, it took away the pain.'

'When you hurt yourself in the garden?'

And now I had to lie. 'Yes,' I'd say.

I never understood what Dr Lewis was trying to get at or how these weekly sessions would help me overcome my 'psychological' problems. Each session ended the same way, with Dr Lewis tearing off the sheets on which she had assiduously written her notes and dropping them in the basket. After about ten weeks, I asked her why she did that and she pointed a finger at her head.

'It's all up here,' she said. 'When you write things down, you remember them.'

She slipped out of her giant's chair and opened the door.

'Goodbye, Emily,' she said. 'See you next week.'

I'd make my way down to the basement and spend half an hour building up my muscles beating the punchbag. It made me strong. I had always been quite good at running and on Sports Day at the end of my last term at The Priory I won several races.

The bus stop was outside the Children's Centre. I'd sit upstairs on the bus and arrive back at Granny's house, where I'd face a cross-examination from Mum. She wanted to know everything that had been said to find out if I had said anything about her, not that I would ever have told the psychologist that my mother beat me.

Children feel ashamed of such things or deny they are happening. The fact that Mum had an uncontrollable temper was something I didn't want anyone to know about, and I can see now, looking back, that Dr Lewis did have an idea that I was being abused, but wrongly assumed it was at the hands of my father. Children have strong loyalties to their parents and abused children can spend the rest of their lives believing that the abuse was in some way their own fault.

I know I did.

Although Dad paid the bills, as Mum was my legal guardian, he was not provided with updates on my progress. I was given no therapy, no information on my emotional state when I started to see the psychologist or my new state three months later when the sessions came to an end. Mum put me through that brief grilling each week, but her interest was fleeting and her mind was occupied with other things: plans that would change our lives forever.

The entire project slid into the past except that I was now on file as a child with behavioural problems who had undergone mental health treatment.

CHAPTER 6

The First Taste

In June I was eleven and in July I left The Priory for the last time. About a week later, one Saturday, I was playing in the garden with Amy when the telephone rang. Granny called us.

'Come. Come quickly, Mummy's on the phone.'

She gave me the receiver.

'Guess what, I just got married,' Mum said.

'Married?'

'Five minutes ago.'

'With Alan?'

'Of course. Who do you think?' I heard her sigh. 'Are you happy for us?'

'Yes, I suppose . . . Why didn't you invite us?'

'I wanted it to be a surprise. Is Amy there?'

I gave my sister the phone and watched her eyes grow big as Mum must have told her the same thing.

The shock of this sudden marriage became even more shocking as we packed our things and moved across town to Alan Briggs's house on the council estate. The house had three bedrooms. Mum and Alan occupied one. There was a small box room for Billy. Amy and I were to share the third bedroom in two sets of bunks with Barbs and Annie.

When we opened our bags, I realised there was no wardrobe. The chest of drawers was stuffed, the top heaped with games in broken boxes and dolls with missing body parts. There were no books on the shelf but a line of stuffed animals, teddy bears, a panda, a pink elephant. There was a jumble of things on the floor and a set of chimes hung silently against the closed window. The air was stuffy and the sheets smelled of pee.

I called Mum to ask her where we should put our clothes and shoes. She came in and closed the door behind her.

'Now you listen. I don't want any trouble from you.'

'I just want to know where to put our things?'

'You've got too many damned things, that's your problem.' She looked around, then pointed at our suitcases. 'Push them under the bed and leave everything there for now.'

Before she had finished speaking, the door was rattling on its hinges with someone beating the woodwork from outside.

Barbs marched in. 'This is our room,' she declared, glaring at Mum.

'I know it is, darling,' she said. 'I was just telling Em she has to learn how to share things.'

'That's all right then.'

Mum didn't call me Emily any more and used Em when 'her' or 'she' or 'that girl' were inappropriate. Years later, in a paranoid moment, of which there were many, I realised that Em could just as easily have been my initials, E.M., a way to push me away still further.

I slid the cases under the bunk and remembered how Mum had always been obsessed with the way we arranged our coats and dresses in the wardrobe, a place for everything . . .

Amy and I followed Barbs downstairs and out into the garden. A garden to me had always meant flowers and fruit trees. Alan's garden was a rubbish dump and there was a farmyard smell that came from the two goats the neighbours on one side kept on long tethers. The stench was present everywhere. It crept into the house and into your clothes. Mum, being delicate, had always been fussy about bad smells, but she smoked menthol cigarettes, which must have helped, and I never heard her complain about the goats.

We sat down that evening with Alan at the head of the table in a tie-dye T-shirt. Mum sat at his side in a crocheted dress that showed her underwear. I helped Barbs, not that there was much to do. There was sliced bread and jam, a banana each and a pot of tea. There was nothing in the refrigerator except some mouldy vegetables and a dozen bottles of beer on the bottom shelf. Alan got a discount from the brewery and, though the fridge was always empty, the bottom shelf was always full.

Barbs wolfed down her food and watched Amy and me to make sure we didn't take more than our fair share. Only Patch ate well. His silver bowl in the corner was replenished twice a day with tins of dog food that he ate slowly, tail straight up, his legs spread for better balance like Alan when he was passing on his worldly wisdom. If dogs are a reflection of their owners, although Patch was usually silent, unlike his garrulous master, you just had to look into his dead eyes to know it wouldn't take much for him to turn back into a wild beast. Amy was terrified of Patch. The dog sensed this and followed her around, feeding off her fear.

That night and in the coming weeks Alan and Mum didn't take much notice of anything except each other. Mum hung on Alan's every word, her blue eyes wide and bright as he told her about cars and football and darts and work; how to bring up children, train dogs, deal with the local council. He was an expert on most things. He called her Gwenny and she purred like a cat as he touched her bare legs beneath the table.

Billy would have liked to have been the centre of attention but didn't know how to go about it. I remember that first night how he kept continually kicking me under the table. I didn't react, unusual for me, and knew he had switched to kicking Amy when she reached for my hand. I held her fingers tightly; she looked back at me and I shook my head. At mealtimes with Dad and Aunt Alice, we talked about what we were doing at school, the music on the record player, how Mozart had composed his first piano pieces when he was five, scraps of facts and ideas that form the jigsaw of our knowledge. At Alan's table, Alan spoke and, when he wasn't concentrating solely on Mum, we listened to long stories that were usually about how someone had tried to do him down but he had ended up getting one over on them. Children, he said many times, should be seen and not heard . . .

'And better, not seen at all.'

Mum laughed as if that was the funniest thing she had ever heard. The bread and jam had gone. Barbs was eating the crusts from Annie's plate. Suddenly, Alan slapped the table with his palm.

'Right, we're off out,' he said, and glanced at Barbs. 'You're in charge. Wash up, put everything away. No misbehaving.'

They left for the pub, leaving us to kill time in front of the television at night and mope about the garden by day, the days glazing repetitively together. Every day, Mum pinned up her hair, dressed in one of her old suits and went to her job in the office at a department store. Alan went to his job loading trucks at the brewery and Amy and I, like square pegs in round holes, tried to slot into our new family.

We were like a troop of primates. Alan was the alpha male, his word was the law and no one ever forgot the rhino-whip hanging on the back of the door. Mum was his dolly-bird. I could see how proud of her he was when his mates came round and they stood at the gate admiring the Jaguar now parked outside, one eye on the car, the other on Mum's legs. Mum had loved her red Mini with the racing stripe, but Alan had persuaded her that we needed something bigger and the new Mini became an old Jaguar Mark 2 that he drove because it was too big for a woman to handle. He kept his Cortina for Mum to drive to work each morning.

Since the chimney incident when I was seven Mum had been offhand with Dad, her tone abrupt, her lips pinched. When she looked at Alan, she had a smile that made her seem younger. She was a beautiful woman. She could have had anyone, but had chosen a man, as she had chosen Dad, old enough to be her father. She was mesmerised. Alan for me was the stone statue in the cemetery, the shadow chasing me in my dreams. But he could be funny and amiable; he had what I realise now was sexual charisma, the psychopath's charm. He was boastful, narcissistic, and Mum and we children were merely extensions of himself and his place in the world. You had to love Alan, admire him, believe his every word, and he was acutely aware if you showed dissent or a moment's doubt.

Alan was a black belt in karate and liked to show off his strength and knowledge. In the navy he'd 'seen the world' and 'learned a thing or two'. In the garden he enjoyed play fights. All of us, the five children, even Mum, had to try to hold him down and he would rise up like a monster from the sea and we'd arrange ourselves so that he could hold us all in his two arms.

'Barbs, got a right thirst on,' he'd then say, and she would skip off back to the house.

She was in charge of bringing him his beer, which he drank in vast quantities, medicinal, he'd say, for the wounds he got serving King and Country. 'Water's bad for you,' he'd add, touching the side of his nose, 'the fish piss in it.' Like Pavlov's dogs, we'd all laugh and Mum would grab his arm and look happy.

The bread and jam we had for dinner, or tea, as he called it, that first night we had most nights. Mum and Alan were both working, but the cost of running two cars and those nightly sessions at the pub where Alan impressed his mates buying rounds meant the cupboard was often bare.

Barbs was always hungry and had beady eyes like a pigeon constantly pecking around looking for crumbs. She taught me how to ask questions in shops while she pocketed chocolate bars, which she was reluctant to share, although she took Mum's advice and shared my clothes, squeezing her plump little body into tight dresses, the vision making Alan sigh and slug back his beer.

'Suppose you wanna be a princess now as well, do you?' he snorted, and Billy fell about laughing.

Billy worshipped his father. He wanted to be like him. He tried to be like him. But he was just a bully. A sneak. He gave Amy and me a pinch or a push every time he passed, asserting his position in the chain of command. We learned to put up with it. There was nothing else you could do. If you complained, Alan called you a 'rat' and you'd be 'sent to your room without any tea'.

Little orphan Annie would often lapse into a trance and stand with a teddy under her arm staring at the world like a goldfish, nose running, clothes messy. Amy talked to her slowly in baby language so that she understood. She helped her wash and I would often see them sitting together on the torn sofa, Annie's finger moving slowly below the words as Amy taught her to read. My sister seemed to know how to do the right thing at the right time and that helped her escape the aggression, which was constant, a push, a jab, a kick, a punch. Mum didn't need to slap me around the head, there was a house full of bullies to do it for her.

I was the opposite of Amy. I had the uncanny knack of doing the wrong thing at the worst possible time. I spoke up when I should have shut up. As Mum had said, I was my own worst enemy. Amy looked like Mum, pale and blonde, the blue-eyed girl who saves the day in storybooks. I looked like the foundling with dark haunted eyes and the beginnings of a squint that made me appear deceitful and would take years to overcome.

Children know intuitively when adults don't like them. I am not sure if Alan liked Amy, as such, if he actually *liked* anyone, but he was aware that Amy took care of Annie and that kept her safe. I was the square peg. I was no longer a little girl. I was a pre-teen full of anxieties, the usual misinformation about sex and a deep yearning to be loved. The house was crowded. We were on top of each other – literally. Four girls in bunks with less space than people have in prison exploded inevitably and often in screaming matches that I, as the eldest, was blamed for. If there was a final straw that would break the camel's back, I was that straw.

Alan accepted Billy for what he was. Annie he largely ignored except to scoop her up occasionally in the garden and fly her through the air like an aeroplane, the display designed more to show his strength and good humour than find pleasure in little Annie's squeals of delight. Like me, she was desperate for attention. The only person in the house Alan had any respect for was Barbs. She had inherited his strong will and ego. She wasn't school smart but street smart. She would argue with her father, but knew how far she could go and exactly when to stop. Billy was her shadow, and I, if I was going to survive, had to fall in with her plans, be it building a playhouse from broken chairs or robbing the local shops. Barbara exercised the female power in the house and Mum was merely an expression of Alan's sense of entitlement. Mum in skirts that showed her knickers was the object of desire every man wanted but it was he, the king of the council estate, who had tamed and conquered her.

Alan was claiming his lost youth in his T-shirt with the words *Peace & Love* in rainbow colours. He played Pink Floyd and the Rolling Stones at a deafening level and did an exaggerated version of Mick Jagger dancing, which always had Mum in hysterics. He liked to talk and often talked about the war. Apart from being a miracle man, he was a 'known hero' having saved several men in spite of his own injuries after the U-Boat attack on HMS *Lark*. If it wasn't for those injuries, he would have become a mercenary, or a secret agent who could be called on to solve international problems.

In 1967, a few years after the Cuban Missile Crisis, people were worried about nuclear war and Alan was 'doing his bit' running the local Civil Defence Corps. One Saturday his volunteers at a summer show demonstrated how they would rescue people from burning buildings. Assuming they would save the women and children first, it was Mum and us children who were strapped into stretchers and lowered with ropes and pulleys down a hundred-foot scaffold, a terrifying experience, but there was absolutely no question of not taking part.

No one said no to Alan. And if they did, he went berserk. If he was frustrated or thwarted or didn't get exactly his own way, his face would go red and he'd clench his fists ready to strike. He was the captain of the darts team at his local pub. One time when his team lost an important match, he came home drunk and I discovered why there were dents in the walls and splits in all the woodwork. We sat at the top of the stairs and listened as he raged through the house punching every surface and karate-chopping the furniture. Next morning, everything was broken, even the table, and Mum had to dip into her savings to buy new furniture.

She didn't mind. She was happy. She wanted to be protected, admired, a little girl. They had become carefree teens and through those warm weeks of August it was like living on the side of an active volcano. There was tension in the air like invisible smoke and a feeling that it was about to erupt.

It erupted one Sunday at lunch.

After two weeks of bread and jam, Mum on Saturday went to the supermarket to buy groceries the way she used to. On Sunday she roasted a chicken with potatoes and vegetables. She carved and served Alan first. He was always served first, and we sat on our hands until his drink was poured. They had discovered Liebfraumilch, and would polish off a bottle at every meal.

We ate what was on our plates and Mum put the remainder of the carcass on a dish in the middle of the table. Barbs grabbed the whole thing and I impulsively tried to grab it back.

'It's mine,' she said.

'No it's not, it's to share.'

'I got it first.'

'What about Amy and Annie?' I reasoned.

'I got it first.'

'That's not fair.'

'Oi, you two. Enough. I'm not going to sit here eating my dinner with you two going at it.'

'I got it first, Dad.'

'But that's not fair, is it, Alan?'

'Fair? I'll tell you what's fair. You can fight over it. Winner takes all.'

'Fight?' I said.

'To the death,' he replied. He stood, finished his wine, and pointed at the remains of the chicken. 'No one touches it, you hear. You two, outside.'

I thought it was a joke, or a game, like when we tried to pin Alan down. But it wasn't. Alan marched out and I just sat there.

Mum beckoned with her finger. 'Come on, then, you heard,' she said.

'But I don't want to fight.'

'You never want to do anything you don't want to do, that's your trouble.'

'But, Mum . . .'

We heard Alan shouting. 'Oi, you could die of old age waiting for you two.'

'Come on, hurry yourself,' Mum said.

She was grinning. She was a bit tipsy. I followed her out. They were all standing there, Alan, Billy, the dog, its mouth open. Amy was holding Annie's hand and Barbs stood in the centre with her fists clenched. The neighbours with the goats were leaning over the fence.

'We're taught at school not to fight,' I said.

'Well, you ain't at your posh school now, are you? In my house, you do as you're told.'

'But I don't want to fight.'

I still expected Mum to intervene. I should have known better by now. Alan stepped forward and bent down into my face. 'It's the only way to find out who's in the right and who's not. Understand?'

I shook my head. I didn't understand. I didn't understand at all.

Patch barked once, and it was like the bell ringing at the start of a boxing match. Alan stepped away and Barbs rushed forward. Before I knew what was happening, she punched me on my cheek, one side, then the other. Tears sprang to my eyes. I was immediately winded. Barbs was box-shaped, with a low centre of gravity. I backed away and she came forward like a threshing machine, swinging her fists. I did try to fight back. I pulled her hair and she butted me across the forehead.

I got a glimpse of Mum as I dragged myself up. She was grinning. Still until that day I had tried to get on her good side, to be the little girl she wanted me to be. I wanted her to love me. But she didn't love me. She hadn't loved me for a long time. I was a nuisance, trouble. I was in the way. Amy had replaced me in her affections. Now Alan had replaced Amy. Mum could only focus on one person at a time and her rejection made me feel like an old mattress ready for the rubbish dump.

Barbs pushed me down again. The dirt ground into my knees as I crawled away from her. I could hear them whistling and whooping. I could smell the goats. I got up again. I swung out vainly, but that only made Barbs move in closer and hit me more. I kept retreating until there was nowhere to go. I climbed up the fence and, as I was about to swing my leg over, one more punch from Barbs sent me flying into the long grass of the common on the other side. The back fence was trimmed with barbed wire and, as I fell, my knee was gashed open.

As I limped onto the common, I could hear them cheering. Alan had set up the fight to prove that, even though Barbara was almost a year younger than me, she had the bulldog spirit, that his children, being his children, were clearly superior. I paused for breath behind the blackberry bushes. My leg was bleeding. My body was bruised. Tears stained my face. I wanted my dad. I wanted to go home. I hugged my knees and stared at the sky. Why did Mum hate me? Why did my real mum die? What happened to my real dad?

I stayed there for a long time, unsure what to do, and then had a brilliant idea. Instead of going back to the house, I made my way across the common towards town. It was more than two miles and it took me almost an hour before I found the police station. I sobbed out my story to the desk sergeant. He wrote down my details, my address and phone number, then a policewoman took me to the outpatients department at the hospital, where I had three stitches in my gashed knee and my cuts were cleaned and dressed.

When I arrived back at the police station, to my utter horror, Alan was standing there dressed in a suit he kept for funerals with Mum at his side in her office clothes. Alan gave me a big smile.

'We've been worried sick about you, darling,' he said. 'We've been out scanning the common looking for you.'

I usually have plenty to say, but I was dumbstruck. Alan was cheerful, charming. He knew how to 'handle things'.

He gave the desk sergeant a shrug. 'Just a couple of girls in an argument, you know what they're like.'

'You made us fight,' I said.

'Come on, darling, you know that's not true.'

'It is true . . .' I looked at Mum and she looked away.

'I'll tell you what,' Alan added. 'Let's go and have an ice cream, then we'll go home and say no more about it.'

'I don't want to go home with you. I want my dad.'

'Come on now, Em, don't go and act all spoiled,' Mum said.

Alan threw out his hands. The desk sergeant looked at me, then back at Alan, then at me again. He folded his arms.

'Sounds pretty good to me,' he said. 'Why don't you get yourself off and have that ice cream?'

'I'm eleven. I'm not a baby. I don't want ice cream. I want my dad.'

I realised I was shouting and would realise later, much too late, that the moment you raise your voice, you lose the argument. Mum's hand flew to her mouth and she sucked air in through her teeth. In a tweed suit with her hair pinned up she looked like the ladies at the Conservative Club, the epitome of modesty and good manners.

'I'm so sorry for all the bother, sergeant,' she said in her best voice, then she smiled at me. 'Stop it now, Em. We don't want to waste any more time.'

Alan leaned across the desk. The two men shook hands, sergeant and petty officer, men of the world, and my world suddenly seemed smaller and more scary. I had been brave going to the police station on my own, but the sergeant must have called the house and Mum and Alan had convinced him that I had exaggerated, that I was seeking attention, that I couldn't be trusted.

I sat in the big leather seat in the Jaguar and Alan drove home without saying a word. There was no ice cream. We marched into the house and straight down the narrow passage to the kitchen.

'Out. All of you,' Alan said. I was about to follow. He pointed at me. 'Not you.'

Mum had that glazed look as she shuffled off with the children. I knew what was going to happen. I'd always known. Alan grabbed me in one big hand.

'Please, please. I'm sorry . . .'

'You, you're trouble, you know that?'

'Please don't hit me . . .'

'Give my family a bad name,' he said, and pushed his face so close I could smell the cigarettes on his breath. 'I've seen it before. You're evil, you're wicked.'

My body had broken out in sweat. Alan was suddenly in a rush. He grabbed the rhino-whip from the door and held me down. I wriggled. I couldn't move. I felt his body tense as he raised his right arm and the whip wrapped itself around my legs, the sound of the lash like hands clapping. I screamed out.

'Mummy. Mummy. Mummy.'

I was a small eleven-year-old girl and he was a powerful six-foot man. I couldn't get away. I knew how to endure pain. But this was like no pain I had felt before. Each time the whip found a new line across my calves and thighs, it felt as if I were being cut in two with a knife. My legs were scratched after running through the brambles on the common and the scratches burned like hot coals. I felt a warm trickle run down my legs. I thought it was blood but it wasn't. I had wet myself.

I could barely breathe. I sobbed.

'Mummy, Mummy, help me . . .'

I called for my mum but the door remained closed. She had chosen me as a baby to be her little girl and that day in the kitchen when she let Alan Briggs beat me with a whip, she had finally cast me aside.

The pain from a beating usually fades by the following day. But the rhino-whip bites deep and my skin was on fire for a week. I lived in constant fear. When we sat down to eat, Alan would glance at the whip, then glance at me. My hands would shake as I looked back across the table and the red stripes on my legs burned brighter.

The whip was black and sticky to the touch, about three feet in length, with a short woven handle that made it easy to grip and ideal for thrashing children. It was like a malevolent presence, a constant reminder that I should be afraid at all times. The very air in the house was charged with hostility and aggression and, four weeks after my mother's sudden marriage, Alan's children gave up what I assumed was their 'best behaviour' and returned to type, short-tempered, easily offended, selfish little bullies.

The following night, Barbs grabbed my bread and jam from my plate and stuffed it all in her mouth at once.

'Yum, yum, yum, yum, yum,' she said, and Alan laughed.

'You're a greedy little sod, you know that.'

'I didn't think she wanted it.'

'I know what she wants,' he added, and glanced at the whip.

Everyone laughed. Billy rocked back so far in his chair it fell over backwards.

'Bloody hell, it's like living in the monkey house at the zoo,' Alan said, and his three children obliged by making monkey noises.

I looked at Mum and she looked at Alan. He was happy. That's what mattered. Amy grabbed my hand under the table, her way of warning me not to say anything, and tears pressed into my eyes as she put her bread and jam on my plate. I had made it my mission to protect Amy. Our roles had reversed and now, when Mum and Alan were out, she tried to protect me from the torrent of rabbit-punches, trips, slaps, sharp elbows.

Even Annie had kicked me in the shins. She knew intuitively that I was at the bottom of the pile and a kick from her cemented her position in the troop. She had learned how to behave watching her father. Just as I had learned from my mother that once you have been beaten, that person, and anyone else for that matter, has an open invitation to beat you again. It is a simple equation. There are tall people and short people. There are those who beat and those who are beaten.

If two men fight in the street and the loser puts up a good show, the winner respects him and they don't need to fight again. It's different with a child. You have neither the will nor the means to fight. The abuser subconsciously loses respect for you and there is no way to win that respect back again. If you beat a dog, it will always cower, it will always have a pitiful look in its eyes. Children are no different. You may be taught as a child to stand up to bullies. But you can't stand up to your own mother. You can't stand up to adults.

That's why I had developed a squint. That's why when the children were playing in the yard I'd sneak off to the bedroom, pull out my suitcase and look at my clothes as if they might give me a sense of myself. I was like Annie's dolls with misplaced parts, fractured, disjointed. I had got into the habit of standing sideways to people as if I half expected a thump or a slap, this stance making me appear shifty and devious. Which I wasn't. My heart was an open wound desperate for someone to notice and care for me.

I kept asking myself why, why, why doesn't Mummy love me? In bed at night I would lie listening to Barbs snoring across the three feet of space between us, my brain churning, turning me at eleven into a different person than I had been when I came home in the Moses basket as a baby. I had been loved and now I wasn't. It is hard to accept, hard to understand. I had been a cheery little show-off on stage and now I was afraid of my own shadow. I had been clever at school. Now I was below average. An abused child becomes a damaged adult and many perpetuate the cycle and become an abuser.

A confused child is unable to articulate their turmoil. It comes out as anger and hostility. As an adult, the confusion turns to paranoia and psychosis. You buy a new dress and a friend says: 'I like you in that dress,' and you analyse the compliment to death. Does it mean she doesn't actually like you, except in 'that dress'? By 'that dress' does she mean your other dresses make you look too fat or too thin? Every word and gesture carries a potential snub or insult. You are never relaxed. You don't go with the flow. You stand midstream like a boulder being battered and spat at by the tide. To capture that carefree feeling you see in others you turn to drink and drugs, abusing them until they turn like a snake and abuse you back. A child is hit and the echo reverberates forever.

CHAPTER 7

Jewellery Box

The following weekend, Amy and I spent two nights in Blackpool with Dad and Aunt Alice. We stayed at the Imperial, a hotel Alan would have called posh and in which Mum would have felt at home back in our touring days.

The contrast of sleeping in a proper bed and eating meals at tables with linen cloths was like stepping back into the storybooks left behind when we moved into Alan's house. We went to see a show at the Opera House. Amy and I swam in the sea. We talked about how they put the name Blackpool in little pink letters through the sticks of rock and decided it was done by the tiny hands of fairies.

I had every opportunity to tell Dad that Alan had beaten me with a whip, but I didn't. Like a prisoner in jail who one day gets two potatoes instead of one, all the bad days are momentarily forgotten. You live in the present. You laugh when someone trips over a banana skin on stage. You join in with the songs. You remember how to be happy.

It was at dinner on Sunday night when Dad dropped the bombshell. Mum was in charge, but she had left this particular task to him. September had arrived and I had been found a place at a new school – a boarding school. My eyes welled up in tears.

'Daddy, I don't want to be sent away to school.'

'It's the best thing, Emily. Don't think I haven't thought about it.'

'Why can't I live with you?'

'I have been to court three times.' He took my hand. 'Your mother has custody. They won't change that.'

'But why?'

'She's your mum. She's married.' He removed his glasses and it was like he had lowered a mask. He looked drawn and worn out. 'The authorities believe you are better off with her.'

'I'm not,' I said, and he shrugged his thin shoulders.

'They don't know that.'

I glanced at Aunt Alice. She was wearing a blue and white striped dress and the faint tan from those two days at the seaside gave her a glow I had never noticed before. I could see in her expression the look I was always searching for in Mum.

'Can you tell the courts you'll look after me?'

'I wish,' she replied. Her lips formed a remembering smile. 'It's not so bad, you know. When I went to school, I hated being away from my family. But in a couple of weeks I was perfectly happy. You have to throw yourself in, Emily. I know you can do it.'

'You can, you know,' Dad added. 'You can do anything if you put your mind to it.'

I looked back at him across the table. Dad loved me. I knew it. I felt it. Just as I felt like a despised and unwanted guest in Alan's house. I should have been grateful to get out, but that night in the Imperial, it seemed to me that Mum was behind the decision and her husband was pulling the strings.

The other children went back to school a few days before me and I spent the time wandering over the common with Patch. The dog panted as it plodded along and, when I stopped to pick blackberries, it looked up at me with that lost expression Billy always had when he was trying to follow a story his dad was telling. Alan respected Barbs but was disappointed with Billy and didn't have the sense not to show it. Like everyone in that house, all Billy needed was for his dad to notice him.

The blackberries were ripe, plump and juicy with skin like velvet, and every time I have eaten blackberries as an adult that summer when I was beaten for the first time with a whip comes back to me. I remember the dog panting, the blustery winds of autumn, and I can picture that little girl, small and far away, a vague blur seen through the wrong end of a telescope. I scratched my arms reaching into the bushes and gave myself a tummy ache by eating too much. Except for bananas, we never had fresh fruit, it was expensive, and Alan said the juice made your teeth fall out, not that it stopped him bringing home the occasional bag of sweets from Woolworths.

On my first day at the new school, I got up at six o'clock. I had a bath on my own, a rare treat, and felt like my old self as I dressed in a new blouse and managed to tie a straight knot in my red and silver striped tie. I zipped up the grey skirt and pushed my arms into a matching grey blazer with red piping around the collar and cuffs. My new pyjamas and gym clothes were packed in my suitcase. My old clothes would join the rubbish pile and Barbs would stain and tear everything by Christmas.

Mum had taken a day off work to drive me across country to Norfolk. Dad had offered, but she had insisted and, grasping at straws, I took this as a good sign. The children were still sleeping and Alan came to the gate to see us off.

'You look like a right little toff in that lot,' he said. He wagged his finger. 'Now, you listen, I don't want you coming back here all high and mighty.'

I smiled. 'I won't. I promise,' I said.

'Saw it in the navy. Poncy officers were a right load of toffee-noses.'

I smiled again. With Alan you had to gauge his mood and react accordingly. He was being funny so I laughed.

'Come here,' he said, beckoning with the same finger, and I hurried forward.

He pulled out a £10 note and folded it into the top pocket of my blazer. My eyes lit up. The cupboard was bare. The karate-chopped furniture was forever being replaced. He wasted money bringing home more clutter and junk for his children. He saw himself as big-hearted, the Good Samaritan who would give a stranger the shirt from his back. But I had an inkling, even then, that this sudden act of generosity wasn't about me, it was about him, the way he needed Mum to see him.

Alan was in an awkward position. He wanted to get as much out of my father as possible, he saw it as 'his right', but resented the fact that dad was from the 'boss' class and could afford to support his daughters, while he, after returning home from the war a hero, was still loading trucks and living in a council house that smelled of goats. He had an ex-wife in a mental institution – why, exactly, I never did find out – and three children who behaved like monkeys. Alan, with his dreams of being James Bond, suffered from an inferiority-superiority complex and I, like a sponge, as children are sponges, was sucking in all his worst qualities. Alan's one great coup was Mum.

'Now, say thank you,' she said.

'Thank you, Alan. Thank you.'

'Off you go then.'

We climbed into Alan's Cortina and the car started after three tries. He guided Mum out from the parking space behind the Jag, measuring the distance between his hands like he was playing a concertina, and gave her the thumbs up before she accelerated away. It was a clear morning, the shadows shrinking in the sunrise. The streets were empty and we were going fast on the main road when steam started pouring out of the engine. Mum pulled over.

'Nothing ever goes right with you, does it?' she said.

'I haven't done anything.'

'Don't use that tone with me.'

It was only because I had been looking forward to having a day alone with Mum that I'd got over the fear of being sent away to school. It was like some dreadful curse that it would all go wrong.

I stayed in the car while she walked back to find a telephone box. I thought she was going to call Alan – he was always fiddling with the cars – but it was an AA man who appeared half an hour later on a yellow motorbike with tools in the sidecar. It turned out that the car had overheated because someone had forgotten to replace the radiator cap last time the water had been topped up. Mum was chatty with the AA man, men always liked her, but as soon as we were on our way she lit one of her menthol cigarettes and stared silently through her dark glasses for the rest of the journey.

We stopped for brunch and arrived at Chadleigh College in the early afternoon. We entered through tall iron gates, the stones crunching and spitting on the gravel driveway as we approached an ornate Georgian mansion with ivy coating the facade like glistening fish scales. I had not cried all the way, but as we stepped out of the car, tears rolled down my cheeks. I felt as if I were being abandoned and the feeling was worse than all the bullying. Mum became all sugary sweet as the bursar came out to greet us. His name, he said, extending his hand, was Lionel Griffiths.

'Stop that, Em, don't make a fuss. I'll write every week,' Mum said in her nice voice, and smiled at the bursar.

She opened the boot to get my suitcase.

'Leave that, I'll have a porter bring it,' Mr Griffiths said grandly, and turned to me. 'Let's go and see your new home. It's all been freshly painted.'

It was a mixed school. The boys lived on the top two floors in the main building. The girls occupied a modern, two-storey block behind trees across the far side of the playing fields. I was shown to my place in a dormitory, the beds lined up with their neat pillows in a way that reminded me of a drawing in a book where Goldilocks enters the house of the Three Bears. We stood in the doorway for a few moments, then Mum left for the long drive home, not with a kiss, but a small squeeze of my shoulder.

'Try to be good,' she said.

'I always do,' I replied, and she raised her eyes to heaven.

As I watched Mum take off with her quick, straight walk, she passed a girl who arrived panting for breath, and Mr Griffiths introduced me to Fee, a senior wearing a skirt a size too small and haircut like Mum's.

Once we were alone, Fee looked me up and down as if assessing a piece of bric-a-brac at an antiques fair.

'Do you smoke?' she asked.

I shook my head. 'No . . .'

'Shame,' she tutted. 'I'm gasping.'

She then took me on a lightning tour to the chapel, which stood on a raised bluff of land containing a war memorial and a small cemetery. I chased her up the hill and down the other side to the boathouse where several boys were pulling skiffs out of the water. We watched the boys for a few minutes, then Fee leaned closer and her eyes sparkled as she told me the school's one strict rule: girls were not allowed in the boys' dorms and boys were banned from entering the girls' building. 'Not that it stops them,' she whispered. This was of less interest to me at eleven than it would have been at fourteen, but I understood the sexual connotations and felt like a grown-up.

At teatime, the entire school congregated in the dining hall. The children sat on benches in four rows at long tables, boys on one side, girls on the other. The staff sat together on the top table, which ran across the width of the room in such a way that they could keep an eye on the pupils. Fee introduced me to Holly and Alison, two girls from my dorm, then went to her place with the seniors. She said something that made them all laugh and, naturally, I thought they must be laughing at me.

After tea, Holly and Alison showed me where to store my clothes in the locker beside my bed, and there was a cupboard at the end of the dorm for suitcases. Above the locker there was a shelf.

'For books,' Holly said, and I turned red with embarrassment.

'I didn't bring any. I didn't know you were supposed to.'

She touched my arm. 'It doesn't matter,' she replied, 'you can borrow mine.'

Holly was tall with milky fresh skin, a ready smile and pigtails tied in red ribbons. Alison, by contrast, was short and plump with rosy cheeks and a high-pitched giggle. She was probably just as kind as Holly, but Holly had the same unruffled confidence as my sister Amy and I instantly wanted her to be my best friend.

The bathroom contained a row of individual showers, which was a relief. I hated anyone seeing my body. There were tiny scars on the backs of my legs. They would go away, young skin heals, but they were fixed in my head and in moments of panic the old itch of healing wounds still comes back to haunt me.

I cleaned my teeth before climbing into bed. I thought about Amy left behind with the Briggs children and wondered if she was going to miss me as much as I missed her. I pictured her that night at the table in the kitchen, the rhino-whip on the door, Mum gazing through her fringe, Billy's blank expression, Barbs eating as fast as she could, their faces blurring as I closed my eyes.

We started the day with breakfast at 7.45 and chapel at 8.30; so many prayers and hymns at a young age turns girls into either confirmed atheists or moral crusaders. The day ended with prep, a new word for homework, then free time before bed at 9.00. There was so much work and so many distractions, the days peeled from the calendar without my noticing. I joined the choir and took up cross-country. There was tennis, music, acting. I learned to sail and would sit at the lakeside with the other girls after tea in the afternoon to watch the boys rowing and racing kayaks.

I pursued Holly, but then so did most of the other girls. It is crucial at school to be a part of the group. Holly didn't try to belong to anything but was at the heart of everything. She was patient, but remained remote, and seemed to prefer being on her own, her head in a book. I wanted to be like that and copied Holly, reading her books so I could talk about them with her.

Every weekend, I went into the village and, using my pocket money, bought a comic, which the woman in the Post Office rolled into a tube for me to send to my sister. One long weekend break, Dad appeared with Amy and we drove to London, where we visited the zoo, Madame Tussauds, the Planetarium. I loved London. The city had a beat, a pull that would obstinately draw me back.

Suddenly it was Christmas and my worst enemy set about ruining everything.

Mum always liked me more when I wasn't at home and did, as she'd promised, write letters most weeks; I still have them. I wanted to do something nice for her. I had seen in the handicraft workshop at Chadleigh the jewellery boxes the boys had made for their mothers for Christmas presents. They were beautiful and looked easy to make. You just had to cut the six pieces of wood that made a box, stick them together and use a strip of gauze as a hinge for the top. The inside and the sides of the box were covered in velvet, hiding the joints and the glue, and seashells were used to decorate the top.

Amy and I were staying for a couple of days with Granny Wheeler. While we had been living with her we were in the way. Now she was on her own she missed us. In the garden shed, there were lots of old tools, including an electric saw. I found a suitable piece of wood, carefully marked out the measurements, and Amy watched as I set the saw in motion.

As I ran the wood towards the spinning blade, the teeth went faster and faster, pulling at my hand. I couldn't stop it. The saw went clean through the top of my thumb, leaving only the fingernail holding it on, and Amy pulled the plug from the wall as I screamed in agony. There was blood everywhere, over me, over Amy, and the kitchen floor as we ran back into the house.

'Hold it in place, Emily, just hold it!' Amy cried.

I wrapped my thumb in a tea towel. The pain was excruciating. My pulse was racing and I nearly fainted. Mum and Gran were out shopping with Auntie Doreen. Amy couldn't reach Dad on the phone and finally called Alan. He adored this sort of situation: he could save the day, as he had saved the lives of his sailors, and complain that I was a bloody nuisance at the same time. He raced over in the Jag and took me to hospital, where I needed about twenty stitches to put the top of my thumb back on again.

If I expected some sympathy from Mum, I didn't get it.

'This is the sort of thing that made us send you away to school in the first place,' she said.

'But, Mummy, I was making you a jewellery box.'

'Jewellery box. Are you stupid? You ruined Alan's day off.'

It set the tone for Christmas. I was back in that prison cell with the other three girls, no locker for my clothes, no place for the new books Dad had bought on our trip to London. One book Mum had said was too young for me but I cherished above all others was *Where the Wild Things Are*, an illustrated story by Maurice Sendak about a boy on his own who must face his fears. That boy was like me, my fears often in my head, the fear of fear, the fear of not being loved and, worse, of feeling unloved.

On Christmas Day we drove to Granny's house and unloaded bags of presents and crates of beer and wine. Mistletoe hung from the door to the dining room. Alan lifted Gran off the ground and planted big smacking kisses on her cheeks.

'My Gwen's a beauty and you know why, don't you?' he said. 'She takes after her mum.'

Granny wriggled and seemed pleased. She was only a couple of years older than Alan and enjoyed having this big male presence in the house. Doreen was there with her boyfriend, Phil, who worked in some office job with the council and looked like a petrified rabbit. He kept nodding at everything Alan said, drank every beer that was pushed in his hand, and agreed that

Liverpool needed a new manager and there had never been a better set of wheels than the Jaguar Mark 2.

There were ten of us squeezed around the table for lunch, Alan at the head in a Father Christmas hat. He was served first. He made sure Phil's glass was constantly refilled with sparkling white wine and told a joke about a missionary in Africa asking some cannibals what kind of beans they liked. I blurted out the answer.

'Human beans,' I said.

Everyone laughed and quickly stopped. Alan sat back in his chair as if he'd just been shot.

'Right little know-it-all, aren't we?'

'A girl told me at school.'

'She knows everything before we do, you know that?' He looked round at his audience. 'Smarter than us, see. We're just the workers paying out so that lot can tell us what to do.'

Everyone was silent. Phil looked nervous. Billy had his mouth hanging open and I don't think he had understood the joke anyway.

'It's only a joke, Alan,' Gran finally said.

'I know it is, darling, that's the thing, see, the joke's on us. The big nobs own everything and keep the working stiffs poor so they can keep it all for themselves.' He glanced at Phil. 'Am I right or am I right?'

'Dead right, mate.'

Alan leaned forward. 'Thing is, this ain't the thirties. I'll tell you this for nothing,' he said, raising his finger. 'Next thing you know, we're going to be out there rioting on the street, demanding our rights.' He pointed at me. 'You lot are on your way out.'

My armpits were wet. My sewn-up thumb started throbbing. Alan swigged his wine and refilled the glass. I knew he wanted to give me a thrashing but couldn't in front of everyone else. He glared at me like I was a murderer. Phil and Amy helped clear the table and Alan was still staring at me when Auntie Doreen appeared back in the dining room with brandy flames swirling about the Christmas pudding. She set it down in the centre of the table and blew out the blue flames.

'Everyone make a wish,' she said.

'I know what I wish for, a quiet bloody life,' Alan said, and it was supposed to be funny so everyone laughed.

Alan found in his pudding a lucky sixpence. He licked it clean and gave the coin to Annie. Phil kept drinking the white wine Alan kept pouring and threw up in the front garden before driving home. Alan fell asleep on the couch with Annie spread-eagled on top of him – she loved her dad – and Mum gave me the silent treatment as I helped Amy bring the dishes into the kitchen.

'That's everything, Mum,' I said when we'd finished.

The kitchen was empty at that moment and Mum slapped me across the face with the wet rubber gloves she was wearing. 'Don't talk to me. Bugger off,' she said, and I had never heard her use that word before.

Alan slept for an hour, then started drinking again. He played Father Christmas handing out presents, unmemorable things that would vanish into the general squalor, and I felt lucky to climb into my bunk that night with the cannibal joke forgotten and my legs unmarked by hand or whip.

★   ★   ★

Dad picked us up on Boxing Day and we went for a walk in the bluebell woods with Aunt Alice. We had to go slowly because Dad's leg was always worse in winter, not that it was cold. On the contrary, it was particularly mild and I missed the annual ritual of building a snowman in the back garden.

Aunt Alice prepared her famous split-pea soup with chunks of goose and boiled ham. While the soup was simmering, she put on a record and the music sent shivers up my spine. I turned up the volume. My heart was thumping. I was transfixed, my fingers literally tingling. Aunt Alice came up behind and put her arm around me. We both stood immobile until the music ended.

'Isn't it wonderful?' she said.

'I've never heard anything so beautiful in my whole life.'

'It's "Für Elise". Beethoven.'

My brow crinkled. ' "Für Elise"?'

'It just means "For Elise".'

The music came to an end. 'Can we play it again?'

'Of course,' Aunt Alice replied. 'It's what they call a baga-telle, a short piece for piano. Your Grandma used to play it all the time.'

I turned to look at her. 'Why don't you play?'

'I did take lessons. I was never very good,' she said. 'You have to find the things that you are good at and concentrate on them.'

'I'm not very good at anything.'

'That's not true. You will be, Emily. Something will come along; it always does.'

She kissed my cheeks. I wondered why Mum was never like that, why Aunt Alice loved me, and why my mother who had chosen me had now rejected me. Mum was becoming like Alan. She spoke like him now, chopping up her words, although she went back to her old accent when she was with people like the bursar at school. If life is a jigsaw puzzle, none of the pieces in my life fitted. Everything was contradictory and illogical. Amy looked like Mum, but had the same personality as Dad. I was more fiery, more needy, like her. Mum saw in Amy the qualities she believed she had, and saw in me the image behind the mirror, a much closer version of herself.

On Christmas Day my emotions had been kicked around like a ball and I had been in constant fear of a beating. Boxing Day was calm, normal, a step back into the past. I read up on the life of Beethoven in the *Encyclopaedia Britannica*. We watched *It's a Wonderful Life* with James Stewart on television. We ate goose-liver pâté on toast for tea and Dad gave Amy and me grown-up watches for Christmas.

CHAPTER 8

Love Letters

Dad drove me back to school. I had endured more than enjoyed the holidays. I was always on edge and the conflicted feeling I had at home stayed with me at school. I tried to join in, but never felt that I really belonged. Most of the girls had been skiing at Christmas. They lived in country houses and had photos of horses stuck inside their lockers.

On half-term breaks, girls took friends home for the weekend. I lay in my small bed at night trying to imagine taking Holly back to the Briggs house and didn't know whether to laugh or cry. The very notion was ridiculous. It made learning lists of French verbs seem equally ridiculous. You can't, as a child, see how your life is ever going to change in a way that such knowledge – that any knowledge – is going to be useful.

Once you get that feeling, study stops being a pleasure and becomes hard work. You fall behind. You get told off. You answer back. You become one thing when you could just have easily have become something else. At school, the children and staff were gentle and respectful. In Alan's house, there was always a feeling that violence was about to erupt – and it did on my first break at home.

Mum and Alan went out to the pub and I was introduced to a new game Barbs had invented. It was a version of chase where you had to move around the lounge without touching the ground, hopping and sliding from the chairs to the couch to the sideboard. If you were caught, you became 'it' and had to tag one of the others.

Patch stood in the centre of the room watching with glassy eyes as we chased over the split and punched furniture laughing and enjoying something we could all join in with. Then disaster struck. As I had known it would. We all scrambled onto the sideboard at the same time and the lamp fell off and smashed to pieces. We stared at the shards of blue and white china and were still blaming each other when we heard the key turning in the front door. Alan strode into the lounge with Mum in her mini-skirt behind him.

'Fuck me! Now what?'

Alan stared at the smashed lamp, then his eyes ran around the room, at Amy, Annie, Billie, Barbs, then me.

'I'll tell you something, girl, nothing like this happens when you're not here.'

'It wasn't me,' I said.

'Yes, it was.'

I looked back at Barbs. I couldn't believe my ears. 'You liar!' I cried.

'Yes, you did,' she spat.

'No, I did not.'

'Liar, liar, pants on fire—'

Alan clenched his big fists. 'Quiet!' he screamed, and looked at Billy. 'Well?'

Billy pointed at me.

'It was her,' he answered.

'We all did it,' Amy then said. 'It was an accident.'

Alan lifted a warning finger and stared at her.

'You, quiet,' he instructed, and looked back at me. 'It might just look like a cheap old piece of rubbish to you, girl, being all posh, but it was a priceless antique.'

'I didn't do it.'

'It belongs to my ex-wife, God bless her, and you've gone and broke it.'

'I didn't. We were playing chase and—'

'I will ask you a simple question, and I want the truth: did you break the lamp?'

'No.'

He stared at each of us, then again back at me.

'Did you break the lamp?'

I looked at Mum. 'Mum, I didn't do it,' I pleaded. 'We were playing and it just happened.'

Alan was shaking now. 'For the last time. Did you break the lamp?'

I glared back at him. 'For the last time, I didn't do it, and don't you dare hit me.'

He laughed. 'Oh, yeah! Why, what you going to do about it?'

'I'll hit you back.'

'You will, will you? Good for you. Come on then.'

'I don't want to.'

'Come on. You heard me. Get over here. Give it your best shot.'

'No, I don't want to.'

'You come here or I'll thrash you in a way you'll never forget, girl. You hear what I'm saying?'

He loomed over me. I gritted my teeth and swung my fists at his stomach and chest. He stood there, hands on hips, a grin on his face. 'Come on, girl, that's what I like to see. You go for it.'

It was useless. My fists were like soap bubbles bouncing off him. I kept up this charade until my arms hurt and my back was running wet with fear and panic. As I slumped back down to the couch, he grabbed me by the hair, wheeled me out to the kitchen and shut the door. The whip was hanging on the brass hook like something alive and waiting. He loved that whip. It was his prized possession.

'Please, please—'

'Break the old lady's stuff, will you?'

He pushed me across the table and held me down with one big hand.

'Please, please, don't. I didn't do it, honestly . . .'

As I kicked and wriggled, he pulled up my skirt and pulled down my knickers.

I sobbed. 'Please don't hurt me, Alan. Please.'

He was puffing for breath. I couldn't see his face. My head was lolling over the edge of the table and he was in no mood to listen as I begged him to stop. He drew back the whip and, lash after lash, as the leather bit into my flesh it felt as if I were being branded by a hot poker. The sheer agony drove the breath from my lungs. It was the sort of pain you can't imagine, and you can't imagine it is ever going to stop. It would just go on and on forever and ever.

I screamed loud enough for my mother to hear, but she didn't come into the kitchen to stop him. She didn't care. She admired Alan. They were soulmates. Bullies find the abused, and they find each other. They form gangs, paedophile rings, hiding their shame by sharing it, making it normal, passing on battered, frightened children to others for them to beat and rape and exploit.

The pain was indescribable, as was the humiliation of being beaten in this intimate way in this intimate place. I was coming up to twelve. I had grown aware those last few months of the faintest flush of my breasts emerging, my fizzing, changing hormones. I wasn't a little girl any more and what Alan was doing was degrading and vaguely sexual.

I don't know how they know, but sadists and torturers know when to stop. They feel it intuitively. I wasn't screaming now. My mother wasn't going to help me and, if the neighbours had heard, they weren't going to call the police. They were terrified of Alan, the same as everyone else. He pulled my knickers up over my scorching bottom and hung the whip back in its place behind the door.

'Now, you just be more careful with other people's things. You hear me?'

'Yes, Alan.'

'It's for your own good, I tell you.'

I had survived before and I would survive again. I was grow-ing psychologically adjusted to being abused. This is who I am, I thought. You just have to get used to it. The girls at boarding school were riding their horses during the half-term and I was being beaten with a whip. Alan was a class warrior. I was a class traitor. I was being punished for all the frustrations and disap-pointments of his own life. A vast wall topped with chips of broken glass runs through the class system in England and I was neither on one side nor the other. I was nowhere.

In three days, I went back to Chadleigh. I didn't want to go and didn't want to stay. I was in the way at home and felt like an outcast at school. When you feel that way, it becomes a self-fulfilling prophecy. You grow sullen, unfriendly, and others react in ways that accentuate your own view of your-self as an outcast. You have to love and respect yourself for others to love and respect you. When you have a low opin-ion of yourself, you're trapped in a vicious cycle you can't break.

Mum had relegated the job of driving me back to school to Dad and I sat on the leather seat for five hours with my bottom stinging. Dad gripped the steering wheel tightly and leaned forward, peering through his glasses as if the road ahead was littered with obstacles. The old Humber held lots of memories – it had a certain smell that reminded me of the past. We sang 'Barnacle Bill the Sailor' and 'On the Good Ship Lollipop'. Every mile that clicked by I considered telling him what Alan had done. But I didn't. I couldn't. I felt ashamed. I felt in some way that I was to blame, that I deserved to be beaten.

We crunched to a stop on the gravel drive. Dad gave me enough pocket money to last the rest of the term and I threw myself into his arms. He held me close in a way that didn't come easily for men of his generation. I was a needy child. He knew that. As I watched the car vanish through the gate, I had this sick feeling that I would never see him again, an anxiety that stayed with me, scratching at the back of my mind. It didn't come to pass, but Dad, against his will, would in the coming years be virtually excluded from my life.

I had been unable to tell Dad I had been whipped, and Mum didn't know Alan had pulled my knickers down to do so. She never even mentioned it. On the contrary, she had got back into the habit of slapping me across the side of the head every time I was within reach. Now she was doing it, Billy copied her, and when she saw him, they would exchange smiles as if it were a private joke. Billy was an idiot, fourteen now and filling out. His slaps were vicious, but I knew I'd get the blame and be called a 'rat' if I said anything.

Each day in that house I was a nervous wreck and each time we sat at the table to eat plates of bread and jam I kept silent. I didn't look at anyone. I tried to keep my expression neutral. Alan talked. Mum stroked the flags tattooed on his arm. His children gobbled down their food like victims of a famine. Annie had finally found a way to get some attention. She had learned a nursery rhyme and would say the first three lines for someone else to complete.

'Hickory, dickory, dock, The mouse ran up the clock. The clock struck one . . .'

Alan – 'And knocked his bloody head off.'

Billy – 'And knocked his bloody leg off.'

Alan – 'What's that? If that's funny, I'm a monkey's uncle.'

More laughter, and Annie starts again.

'Hickory, dickory, dock, The mouse ran up the clock. The clock struck one . . .'

Alan – 'And kicked him up the bum.'

Barbs – 'And spanked Emily's bum.'

'Hickory, dickory, dock.'

Peals of laughter.

'Nice one, Barbs,' Alan said, and looked at Billy. 'See, that's funny, what you said's not funny.'

Billy glared at me. Alan glanced at the whip and Mum grinned. He must have touched her legs under the table and she shivered like a snake. In her eyes, Alan could do no wrong. They had become co-dependent. She needed him to make her feel beautiful. He needed her to show the world he was special, potent, important. They lived in their own private universe and believed those things that were absent from their lives, the shabby house and poverty, the lack of direction, were due to some force beyond their control. For reasons that were mad, twisted and illogical, I had come to represent that force. I was the cuckoo in the nest, the intruder preventing their well-being and happiness.

Annie, with her new-found confidence, had taken *Where the Wild Things Are* and pulled out all the pages. I didn't even tell anyone.

I had books now to put on my shelf in the dorm. I unpacked my underwear and gym clothes. I put my suitcase in the cupboard and it was time for tea. In my school uniform I was identical to all the other girls. That made it easy to hide in plain sight. Luckily, my squint had grown so bad, no one caught my eye.

The following morning, Holly had just entered the bathroom when I came out of the shower. She noticed the stripes of red and blue bruises on my backside.

'Emily, what's happened?' she said, and rushed towards me.

I instantly covered up with the towel.

'Nothing,' I said.

'Your bottom's all red and bruised.'

'It's not . . .'

She held my elbows and spoke kindly, but forcefully.

'Emily, look at me. Tell me. What's happened?'

This moment of kindness was almost as painful as the beating and I burst into tears. I needed a good sob and cherished the touch of Holly's arms around me.

I sobbed and it all came gushing out like poison as Holly held me.

'Emily, Emily, slow down, I don't understand.'

She stared into my eyes.

'My stepfather beat me with a whip,' I said. 'A rhino-whip.'

'What? That can't be true.'

'It is true. He hit me with a whip.'

'But why?'

'His lamp broke, and it wasn't even me.'

'He hit you with a whip because a lamp got broken?'

I nodded.

'But that's not allowed, Emily. Adults can't do that sort of thing.'

I nodded again. 'He did though.'

She took a long breath and looked at me sternly. 'We have to call the police—'

'No, no, we can't do that—'

'Why not?'

'I did once. I went to the police station after fighting with Barbara, my stepsister, and the police blamed me.'

I cried again and she hugged me some more. I had wanted so much to be best friends with Holly Greenly and now there I was, in her arms, the centre of attention, happy for a moment.

'You can't let him do it again, Emily. It's not right. It's against the law,' she said.

'I know, but there's nothing I can do. Nothing.'

She dried my tears with her towel. Her eyes grew brighter and a smile lifted her pretty lips. 'You must forgive him, Emily. Tell God what happened in your prayers. He knows what to do,' she said. 'I'm going to pray for you.'

Her words made me feel better that instant, but the feeling didn't last. If anything, it made me feel more remote, more of an outsider. Holly had God on her side. He wasn't on mine.

Squinting, occasionally stammering, standing in the shadows with an unnamed part in *Romeo and Juliet*, seeing pity and kindness in Holly's eyes, I managed to get through the rest of the school year with only one incident that spilled into the summer holidays.

One day, I was passing the music room when I recognised my favourite piece of music. I entered, softly closed the door, and watched a boy playing the piano. His name was Richard Symons.

' "Für Elise",' I said.

'It's one of my favourites.'

'Mine, too.'

As I had become a girl no one noticed, Richard, with his red hair and freckles, was a boy none of the pretty girls ever talked to. It created the perfect ingredients for a friendship that consisted of discussing music, sharing books, talking about our lessons. It never went as far as kissing, although once or twice we did hold hands when no one was looking. Having a boyfriend was good for my self-esteem and, as a result, I started to do better in class, and even stopped squinting.

We were miserable when we broke up for the summer and immediately started writing daily letters that showed from the safety of distance all the love and passion we would never have dared express in person. We trawled through Shakespeare's *Romeo and Juliet*, the play I had performed in and studied that year, and quoted our favourite lines.

Richard wrote:

> O, she doth teach the torches to burn bright!
> It seems she hangs upon the cheek of night
> Like a rich jewel in an Ethiope's ear;
> Beauty too rich for use, for earth too dear!

And I responded:

> From forth the fatal loins of these two foes
> A pair of star-cross'd lovers take their life;
> Whose misadventured piteous overthrows
> Do with their death bury their parents' strife.

Richard had turned twelve in April; me in June. These were childish love letters, the result of two lonely children finding friendship with no deeper significance. Richard's mother didn't see it like that. His father was someone important in the government; she was a patron of the Royal Ballet. She didn't write to my parents. She complained to the school and went to the police.

The police in Kensington, where they lived, sent my letters to the local police and they, with orders from London, came knocking on the door at the Briggs' house. I was playing on the common with the others when Alan's voice boomed like a cannon over the long grass.

'Emily MacKenzie. Emily MacKenzie. Get in here.'

When I heard that voice, my first instinct was to run away. But I had done that before and it had got me nowhere. I scooted back to the house as fast as I could. Mum was still at work and Alan, home from the early shift at the brewery, stood in the lounge with the same sergeant I had met before.

The sergeant outlined the story. He made light of it. I'm sure he could see it for what it was. Not Alan. I could see his joy in the set of his jaw, the brightness in his eyes. It proved my story about him making me fight with his daughter had been a lie. He shook his head despairingly.

'I suppose that's what you fancy doing, is it? Burying your parents?' he asked. 'Star-crossed lovers with, what's that, fatal loins. Bloody disgusting.'

The sergeant folded his arms and glanced around at the punched walls and split furniture.

'Storm in a teacup, Mr Briggs. Waste of time if you ask me.'

'Hope you're right. You know how it is, from little acorns?'

Alan fancied himself as a wise man who could see into the future: Liverpool's going to lose two-nil at Tottenham, mark my words. Wind from the west, put on a vest. At Christmas he'd been right when he warned that the workers were going to take to the streets in mass protests. Five months later, in May 1968, the Paris Riots were the beginning of a rash of student and worker unrest across the world.

He nodded shrewdly as his eyes moved from the sergeant back to me.

'Go on like this, girl, and I'll tell you what, you'll end up a prostitute.'

I wasn't exactly sure what a prostitute was. As a child of twelve, his prediction was absurd, as was it coming to pass in a little over three years' time.

CHAPTER 9

Growing Pains

Holly had been right. I should have gone to the police when Alan Briggs beat me with his rhino-whip. But I was afraid Alan would deny it and Mum would explain in her nice voice that I had done it to myself – impossible, of course, but you don't think that way as a child.

I look back on that beating as the event that changed my life. Had I gone to the police and shown them the bruises, Alan would have gone to prison and everything would have been different. Our journey through life isn't a winding road but a maze, easy to get lost and, with one wrong turn, you might end up anywhere.

I never saw Holly Greenly again. Nor Richard Symons. His mother threatened to withdraw her son from the school if I was attending. Like Eve in the Garden of Eden, I was the temptress, 'sexually precocious', the root of the problem. As I would come to see, from love letters to rape, girls more often than not are made to shoulder the blame. Romeo had to be protected and I was found a place at an all-girls' boarding school.

After the police came to the house, Mum, in a rare act of self-assertion, insisted on dealing with me herself. She had tried the cane and the slipper, but preferred the intimacy of her bare hands. With Alan nodding his approval, she knocked me around the lounge, slap after slap, the sound a lot worse than the pain. You end up red, not bruised, and the sting goes away quite quickly. A whipping makes you feel less than human. A slapping is just demoralising. If you feel bad about yourself, you can even get to enjoy it.

I was grounded for a week, seven long days in that cramped bedroom with four bunks and the smell of pee. Annie, now seven, still wet the bed. My fault. Not only was I a bad influence, I had 'terrified the child' giving her that 'disgusting rubbish' *Where the Wild Things Are*.

After my week in solitary, I went on holiday with Dad, Aunt Alice and Amy. The contrast was like ice and fire, totally schizophrenic, from the farmyard odours and 'Jumpin' Jack Flash' by the Rolling Stones blaring from the stereo, to the Dickensian calm of Broadstairs, the little seaside town in south-east England, about the furthest distance you can travel from our home in the north-west.

This was to be our last holiday together and it stays in my memory like an old black and white film, more dreamlike than real. We stayed in a hotel facing Viking Bay with its long beach and the white chalk cliffs home to hundreds of seagulls. There was a Punch and Judy show every afternoon at four o'clock and the striped windbreakers protecting the deckchairs spread out across the sands like the flags of the United Nations. The old town meanders down to a promenade that leads along a jetty and up a steep hill to Bleak House, where Charles Dickens wrote his books. To add to the Dickensian flavour, there were people walking around in Victorian costumes. The sweetshop sold humbugs and treacle toffee, and we went every day to have scones with strawberry jam and cream at The Olde Tea Shoppe.

The purpose of this journey, apart from the holiday, was for me to visit my new school, which was situated four miles around the coast in Westgate. Like Chadleigh, the classrooms and offices were in an old manor house with gargoyles peeking over the roof. There were new dorms built in a square around a lawn, a new sports hall and an indoor swimming pool. The school 'felt' right. I felt lucky to have a place there and at twelve I didn't have the same fear I'd suffered when being sent away to board the first time.

I was introduced to Miss Jane Horsley, the principal, who was young and modern in a dark-red trouser suit and round John Lennon glasses.

'You will be very happy here, I assure you, Emily,' she said, her eyes magnified behind her glasses. 'We have outstanding hockey teams at all age levels and one of the highest Oxbridge intakes in the county. If you want to succeed, this is the place to be.'

Dad gripped my hand and I smiled back at Miss Horsley. 'Thank you, I do,' I said.

'Then I shall look forward to seeing you in September.'

In Miss Horsley's study with the sun shining on the

bookcases and Dad at my side, the bedlam of the Briggs house was forgotten. This was my chance. I saw myself in that same black and white movie, head down over a desk, a list of French verbs in front of me and a voice whispering you can do it, you can do it. This was my desire, my dream. But there was another voice, the realist in me saying no you can't, you won't, you'll mess up. You always do. When I was with Dad and Aunt Alice, I was like them, considerate, courteous, a bit old-fashioned. The moment I fell under Alan's shadow, I became boisterous like Barbs, sly like Billy, as gormless as bed-wetting Annie. I was still trying to please my mother and still being slapped around the head for no other reason than she enjoyed it.

Dad drove slowly back around the coast. He patted my leg. He was happy. That made me happy. I was a mirror reflecting the feelings of those around me without always being conscious of my own. The beatings eat away your confidence, reshape you. You become a follower. You do things others want to do in the hope they will like you and, if they don't, you become sulky and aggressive. You stop being you and become the person you imagine others want you to be.

It wasn't like that when I was with my dad. He had adopted me as a baby and I didn't have to do anything or be anything for him to love me. He was loyal, indulgent, supportive and, if he had one failing, it was failing to go back to court a fourth time and a fifth time, enough times to convince the authorities that Alan and my mother were not fit to have me in their care.

I didn't think that then; they are adult thoughts. I sat in the front seat wearing the smart skirt and white blouse appropriate for the interview. The sun was shining. I was alone with my dad and, for a moment, just a moment, I didn't have a care in the world.

The positive, optimistic me remained on display when I chatted about the school over tea with Aunt Alice and Amy. Dad was wreathed in smiles. The air on the south coast was good for him. He had bought a bathing costume and, after swimming every day, his limp had almost vanished.

'The school's wonderful,' he said. 'And don't forget, in three years, Amy, you'll be old enough to go, too.'

Amy threw up her arms. 'Whoopee!' she cried.

. Three years is such a short time when you say it quickly and such a long time as a child.

The holiday was such a success, Dad called Mum to ask if we could extend it and tour the south coast, then make our way back north going through Wales. Mum had the final say, but Alan 'knew a thing or two about bringing up children' and she told Dad she would have to discuss it with him first.

This would have been tricky for Alan. He was determined that I, the disruptive influence in the house, should receive the discipline I needed, but it was convenient for him to have me and Amy out of the way so my mum could concentrate on being a real mother to his three children. He must have come to his decision at the pub. Mum called the hotel late at night to say yes, and Dad gave us the good news at breakfast.

With the extended holiday and a week staying with Granny Wheeler, I spent little time roaming the common behind Barbs and arrived at boarding school with my confidence running high and landed immediately on my feet.

I was the new girl in a dorm with five other girls including Roberta Raimondo, Bobby for short. Half Italian with glossy dark hair and big green eyes, she was already thirteen with breasts peeping out of her blouse, the buttons of which were forever popping open and members of the staff were forever telling her to do up again. She had long legs in short skirts she made shorter by rolling up the waist, and the way she raised one shoulder as she talked was so cute everyone copied her. The other girls in the dorm adored her and, what was more important, as I was accepted by Bobby, I was accepted by them all.

In the classroom, Bobby gazed at the teacher as if, at that moment, there was no other person in the world and what they were saying was the most interesting thing she had ever heard. She was good at sports. I was a fast runner, and on the hockey field we became experts at stroking the ball back and forward between us. When we made a goal, she would throw her arms around me and kiss my cheeks, the first kisses that ever meant anything to me. When Bobby focused on you, you felt the full force of her personality and life just seemed to be so much brighter.

Saturdays we didn't have to wear our school uniforms. Dressed not unlike my mum, we took the bus to Margate, a seaside town like Broadstairs, but different, not Victorian, but brash with boutiques, coffee bars and a pier with a fortune teller and hippies handing out flowers and playing guitars.

In 1968, underwear was big news: while some women were burning their bras in protest over beauty pageants, the Wonderbra had come to a new shop in the high street and, with Bobby's encouragement, that's what I spent my pocket money on, not that there was anything very much to uplift. I learned how to put on make-up and eyeliner and hiked up my skirt to show my skinny legs. With Bobby's blouse open to the verge of criminal indecency, we made the local girls green with envy when we sat drinking frothy coffee and the boys couldn't take their eyes off our table.

The coffee bar had a chrome jukebox with flashing lights and rows of buttons like a spaceship. Boys in baggy bell-bottoms and tight T-shirts with silhouettes of Bob Dylan and Che Guevara would ask us what we wanted to hear and swivel their hips as they fed their money into the machine. Our favourite song was 'Born to Be Wild', by Steppenwolf, because it was just how we felt. We raved over Jimi Hendrix playing 'All Along the Watchtower', and, of course, the big hit that year, beloved by my stepfather, was 'Jumpin' Jack Flash'. With bra-burning and students marching against the Vietnam War, there was revolution in the air and the birth of what would become known as youth culture. We were too young to be a part of it, but just as a rising tide lifts all boats, we were carried along on the current.

While I was with Bobby and the others – Abigail, Sonia, Julie and Christine – we were secure in our private world which consisted of talking about pop music and film stars, rating the local boys, and spreading gossip about older girls in the school who had 'done it'.

In Italy, everyone was 'doing it' at thirteen – like Juliet, Bobby said, and I had a moment in the sunshine:

> From forth the fatal loins of these two foes
> A pair of star-cross'd lovers take their life;
> Whose misadventured piteous overthrows
> Do with their death bury their parents' strife.

Bobby clapped her long hands.

'That's brill, Emily, say it again,' she said, and I did.

I told them all about Richard Symons, the 'concert pianist', the 'genius', and I loved having those five pairs of schoolgirl eyes hanging on my every word.

'Did you do it?' Bobby asked in a whisper, teasing out a lie.

'Not quite,' I said. 'But he was a great kisser.'

I linked arms with Bobby as we strolled back up the high street. We passed the Clock Tower, then wandered along Margate's golden mile of amusements and pubs where men stood outside with pints of beer making rude comments that made us blush and giggle. We were young girls growing up with the usual impatience and ignorance. Being sexy was important and sex was like an unexplored land glimpsed after a long voyage from the rails of a ship, scary and seductive at the same time.

Apart from being at the heart of the gang, there was another plus. I was doing well in my schoolwork. I probably spent too much time worrying when my breasts were going to grow bigger and whether I should ask Dad to send me an extra £5 to buy the new miniskirt I couldn't live without, but I didn't find it hard to concentrate in class and my report at Christmas was lit by a couple of As.

I am not sure who made the arrangement, but when the term

ended Abigail's father picked us up from school. They were driving back to Banbury, in Oxfordshire. On the way he took me to Euston Station and put me on the train. I travelled by myself, a sign of my coming of age.

What I remember most about that Christmas was the day I got the train back to school, which I will come to.

Billy had shot up and had hair down to his shoulders. He found any excuse to 'accidentally' touch my chest, an improvement on being pushed and punched all the time. With me in minis and a flash of blue eye-shadow, not uncommon with girls of my age on the council estate, Barbs was conscious that I had entered a new phase and I got on her good side by letting her wear my new clothes and showing her how to put on make-up. Just as Amy had eased her way into the troop by taking care of Annie, I learned from my clever sister and took Barbs under my wing.

Mum didn't seem to notice that I had suddenly grown up from being a little girl, she was too busy still trying to be one herself. But Alan that Christmas began to look at me differently, in the way he and his mates looked at second-hand cars. One day when we were alone in the kitchen, he patted my bottom and said I was 'filling out nicely'. His lips turned in the sort of half-smile people have when they come to a decision and I couldn't work out if he was just being nice or if this friendly new face had some deeper meaning.

As for Dad, he was far less approving. Against his better judgement, I persuaded him to buy me several new Saturday outfits, velvet hot pants, a multicoloured Go-Go dress, heart sunglasses, a little hat like Donovan wore and a ban-the-bomb symbol on a chain. He looked at me and shook his head.

'You don't want to grow up too quickly, Emily,' he said.

'I'm not, Dad. I just want to fit in.'

It was what he wanted to hear. 'You're happy at school?' he asked, and I shook myself in bliss.

'I love it, Dad, it's really fab.'

He smiled. Everything was all right. I didn't squint any more. The comments on my school report were encouraging and revealed my 'artistic aptitude'. I was competent at drawing, I'd got an A in English literature, I was 'actively involved' in the theatre, and had shown 'moments of flair' on the hockey field.

The holiday passed with the customary bipolar Christmas Day with the Briggs brood and Boxing Day with the MacKenzies. Aunt Alice gave me a Parker pen and my own personalised stationery from Tiffany's, consisting of postcard-sized cards with my name on the top and envelopes with pale blue lining. She had stuck stamps on the envelopes.

'Now you have no excuse not to write home and tell us everything.'

I looked back at Aunt Alice with her neat grey hair in a pageboy and wished she was my mum.

On New Year's Eve, Mum and I worked together applying make-up to the tense little faces of Barbs, Amy and Annie. Modifying things from the piles of junk, I helped them dress in my own version of the Swinging Sixties and put on my wine-red hot pants for the first time. I pushed some cotton wool in my bra and wore a T-shirt, the Donovan hat and the ban-the-bomb badge on a long chain.

'Blimey, look at her – it's Twiggy with tits,' Alan said, and everyone fell about in hysterics.

I was the centre of attention, but in a good way. Mum blew out her cheeks and shook her head, but Alan was happy and that's all that mattered.

They quaffed their Liebfraumilch like it was water. Billy got a clump when he was caught drinking one of his dad's bottles of beer, and Alan, if our eyes met, had the same smirk he'd worn when he'd said I was filling out nicely. We watched *The White Heather Club* on BBC Scotland. The bells chimed at midnight and we joined hands to sing 'Auld Lang Syne'. There were lots of hugs and kisses and 1969 began with a moment of good cheer I was certain would last the whole year.

In my bunk before I went to sleep I made a New Year's resolution: Work hard and play hard.

Again, I was taking the train to Euston alone. Alan drove me to the station and heaved my cases into the carriage. 'What you got in there, gold bars?' he said, and he was being funny so I laughed.

Mum wasn't there, she was at work, which made it even more surprising when he tucked another £10 note in my blazer. He put his arms around me and held me really tight. He kissed my cheeks, so close to my lips I could taste his roll-ups. With his body pressing against me, it felt as if the shadow in my dreams had become real and solid; this huge man, so tall I wasn't sure if the lump I felt in my chest belonged to me or him.

'You work hard, girl, you'll do all right.'

'Thanks, Alan, thanks for the lift.'

'You're welcome, darling. Do anything for you, I would.'

The whistle blew. He ran his hand over my hair and stepped off the train as it was about to pull away. I waved from the window, then sat with a book, not that I could concentrate. I was confused. Why did Alan like me all of a sudden? He'd given me £10. *You're welcome, darling.* He'd kissed me, and he'd never done that before. I was aware that it was something to do with me growing up and decided that being an adult was going to be so much better than being a child. I was nearly thirteen, a teenager, and couldn't wait for my birthday.

CHAPTER 10

Alan's Last Prediction

I had to change trains to get to Banbury, where I spent the night with Abigail's family and her dad drove us to school next day. We tried on each other's clothes as we settled back into the dorm and were amazed that we both had the same wine-red hot pants. Julie, Christine and Sonia arrived one after the other. By lights out, there was still no sign of Bobby and that night the empty place in the dorm was like a void sucking out our sense of well-being.

We trailed from class to class feeling gloomy. Miss Horsley, the head, told us she had been unable to reach Bobby's family and we started to believe she had been kidnapped by the Mafia – it was the sort of thing that happened in Italy all the time – or she had been sold to a harem as a slave girl. We had vivid imaginations and suspected an evil plot.

That first Saturday when we sat in the coffee bar in our Christmas clothes, it was practically empty and none of the boys asked us what music we wanted on the jukebox. Margate in winter was like a town after the plague. Shops were boarded up, the sea roared as it lunged at the beach and the survivors walked bent over against the force of the wind. Nobody wolf-whistled and we got the bus home in the rain.

Bobby appeared a week later with her green eyes bright as jewels and that air people have after training hard for a race and finally breaking the winning tape. She was more self-assured, if that were possible. There had been a family crisis, she told the school, but she told us, whispering furiously, that she had fallen in love with a boy named Alberto and had fixed it so that she could stay in Italy to be with him until he went back to school.

We had to wait for lights out to hear the full story. Bobby had gone with her family on New Year's Eve to stay at a villa in Lucca belonging to the Battelli family. She had danced all night with Alberto, who was fifteen 'with big watery dark eyes and the most kissable lips in the world'. He was skinny and hand-some with masses of jet-black hair and looked like Keith Richards. The villa had 'hundreds' of bedrooms and she was tucked up in bed 'after an entire bottle of Prosecco' when she heard the sound of the door opening.

'It was him?' Sonia murmured.

She nodded. 'His hair was all messy and he looked just so beautiful,' she said, and sighed at the memory.

'Then what happened?'

Bobby's eyes had grown misty. We gripped our hands and held our breath.

'He said, in a real soft voice, we can't let this moment pass . . .'

'Oh my God!'

'What did you do?'

'I just, like, stared into his eyes and . . . pulled back the covers.'

The blood drained from my veins. My heart was crashing away like the waves on the beach. I held myself and gasped, but Christine was practical, like my sister, and broke the spell.

'Did he turn the lights on?' she asked.

'No.' Bobby shook her head. 'We had the light of the moon.'

'That's so romantic,' I said.

'It was, Emmy. It was absolutely fab.'

'Did you do it?' Christine now asked, and I was glad she did.

Bobby looked at us each in turn. 'There's more than one way to, you know, to do it,' she replied.

I wasn't entirely sure what she meant and none of us wanted to ask. Bobby knitted her fingers together and we pulled closer around her small bed.

'I thought it was a good idea to save it, you know, just in case,' she explained. 'And Alberto was, like, really cool.'

Christine continued to look puzzled. 'What do you mean?' she asked, and Bobby shrugged and looked serious.

'Well, you can't just lead someone on and stop – it's not fair.'

'You just kissed?' asked Sonya.

'Nooo. We didn't just kiss.' Bobby took another long breath and her eyes grew big. 'We did a *soixante-neuf*.'

'*Soixante-neuf*?'

'Sixty-nine,' I said, proud of my French.

'But . . . what's it mean?' Christine asked, her brow crinkling.

Bobby looked coy now and gave a little shrug. She then made shapes with her hands to demonstrate. 'It's when he kisses you down there, and you kiss him, down there.'

It took a few moments to work this out.

'Just kissing?'

'Well, at first,' Bobby said. 'But you sort of get carried away. He put his tongue inside me and I put his *pene* in my mouth.'

We all blushed and shook and felt a mixture of envy and repulsion. The very idea of touching a man or a man touching me in that way seemed silly and unnatural. I had watched dogs on the common doing it. We knew where babies came from and how they were made, but it was theoretical and the very idea that sex included the act of *soixante-neuf* seemed bizarre.

'What's it like?' Sonia finally asked.

'It's . . . dreamy. It's fabulous. You want it to go on forever and ever and ever.'

The dorm warden gave three sharp knocks on the door.

'That's enough for the night!' she called, and we scurried back to our own beds.

'Nighty night.'

'Nighty night.'

'*Buonanotte.*'

I pulled the blanket up tight beneath my chin. I was confused by what Bobby had told us and realised now she was back just how much I had missed her. Next time we went to Margate she would be there and I made a bet with myself that it wouldn't be raining – which it wasn't. It was one of those clear winter days, the sky going on forever. We walked along the hard sand where the tide had gone out and watched the seagulls digging for worms and crabs.

Bobby talked about Alberto. His father wanted him to go to a military academy, he wanted to be an actor and was going to run away to join a commune in India if he didn't get his own way. It was all so exciting and wonderful. There was a great big marvellous world out there and Bobby was the shining glass through which I viewed it that bright January day.

It was that same day when we were struck by the amazing coincidence that it was 1969 – the year of *soixante-neuf*. We started to draw the number 69 endlessly in our notebooks, on the mist coating the windows, and once we made a giant 69 sandcastle on the beach. I loved the fact that 6 and 9 are the same shape, they slot into each other and become each other's opposite when they are upside down – the perfect symbol for the changes we were going through in a world similarly changing. During French lessons, we contrived to use the number *soixante-neuf* whenever we could, then turn to each other with furtive smiles. We all pledged to try a 69er with our boyfriends not, with the exception of Bobby, that any of us actually had a boyfriend. It didn't matter. We were the 69ers, united we stand, friends forever.

We were members of the drama club and were all cast in *Androcles and the Lion* by George Bernard Shaw. In Shakespeare's time, female roles were taken by men – in our school, the male roles were performed by girls – the lead roles like Androcles and Lavinia played by sixth formers who got into trouble for showing too much passion in their romantic scene. Bobby and I were cast as gladiators.

At the dress rehearsal, wearing matching make-up and costumes, Bobby's mouth fell open in that way she had of showing dizzying surprise.

'Emily, we're twins.'

We turned to the mirror. We were dressed in togas, strappy sandals and breastplates made of papier mâché. My hair had grown long, nut brown, the same as Bobby's. She was taller than me and our eyes were different, hers were green, really striking, mine were big and brown, but they looked the same in the bright lights of the changing room.

I stared at our reflection, two young girls, skinny and cute. I so much wanted to be like her. But Bobby was more than pretty, she had presence; she turned heads wherever she went and came from a world so different from my own, different from most of the girls. Abigail's dad had some position with British Rail – 'I run the trains, I don't go on them,' he once said. Christine's dad was a dentist, and Sonia's was a high-ranking policeman. Bobby's parents weren't anything, they were just rich, and that meant she had everything she wanted except they were not always there for her.

At the end of term we performed *Androcles and the Lion* – 'Shavian drama adroitly interpreted' said the local paper, and we all went home for Easter – except Bobby was left behind. She had been exchanging love letters with Alberto since Christmas and was dying to go back to Italy to see him. But her parents were on safari 'killing innocent animals' and she had to stay with her surrogate family in Broadstairs.

I was still in the dorm when we were told Abigail's father had arrived to pick us up. Abigail went running out and I gave Bobby a hug.

'I'm going to miss you, Emmy,' she said.

'I wish you could come with me.'

She gave a little shrug.

'It's OK, we'll be friends for the rest of our lives,' she said, and I don't recall ever feeling so happy as I did that second.

I felt confident arriving back at the Briggs house that the customary slappings and beatings had come to an end, which turned out to be correct. I roamed around the common with Patch and the girls, stayed out of Mum's way, and was relieved that Billy had a holiday job clearing out an old warehouse at the brewery.

Mum was in her mid-thirties but was still girlish in her short skirts. Alan was cheery and one early evening when he had to drop off some records at a mate's house across town, he asked me if I wanted to go with him for a ride. I actually didn't but grinned eagerly and ran out to the car like the chosen one.

He drove with his right hand loose on the steering wheel and his left arm along the back of my seat.

'So, how's school going then, darling?'

'It's great. I really like it.'

'You're doing all right. I'll tell you, you're right grown up now.'

'Thank you.'

'Never used to do a damned thing you were told. You remember that?'

It wasn't always easy to work out whether Alan was asking a question or making a statement that sounded like a question.

'I suppose,' I replied.

'That's all changed, though, innit? When you're told to do something, you know it's for your own good.'

I nodded.

'Am I right, or am I right?'

'You're right,' I replied, and we laughed.

He dropped off the records. I stayed in the car. His mate invited him in, but I saw him shake his head and he bowled back down the garden path like a cowboy in his jeans and denim shirt. The colour was bleaching from his hair, but it was still thick and he wore it combed back in two waves that bounced as he was walking. He started the Jag and turned with a grin.

'This is nice, innit, just the two of us?'

He drove back a different way and stopped in a lay-by under trees on the far side of the common. I thought to myself, why are we stopping? But I sort of knew why. Alan didn't say anything. The silence hung in the air. My heart was pounding. He rolled a cigarette from his tin of Old Holborn, but didn't light it. He put it on the ledge under the clock on the dashboard, then lowered and pushed back his seat.

'I'll tell you something, darling, you're growing into a right little cracker, you know that?'

I had moved as far away towards the door as I could. I hadn't thought about it or planned it. It just happened. I had a hollow feeling in my tummy. I tried to keep my features neutral and behaved as if stopping here in the twilight was normal.

'You're not nervous are you, darling?'

'No,' I replied, but I was. My mouth was dry and I was biting my lips.

Alan was stroking himself through his jeans.

'We ought to get to know each other a bit better – you being away at that posh school all the time – you know what I mean?'

I nodded again. He grinned.

'Come here, come on. Come here. Give us your hand. I won't bite.'

I gasped for air. I was terrified.

It was all so quick.

He took my hand and guided it over the lump growing big in his trousers.

'That's it. That's nice. Very nice. You're a good girl.'

I was a child still with childish thoughts. I could recall playing with dolls in the bedroom with Amy and Annie. I knew this was wrong and I knew, too, there was no way to stop it. I was petrified of Alan. I always had been. You had to do whatever he wanted you to do and I thought, even then, that there was some grotesque inevitability that I should be there in my grown-up clothes doing this grown-up thing.

He unbuckled his leather belt, lowered his zip and lifted himself up so he could lower his jeans and underpants. 'There, that's better, more room,' he said. He took my hand and wrapped my fingers around his penis. 'Go on, that's my girl, up and down, just slowly. Come on, on your own.'

It was horrid. It was like something alive in my hand, sweaty and sticky, like the handle of the rhino-whip. He started puffing and panting.

'Yes, nice. Very nice.'

He reached over to drag me closer and pushed my head down. I remembered what Bobby had told us that night in the dorm. I knew what Alan wanted me to do. He wanted me to suck it. But I couldn't. I gagged just at the thought of it. I tasted bile in my throat and pulled away.

'Come on, girl, you've got plenty of mouth on you.'

'I can't. I don't want to.'

'It's all right, darling. It's perfectly natural. It's what girls do when they're all grown up.'

'I'm not grown up—'

'Come on, do it. Put it in your mouth,' he said in a harsher voice.

I shook my head. Tears were running down my cheeks.

'I don't want to.'

There was a pause, a long frozen moment. He was thinking, calculating. I could almost hear the cogs and wheels of his mind clicking and spinning.

'All right, then. You just carry on. You're doing all right, darling.'

I'd moved away. He took my hand again. I held on tight like I was holding a hockey stick and continued jerking the loose skin up and down the length of his penis. He started sighing and gasping again.

'Nice. Very nice. Come on, quicker, girl, quicker.'

I went faster. It was like pumping up the tyre on a bicycle. He let out a terrible groan like he was dying, then exploded in a jet of thick creamy guck that covered my hand and spurted over his stomach, pearly white in the dim glow of the lights streaking by on the main road.

'Oh, fuck, yeah. That's nice. Lovely. You're a right little smasher, I'll tell you that for nothing.'

He sat there for a moment, playing with himself, then wiped away the mess with a cloth he used to clean the inside of the windscreen. After pulling up his jeans, he put the seat upright, opened the window and lit his roll-up. He took a long drag and the way he blew the smoke from his nose in two curling tusks reminded me of the mammoth I'd seen with dad and Amy at the Natural History Museum in London. He stroked the back of my hair.

'Let me ask you something – that wasn't so bad, was it?'

I shook my head. 'No.'

'You're growing up and it's nice, you know, with people you like. You know what I mean?'

'Yes,' I said.

'I like you, darling. You're a good girl. You're going to do all right.'

He took another drag on his cigarette, started the car, then placed his huge hand on my leg.

'Not a word,' he said. 'Not to your mother, not to anyone. This is just between us. Our secret. You understand?'

I nodded my head.

'Let me hear you say it.'

'It's just between us. It's a secret.'

'That's my girl. You all right? First time, it was quite nice, ay?'

I nodded again. I'd agreed. It was my 'first time' and it was 'quite nice'. This was our private, secret thing. I wasn't a victim. We were co-conspirators. He slid the car into gear, pulled away and drove slowly home with a big grin on his face.

Two days before I went back to school was one of those frequent occasions when there was no food in the house. I was watching TV in the lounge and heard Mum and Alan in the hall.

'You got any change, Gwenny? I'll pop out and get some fish and chips.'

I heard the clasp snap on Mum's bag, then Alan poked his head around the door. He pointed his finger at me like a gun.

'Tell you what, I'm going to go and hold up the chippie. I need a lookout,' he said.

I didn't understand for a moment.

'Come on then, get cracking. You know what they say, chips wait for no man.'

Sweat prickled in my armpits. 'I'm watching something,' I replied, and Mum squeezed in beside him.

'Why don't you just do as you're sodding well told?' she yelled.

'Leave it out, Gwen, you're making my bloody ear ache,' Alan said, and smiled at me. 'Come on, you can keep an eye on the car.'

I looked into Alan's eyes and what I saw were two black holes like empty space sucking me in. I was trapped. I couldn't say no. I knew what was going to happen, like you know when you're reading a book that the little girl who gets stuck up the chimney will be rescued by her daddy. You know, but you keep reading because you are mesmerised by the story and half hope there will be a twist, a surprise ending.

'Come on, then.'

I followed him out. Alan drove as fast as he could. He raced into the fish and chip shop, barged in the queue and came out with a parcel wrapped in newspaper that he put on the floor behind the seats. He stopped in the same lay-by. The smell of fat and vinegar made my stomach churn. I felt small in the big

Emily MacKenzie

leather seat with my short skirt and love beads around my neck. The car lights swished by and, in under a minute, his trousers were down and his penis was in my hand.

'Very nice. You know something, you're getting good at this.'

Having forced me into a sex act with him once, I had known by his little winks and nods in the days that followed that Alan couldn't wait to do it again. He couldn't stop himself. I was completely helpless, totally vulnerable, a white wall screaming out to be scribbled on and vandalised. There is something in men, some men, that makes them want to obliterate and profane anything that's pure and weak. Rapists will piss on their victims. It makes men without power feel powerful and potent. I was fresh prey. Alan was the king of the jungle claiming what was his. He provided the roof over my head. He knew how to bring up children. I owed him. He wanted this. He deserved it. It was his God-given right and, more than that, he had made himself believe that it was something I wanted as well.

First time, it was quite nice, ay?

That's what he'd asked and I'd nodded my head, become complicit. We were in it together. That's what he wanted to believe and I let him believe that although the experience for me had been terrifying, degrading and repulsive. Later that night, I had thought about going to the railway station and throwing myself under a train.

This time, the second time, I knew what was going to happen. That made it no less degrading and repulsive, an assault on my mind more than my body. But it was less terrifying. I didn't want to kill myself. I wanted to be back at school with

Bobby and the girls. What had been shameful and abnormal was anticipated and would, if it continued, become normal. Knowing what was going to happen, I shut down my feelings. I closed my eyes. Like an automaton, I slowly ran the loose flesh up and down the length of his hard cock and thought: thank God it's me in the car not Amy.

Sex with a child is addictive. We didn't know the word grooming then, but that's what Alan was doing. He wanted me to believe that this was acceptable, that I was a 'good girl' doing the right thing because that's what my stepdad expected of me and, like a new game with new rules, I would come to enjoy it as much as he did. This attitude is perverse, distorted in the mind of the abuser, and confusing in the mind of the child. It's like being in a foreign land where you don't know a word of the language and there is no one to turn to for help. I knew it was wrong, and I knew that if Mum ever found out, she would blame me. I was trapped in that car, completely alone, with Alan's cock in my hand and there was nothing I could do except jerk at that hard lump of flesh and remember that this wasn't as painful as having a rhino-whip across my back.

The lights from a lorry lit the inside of the car. His face looked twisted as I glanced up. He didn't say anything. He cupped the back of my head with his big palm and pulled me down into his lap.

'Down you go, girl, come on. You can do it.'

I wriggled, but he held the back of my hair tight the way Mum used to do when she ran me up the stairs slapping the backs of my legs. I felt his cock brush over my lips as he guided

135

it towards my mouth and my mouth opened as if I had lost the will to stop it. I sucked the top like it was a lolly and he sighed.

'That's my girl, that's lovely, really nice.'

He still had my hair scrunched up in his hand and eased my head up and down, up and down.

'That's lovely. You're a right little cracker.'

He held me in the same position as he started to masturbate himself. He was panting for breath and then the sticky stuff splashed over my face. It was warm and smelly. He sighed and continued to jerk up and down, pumping out the last dregs. As I sat back up, he rubbed the stuff over my lips and teeth.

'There, get a taste of that.'

I cringed and screwed up my face. It was like bitter yoghurt with salt.

'See, it's nice, darling?'

I shook my head. 'I don't like it.'

He leaned closer.

'You'll get used it. You're going to be swallowing down plenty more.' He stared into my eyes. 'Take my word for it. Don't ask me how I know, but I know.'

CHAPTER II

Friends Forever

Bobby was so miserable because she had been unable to go back to Italy to see Alberto, I concentrated on her problems without dwelling on my own. Thinking about what had happened with Alan made me feel sick. So, I didn't think about it.

I was happy to be back at school and a smile spread over my lips that night as Christine started our customary ritual.

'Nighty night.'

'Nighty night.'

'*Buonanotte.*'

I slept without dreaming of shadows and wrote the following day to Aunt Alice on one of my cards to tell her there was an 'army' of bluebells under the trees and it reminded me of our walks in the bluebell woods. The spring tides battered the pier, but the days were warmer, and I felt as free as the clouds as I raced in my blue skirt and plimsolls across the hockey field brushing the ball back and forth with Bobby.

On Saturday, we got the bus to Margate and found a vacant booth in the coffee bar. The benches were red vinyl and made squelching noises as we squeezed in with frothy coffee in tall glasses with long spoons. We were dressed to kill with little hats and love beads. The jukebox played the latest releases – 'Get Back', by the Beatles; 'In the Year 2525', by Zager and Evans; 'Let the Sunshine In', from the musical *Hair*, and we were all jealous because Julie had seen the show with her parents.

A boy of about sixteen strolled up looking cool in an Afghan coat and hair down to his shoulders. He leaned over Bobby.

'Hey, man, don't you think this place is a drag?' he said.

She glanced back with that little shrug she had. 'Not particularly,' she replied.

'You wanna go down the pier or something? You know, like, get out of this place?' he added, and it sounded like a line from a song.

We were all holding our breath, wishing he'd asked us. Bobby had been smiling, but now her green eyes grew misty with tears.

'I've got a boyfriend and he'd go crazy if I did,' she said, and the boy wandered back to his mates looking pleased with himself.

It was just a little exchange, it had happened before, but this time it had a profound effect. Bobby wasn't putting it on. The tears were real.

'I've got to see Alberto,' she moaned. 'I really, really miss him.'

'What can we do?' I asked her.

'You've got to help me.'

'But how?'

She wiped the tears from her eyes with her fingers. She leaned forward and I wasn't sure then, and would never know, if what she was about to say just sprang into her head or whether she'd been planning it for a long time.

She lowered her voice to a whisper. 'I'm going to burn the school down,' she said. 'Then they'll have to send me home.'

At first I thought she was joking. I looked at the others. They were all nodding in agreement and I did the same.

She looked round the table. 'Are you going to help me?'

Christine shook her head. 'What if someone gets hurt?'

'We'll do it when the school's empty.'

'Yes, but . . .'

Bobby waved away the interruption. 'It's not only for me. It's . . . it's bigger than that. It's about time we made our voices heard.'

'But why?' Christine asked, and Bobby pointed at the ban-the-bomb badge I was wearing.

'There's going to be a war. Not like before. With atom bombs. We all know that. Tomorrow we might get blown to bits by the Russians. We've got to live for today.'

'Far out,' I said, and Bobby grinned.

'Learn from yesterday. Live for today. Hope for tomorrow,' Sonia quoted; she was the clever one. 'That's what Albert Einstein said.'

We stared back at her as if Einstein had given his approval. We joined hands across the table. All for one, one for all. We made pledges and giggled when Bobby grew a foam moustache drinking down her coffee in one long gulp.

'Friends forever,' she said, and she was looking at me.

'Friends forever,' we chorused, and I took another turn in the labyrinth.

Burning down the school would make a statement. It was rebellious, daring, true to the age. It was what the singers in 1969 were singing about. It would free Bobby from boarding school to be with Alberto. That's all that mattered. At twelve, you don't understand irony. It never occurred to me that if there was no school, I wouldn't be liberated, I'd be imprisoned in the front seats of Alan's Jaguar with my mouth open.

I don't think Bobby had a plan of action. If she did, she didn't share it, but now the idea was in the air it became linked in our minds with the Vietnam War, student demonstrations, a world in crisis. The idea never had any substance or preparation, but started to sprout wings of its own accord. It became real. It's like advertising. If you hear enough times something is good for you, you start to believe it is good for you. Groomers use the same technique.

The weather through the spring was running hot and cold, windy one day, still the next, as if it wasn't sure what it was doing. Julie turned thirteen on May Day and the following Saturday the senior hockey team was playing a cup final match at our school against the sturdy cup holders from the Medway. All the corridors got a fresh coat of polish. The ground staff put up marquees and erected benches for visiting parents and dignitaries. The trees rustled and the gargoyles on the roof stared down with knowing little faces as we filed past the main building into the hall for breakfast.

It was soon going to be half-term. During grace, I decided in that quiet moment to write a note to Dad to ask if he could take Amy and me away for a few days. I couldn't tell Mum what Alan had done, but if I told Dad and Aunt Alice, they'd believe me. They'd be able to do something to stop him doing it again.

Amen, I said, and shook my head to shake Alan out of my mind. I ate Weetabix, toast and scrambled egg. My throat was dry and I drank three big glasses of orange juice.

As we left the dining hall, caterers from Broadstairs arrived in two green and yellow vans. They laid out prawn vol-au-vents and sandwiches on long tables and pessimists pointed at the clouds saying it was going to rain, which it didn't. The rival team appeared in a coach and the staff told us to give them a cheer, which we did half-heartedly. Everything happened quickly. It was like a stone had been dropped from a bridge and gravity was pulling it down. The sun was suddenly hot, baking my skull, and I never did get round to writing that card.

By two o'clock, all the girls were in uniform, Che Guevara miniatures in our dark berets. I had that feeling I'm sure suicide bombers must have, nervous, exhilarated, unsure if I were doing the right thing, but the clock was ticking and there was no way to stop it. It was more important to be a part of the group than to stand alone and voice some last-minute doubt. I'm sure the others were thinking the same as me. I recall even now their tense faces, their tics and glazed stares, the uneasy looks if our eyes met for a moment. We were burning down the school because we were friends and knew subconsciously it would end the friendship. We remained at the back of the crowd until the whistle announced the commencement of play.

'Time to go.'

Bobby tapped our shoulders, and we slipped off one at a time to the car park.

Two things that were different in 1969 was that most people carried a spare can of petrol in their boot, and, as there were no electronic gadgets to secure the doors, few drivers in the safety of our school had bothered to lock their cars. We popped open the boots and it wasn't long before we had six cans of petrol. I heard a cheer.

'Someone's scored a goal,' I said, and Bobby grinned as she threw up her shoulders.

'Who cares?'

I grinned back and we sneaked around the main building to the side door. We followed in a line. I don't know if the others were afraid. I'm sure they were. I felt a sort of relief. I was hitting back at parents and oppressors; the fat police sergeant who refused to believe me when I told him Alan had made me fight with Barbs, my mum for hitting me, Alan for all the things Alan had done, thrash me with his whip, stick his penis in my mouth. We were swept along that day by the sheer force of Bobby's personality and the momentum of what we were doing.

We followed her down the wooden steps to the basement. After she'd tipped petrol all around the boiler, there was a moment's pause. We were connected like links in a chain. We were the 69ers. All for one, one for all. We were suddenly in a panic and Bobby pressed on before the pause extended and we stopped altogether.

Christine was the sensible one. Her hands were shaking. Bobby grabbed her can and emptied the contents on the floor below the electricity and gas meters.

'Come on,' she said, 'empty out the petrol as we go.'

That's what we did. We left a trail up the steps from the base-ment and along the corridor to the back of the building. Bobby had some matches and we watched with big eyes as she stood at the door.

There are few moments in life when our destiny changes course, when fate is truly in our own hands and the decision we make will change everything. I believe I have been in that posi-tion more often than most people and every time I have made the wrong decision.

Bobby lit a match and I was tempted to blow it out as it flared.

I didn't. I watched as she threw the lighted match into the stream of petrol. It ignited immediately and flames raced like a blue snake back along the corridor and down into the basement.

There was an enormous explosion. Red and green flames leapt into the sky and there was a volley of smaller blasts like fireworks going off. We raced back to the top field and mingled with the rest of the girls. I watched Miss Horsley set off, sprint-ing in her heels, and I thought she was really brave as she ran through the smoke and disappeared through the main doors into the flaming building. By the time she came out, the east wing was almost destroyed and I could hear bells and sirens wailing in the distance.

In no time, the fire brigade, police and ambulance were screaming up the drive. Hoses were soon aiming arcs of water into the flames. The hockey match had been abandoned and the staff ushered the girls into the new sports hall.

It took Jane Horsley about ten minutes to find the culprits. She could smell the petrol that had splashed on our shoes and socks. She found Abigail first and guessed that all the girls from our dorm were responsible. She called out our names, and we stepped forward, ashamed now, the rebellion over before the flames were quelled.

Our families were called and, to allow them time to all get down to East Kent, they set up a meeting for four o'clock the following day.

We were interviewed individually by the police. I told the truth about what we had done and why. I am sure the others did the same. We were confined to our dorm, our last night together. It was my time to start the ritual.

'Nighty night.'

'Nighty night.'

'*Arrivederci,*' Bobby called, and I didn't know what it meant.

During the day we watched parents arrive to take their daughters home. It was almost half-term, and they would have an extra few days' holiday. The old mansion house that had stood on the grounds in Westgate since 1830 was half-destroyed. I have no idea if they rebuilt it, keeping the past alive, the English way, or if it was pulled down to build something new to match the sports hall and swimming pool.

We were interviewed again by the police, two detectives without uniforms this time, and I told them exactly the same story.

'You did it so your friend could go back to Italy to be with her boyfriend?' the older one asked.

I nodded and said yes.

'Bit of a stupid thing to do, wasn't it?'

'Yes, it was. I wish we hadn't done it.'

'No good wishing away the past, is it?' he said, and he sounded a bit like Alan.

I left the room and it was Abigail's turn.

The six of us were kept together on a table away from the other pupils for breakfast and lunch. We didn't say very much to each other. There was nothing to say. The full force of our stupidity had come down on us like a fall of snow. Our uniforms were confiscated because we had shamed them and, after packing our cases, we put on our Saturday clothes. By the middle of the afternoon, our parents had arrived and we were taken to the sports hall where tables had been set up next to the changing rooms.

We sat on a row of six chairs by the door, little girls dressed as adults. The police mingled with our parents at the opposite end of the hall. Alan wore his funeral suit and Mum was in her office clothes, but you could tell, even from the distance, they weren't like the other parents, men with military short backs and sides, their wives in spring dresses. Sonia's dad was an Assistant Chief Constable. He had come in his uniform with two rows of medal ribbons on his chest and a peaked hat that he held tightly under his arm. He shook hands with the local police chief. They drank tea and ate biscuits.

Bobby's parents had been unable to come to England in time, but a man and a woman from the Italian Embassy appeared and what I remember was the way the woman raised one shoulder as she spoke, just like Bobby. The man was immaculate, like a film star, and I saw Mum laughing when he talked to her.

There was a quiet moment. Chairs scraped on the wooden floor. Miss Horsley came forward and made an announcement, her blue eyes intense through her round glasses. She told us the school didn't want to make the scandal any worse than it already was and had decided not to press charges. The police, in turn, had come to the same decision.

'I am sure you are aware of the gravity of what you have done,' she said, and we stared down at our shoes. 'And I can assure you of this, you are extremely lucky not to be facing the juvenile court and a spell in reform school.'

We were lucky. We knew that. Although there would come a time when I would look back and question what part luck had really played.

Bobby was the first to leave. She waved over her shoulder and I never saw her again. Sonia left, white as a sheet, her hand held by her father, her mother trotting along behind them. Julie was next, Christine, Abigail with her mum and dad, who glanced back at me and shook their heads. I watched them climb into their nice cars and pull out of the car park. The police left. Alan and Mum sat hunched over a table and I could see Alan making his points, waving a finger. I sat frozen to the chair in my black and white skirt and white top. Did they think I was the ringleader? Had my friends all ganged up on me?

Finally, Alan and Mum stood and shook hands with Miss Horsley. They made their way towards me. I was sitting close to the door. I stood to leave with them.

'Not you,' Mum said, and held up the palm of her hand as if to defend herself from something evil.

'But, Mummy . . .'

'You heard what I said.'

Alan stopped, looked at me for a moment, then looked down. It was just an act. We both knew that. They left and I watched through the window as he put his arm around her as they approached the car park. Alan opened the door for Mum to get into the car and the vehicles vanished up the long drive.

Miss Horsley was standing beside me now. Tears streamed down my face.

'It wasn't me. It wasn't my idea,' I said.

'I know.'

'But why? Why?'

'Come and sit down, Emily.'

'Why can't I go home? Why?'

We sat at the far end of the room. There was a lump in my throat. My bones hurt. My hands were trembling.

'Your father—'

'He's not my father.'

'Your stepfather and mother say you are a disruptive influence and they have four other children to worry about—'

'But I'm not—'

'That's what they say, Emily. They don't want you to return home . . .' she said, and I stopped her continuing.

'But I can go home to my dad. It's what he wants,' I said, and she shook her head.

'It's too late for that. I have contacted social services and a place has been found for you—'

'Social services?'

'Your mother has placed you in voluntary care.'

CHAPTER 12

Running Away

The first time I ran away was two weeks after my thirteenth birthday in June. It was no coincidence that this failed attempt at escape, if that's what it was, came a few days after another first: the first time I was abused by a man in a children's home and realised that there was nothing I could do about it.

If you are in care and find yourself alone with a man who molests you in some way, you can't defend yourself and you can't stop him. You know, as he knows, that if you tell anyone, it will be your word against his. His story will almost certainly be believed; in care you are automatically considered untrustworthy, and you suffer the double indignity of being abused and being shown to be a liar. You can't stop the assaults. You can't tell anyone. So what you do is close down your emotions, you bury the shame in a private place where it festers and decades later you still can't talk about it.

Institutions function primarily for the people who work in them, not for those they are supposed to be serving, in this case, vulnerable, maladjusted, frequently abused and mistreated children.

The fact that the system is riddled with faults dawned on me as the twelve-seater van lurched out of the gate at my boarding school and headed up the Thanet Way to the A2. Social services should have sent me back to the north to be close to my parents, but there was no inter-agency coordination, no sense of what might be best for me. I was twelve, frightened and felt unloved and discarded. None of these things were taken into account. I had been placed in care in Kent and in Kent I was to remain.

A tall thin social worker who was annoyed at having been called out on a Sunday was at the wheel of the vehicle that drove me from Westgate to the heart of the countryside without a single word passing between us, just the hymns she sang along with on the radio. We pulled up outside a Reception Centre, a steel and glass building generally called a 'holding bay', a half-way house on the outskirts of a village surrounded by fields and wetlands.

'Here we are,' she said, her first words, and I stepped from the vehicle with that hollow sense of being halfway between nowhere and nowhere.

Orange streaks lingered in the sky and the trees looked haunted on the horizon. I entered the building in my short skirt and white boots, dragging my case, and was sent straight to bed in a room that smelled stuffy and contained four steel cots set out in a line below narrow windows.

I didn't sleep that night. Snatches of the day reeled through my head like movie clips: Bobby waving over her shoulder without glancing back; the way the Italian woman from the embassy had glided by in stilettos; Mum holding up a defensive hand and saying 'not you' as she left the sports hall. No two words in that context could have been more unkind, more uncaring. Not you. Everyone else can go home. But not you. You're nothing. You're on the scrapheap, garden rubbish, unwanted.

Mum left, shaking her head, and Alan paused in the doorway, the light behind him, his chill gaze like a death mask. He had left scars on my bottom with his whip. He had plunged his cock in my mouth. If this was a game, a test of wills, he had won. Alan Briggs was the Miracle Man. He had a powerful sense of self-preservation and was conscious of two things: he wouldn't be able to stop himself abusing me again if I were at home and would, by the law of averages, eventually get caught. Now, the past was left behind, the unbearable temptation of a nubile twelve-year-old was out of reach and he could play the role he believed he was born for, the hero protecting the other children from my bad influence.

These are adult thoughts, years in forming, and that night I lay in a strange bed with a broken heart and bitter tears staining my cheeks. I had been abandoned again. My real mother had left me for adoption and my adopted mother had left me to be taken away to a fate she couldn't have imagined.

I sniffled and pushed my head under the pillow. Why wasn't I like the other girls – Abigail and Sonia, Christine and Julie – normal girls with proper mums and proper dads with proper jobs? Why was my mum my guardian, not my dad, who paid the bills? Why, when he wanted me to be with him, did the authorities, the county court and social services, say I couldn't be? I should never have taken part in burning down the school and now, that second, the smell of smoke in my hair, I felt like burning down the Reception Centre with me inside it.

Days in children's homes start early. The sun was bright through the uncurtained windows when I woke up. I slipped from the covers and stood in my pyjamas looking out over a vast quilt of fields trimmed by hedgerows, ripening crops in shades of green and yellow, with the trees in the distance less frightening in daylight.

I found my way to the bathroom where I bathed my swollen eyes in cold water. I hadn't eaten anything since lunch the previous day, but wasn't hungry. I felt sick. There was a tight feeling in my stomach and, as I glanced at myself in the mirror, I noticed the twitch was back.

There were twelve children at the holding bay, five boys and seven girls. I was the eldest. At first, it wasn't so different from being at boarding school, except we walked the two miles every day to the local school, where the fact that we were 'in care' marked us as if we wore a scarlet letter. Parents would tell their children to stay away from us; we were ruffians, prone to violence and had head lice, which wasn't entirely inaccurate.

There were other differences that quickly became apparent. At boarding school, girls are generally confident, exuberant and well mannered; privileged and aware of it. At the holding bay, the children were insecure, inconsiderate and easily offended. The first morning when I sat down for breakfast, a tubby girl named Jeanie clenched her fists, turned bright red and started shaking in fury.

'Oi, you, what are you doing there? That's my place. I always sit there. That's my place,' she cried.

I moved before she blew a fuse. Mrs McCann, the stocky warden, directed me to another place at the long table and turned to Jeanie.

'There, you see, Jeanie, it doesn't need all that shouting.'

'But what's she doing in my place?'

'Emily's new. She didn't know.'

'But it's my place.'

'Well, you've got it now, haven't you?'

She sat down, shaking, baring her teeth. The way the others ignored her, I realised the explosion wasn't unusual.

There was a stack of toast on a plate, bowls for cereal and tea steaming in an enormous metal teapot. It looked too heavy to lift, although Mrs McCann in a short-sleeved blouse had beefy arms and successfully went around the table pouring thick black tea into white enamel mugs. After adding milk, I took one sip and felt my teeth rotting in my gums it was so sweet.

'Could I have tea without sugar?' I asked.

There was total silence. It was like I was Oliver Twist and had asked for more. Mrs McCann glared back at me with the same expression Jeanie had worn when she found me in her place.

'What did you say?'

'I don't take sugar.'

'Don't take sugar! You do now – everyone does.'

'But I don't like it.'

'Then you'd bloody well better learn to like it.'

Sugar had been added to the pot while the tea brewed, something I had never seen before. I watched the steam rising from my chipped mug and I remembered tea with Aunt Alice, the wafer-thin porcelain with the manufacturer's stamp on the bottom of each cup and saucer, milk in a jug, sugar in a bowl, slices of lemon on a plate. There was always a choice and, in choosing, you acquire your own tastes and that forms your personality, that sense of being you. That was another difference with boarding school where everything is designed to develop your individuality. In care, the system is the opposite, everything contrives to crush individuality and turn you into a clone.

When I shared the dorm with Bobby and the girls, I had been aware in a vague sort of way that I didn't come from the same solid background as they did. When I was with them, I behaved like them. I wanted to fit in and did fit in. At the halfway house, I had to adapt, and adapted so well I became uncertain if I was a bright, confident girl now behaving like a disturbed child with emotional problems, or if I was a disturbed child with emotional problems who had been acting as if I was a bright, confident girl with a future when I was at private school.

The staff at the home were by and large indifferent and let us do whatever we wanted as long as we didn't make a noise or break anything. We were 'on hold', which is like being in purgatory, neither one thing nor the other, and some other warden or social worker up the line would 'put us straight'. Like the children, the staff, too, all seemed to have a chip on their shoulder. The simplest question was met with either suspicion or derision. Everyone was on edge and constantly looking for sleights or sarcasm. Every question was answered by a question.

'Can you pass me the milk, please?'

'So you want milk now, do you?'

'I can't seem to find my book.'

'What, someone's a thief, are they?'

'What time is it?'

'Time you bloody well shut up and stopped asking.'

This attitude was mystifying. I was in a daze, permanently confused, lonely. I couldn't understand the unfairness and stupidity of sending me into voluntary care when I knew Dad and Aunt Alice wanted me to be with them. I tried to explain this to Mrs McCann, but she was always too busy to listen. 'You think I'm here to deal with you and nothing else?' I felt lost, unloved, forgotten, and these things eat at your mind. You don't have to be born with mental health issues for them to develop and, if they develop through ill-treatment and neglect as a child, it leaves a scar you can never stop scratching and remains present like a shadow when times are better. Physical, sexual and psychological abuse have no cure and never go away.

For the first few weeks I kept to myself. There was a good library and I read book after book, living in those comforting middle-class stories where everyone was agonisingly courteous and it was still 1950.

After breakfast and regulation teeth cleaning, the one thing the staff were strict about for some reason, we trooped off to school. The younger children filed into the red-brick primary and I walked across the playing field to the new secondary mod with a boy the same age as me named Doug Mortlock, who obviously liked me and I ignored because he liked me.

It was my third school in two years. The syllabus was different and, where I had found it easy to catch up and do well at boarding school, I now found it just as easy to fall behind. When expectations are high you can, as a child, rise to them. When there are no expectations, it's easy to become listless, bored, apathetic. I was all of those things. At first, I behaved like Bobby, peering back over one shoulder when I was asked a question, but what was charming on her seemed condescending or just plain silly when I tried it. Like a chameleon moving out of the sun, I changed colours and took on another aspect of myself, my own worst enemy.

I had two pleasures that kept me sane – cross-country running and working in the garden at the home, a haven of flower beds and rambling roses that had climbed over the tool shed where Harry, the gardener, played classical music on his transistor radio. Like running, when there's earth beneath your nails and you are down on all fours pulling weeds, you stop thinking, your anxieties fade and you feel in touch with something uplifting.

Harry was chatty and funny. In his tweed jacket and corduroy trousers held up by a thick leather belt, he reminded me of the countrymen at home when I was little. He had red hands, a ruddy face and twinkling eyes like the Father Christmas in the department store where Mum worked.

One time when 'Für Elise' was on the radio, I told Harry about Richard Symons; my 'first boyfriend', I said, showing off, echoing the half-truths I'd told the girls at school.

'Was he handsome?'

I shrugged as I thought about it. 'Yes, I suppose so.'

'Not as handsome as me, though?'

I giggled.

Another time when I was wearing a miniskirt, he shook his head as he studied me.

'Blimey, don't your bum get cold in that?'

I'd heard this line before. 'No, it's just the fashion,' I replied.

'Thing is, Emmy, it's not how long your skirt is what matters, it's how short it is to take it off.'

He sounded serious and I wasn't sure whether or not he was being rude. I was entering the adult world, but it's like you've won your certificate for swimming two lengths of the pool and now you're confronted by the English Channel. We took the tools back to the shed to hang on their hooks. Harry had a calendar showing models in bathing costumes, one for each month. He took it down from the shelf and flicked back to April. He pointed at a girl in red bikini briefs hiding her breasts with her arms and staring modestly at the camera.

'I noticed the other day, look, you're the spitting image – you could be sisters.'

There was a similarity. Like Bobby, my hair was over my shoulders, long and thick, and I had the same wide eyes and wide lips as the model.

'You could do that job,' Harry added, and I felt grown up and happy for the first time since I'd arrived at the holding bay.

The following day, as I was putting the tools away, the light darkened as Harry stood in the doorway. He closed the door and the breath caught in my throat. Dust motes floated in the air and my heart was racing in time to the strings and flute on the radio. I tried to move away, but it was like my feet were stuck in cement and I just watched in disbelief as he unbuttoned his trousers. He reached for me, pulling at my skirt, and started to masturbate as he ran his hand inside my knickers.

'Come on, touch it,' he said. 'Touch it.'

I didn't. I held my arms rigidly at my sides and his sperm spurted onto the floor and dripped on my bare leg.

'There, that's nice,' he said, puffing away.

He was big like Alan and said the same things as Alan. Would they all say the same things? Are men programmed to grab little girls and say that's nice as they shove their penis in their hands? I pulled away and ran out. The garden had been my sanctuary. Now it was poison.

I bolted across the field and along the deserted railway lines. I did this run every afternoon, only now, I wasn't just running, I was running away from something. The landscape in the Medway was different from where I grew up, gentle, more rounded. I knew the names of the trees – aspens, ash, alders, the elms and oak. There were patches of heather, buttercups and marsh violets, the same wildflowers I had pressed in my project book as a little girl with Grandma.

It felt as if there was no connection between that little girl and me running for my life. Why did Grandma die? Other children had grandmas. Then I remembered, I had Granny Wheeler, and she had spent two years slapping me around the head. She never hit Amy. Just me. I couldn't understand why. Was I a 'bad seed'? Was it all because I had pushed Amy up the chimney to search for treasure? Was it all my own fault?

The word why, why, why escaped through my lips with each breath. I ran into the wind, tears streaming down my face.

I had thought Harry just liked me for me and never had any idea of what lay beneath his flattery. I couldn't understand how a man who listened to classical music would also sexually assault a child, that evil people, the pimps and groomers, the beaters and abusers also enjoyed fine things, they felt pain and were moved when they heard 'Für Elise'.

I had turned thirteen a week before. I didn't even get a card from Mum. Dad had sent me a postal order for £20; he sent £5 every week with a note, a huge sum that made me richer than anyone else at the children's home, not that it was money I needed. I ran through cornfields and over hedges, running to escape from being me. My tears dried and I suddenly had a fantastic idea.

I would run away.

As the thought hit me, I felt a wave of relief and sprinted home as fast as I could. Like the time when I took Amy on that fateful journey to the Little Red Riding Hood cottage, I didn't want to go on my own and studied the other children around the table at dinner that night. My eyes lingered on Doug Mortlock, my companion in senior school, the boy I always ignored. He was a few months younger than me and big for his age. His father was dead, his mother had fallen ill with some incurable disease and he was in care, not because he had done something stupid or criminal, but because there was no one to look after him.

Before bedtime, I told Doug I planned to run away and he immediately agreed to come with me. He didn't have anywhere to go but then, neither did I, but it was the running away that appealed to him.

We needed equipment, I can't think why, and the following evening we took some jam from the kitchen and smeared it on the tool-shed window. We covered the jam with a sheet of newspaper, then hit it with a rock. I'd seen this done on television and the glass broke cleanly without a sound. When we did it, there was an almighty eruption of shattering glass and we set off across the fields empty-handed.

We were picked up about three miles from the home by two local bobbies in a panda car. They drove us back, had a laugh with Mrs McCann, and we were sent straight to bed. No one thought to ask why we had run away. No one asked if we had problems at home or if we were unhappy and, if we were unhappy, why we were unhappy. Mrs McCann, her assistant, Mrs Tucker, and their staff of several part-timers spent most of their time making tea, drinking tea, eating biscuits and chatting. They weren't unkind. They were lazy, neglectful and did not provide any sense of homeliness, care or security.

For Doug, I suppose it was fun running away. For me, it was different. I was running away from the vision in my head of Harry in the tool shed unbuttoning his trousers, from the shadow of Alan Briggs, from some unbearable inevitability. While you are running away there is no past and no future. It's like swimming under water. There is a moment when there is just the present and the pain of memory is suspended. Aunt Alice had said I was going to be good at something. I just needed practice.

We ran away three more times, once more fleeing across the fields and once on bicycles. On each of those occasions, we were taken home by the local police, who seemed pleased to

Emily MacKenzie

have something to do in rural Kent and enjoyed dropping by to have a cuppa with Mrs McCann. The last flight we made was by bus, which took us to the nearest town about twenty miles away and I remember sitting there certain that all the other passengers knew we were runaways. This was just paranoia and we arrived in the high street as the shops were closing.

Doug was a growing lad. He was starving and I had a brilliant idea, like the brilliant idea of helping Amy climb the chimney in search of treasure, or stealing things from the other girls' bags at The Priory, or, the most brilliant of all, setting the school on fire. My plan was to hide in Woolworths until it shut, then we would be able to fill up on sandwiches and sweets.

'Brilliant,' Doug said.

Now he'd acknowledged my brilliance, we had to go through with it and it was actually a lot easier than I'd thought. We crouched behind a counter and remained there hyperventilating from a mixture of fear and excitement. Suddenly, the lights went out. The doors snapped shut and we looked at each other knowing instantly that what we had done wasn't brilliant at all. It was totally stupid.

'Now what?' Doug said.

'Well, you were hungry, not me.'

'I'm not any more.'

'Well, it's not my fault.'

'Then it *must* be Jeanie's fault,' he said and grinned; Jeanie was always angry, always breaking things and, after any mishap, we tended to all look at Jeanie as if she were to blame.

We searched the building and were surprised to find an open window in the stockroom. Doug climbed up on a chair and discovered why: the back of the building was on the Medway – literally; there was no path, just an eight-foot drop down to the murky grey river.

'Can you swim?' I asked.

'Better than you,' Doug said.

'Well?'

He shrugged. 'I'll go first, make sure you're all right.'

He climbed up on the chair, swung himself onto the window-sill and pushed off into the river. I heard the splash, then he called out.

'Come on then.'

I followed and the water was freezing, even though it was the end of June. We swam across to the far side and scrambled up the bank. Doug took off his clothes to wring out the water. I was too embarrassed to do that and sat there shivering.

We were pleased to get picked up by the police this time. They took us back to the station where we dried off in front of an electric fire. We admitted that we had hidden in Woolworths and were told this was still considered breaking and entering, even though we hadn't broken anything. These were city cops, not local bobbies, and not so friendly, although they did give us mugs of tea – I took mine without sugar – and blankets to keep warm.

We were returned to the halfway house and were told that if we ran away again, there would be grave consequences, a warning I never took seriously.

CHAPTER 13

A Bag of Sweets

The school holidays arrived and the children where possible were found places to go until the new term started. Doug went to stay with an aunt. Mum didn't want me at home and refused to allow me to stay with Dad. Why she chose to punish me in this way and why the authorities agreed was a mystery that I thought about incessantly in the coming months as that cruel decision condemned me to a fate far worse than being put into voluntary care in the first place.

Only two younger children remained at the holding bay. Most of the staff were away and, when it was bedtime, I got into the habit of offering to make sure the little ones cleaned their teeth and went upstairs with them while the night warden made herself a fresh pot of tea. Once the children were tucked in their cots, I dug out the make-up and eyeliner from my suitcase and dressed in the outfits Dad had bought the previous Christmas. The staff rarely checked the dorms at night, but I pushed a couple of pillows under the bedcover just in case, slipped out the back door and wandered into the village on my own.

There must have been about a dozen pubs dotted around the high street, but older children from school always met in the same tumbledown old coach inn that stood on the outskirts of the village. The landlord wore glasses that were so thick they hid his eyes and, as long as you could pay for your drinks, never asked anyone their age. Out back there was a garden with woodwormy furniture and it was here, beneath the weeping willows, where I learned to smoke. I discovered I enjoyed dry white wine, not sweet wine like my mum, and, after just one glass, I felt relaxed and confident.

As I was accepted by the boys in the garden, I was accepted by the girls. There were strict rules over who was whose boyfriend, or projected boyfriend, and who it was acceptable to let chat you up and who it wasn't. I learned the rules and one boy walked me back to the home several times. I can't remember his name, but it was with this boy that I had my first real kiss and when I climbed into my bed that night his taste on my lips made me feel good about myself for the first time in ages.

I ran next day for hours. I took a long bath and, after I had put the little ones to bed, I dressed in my velvet hot pants, yellow All Star basketball shoes and a tight yellow top. I used blue eye-shadow, flicked mascara on my eyelashes, applied pink lipstick and balanced my heart sunglasses on the end of my nose. I stood back and studied my reflection in the mirror. If there was a moment in my life when I looked my best, it was probably that moment. I turned sideways and pouted like the April model from Harry's calendar. My legs were tanned and my brown eyes looked big and shiny. I stared at myself over my shoulder.

'Roberta Raimondo, eat your heart out.'

I strolled into the village as the sun went down behind the trees on the horizon and darkness gushed across the landscape like a tide. I had not made any plans to meet the boy who had kissed me – he had become my 'boyfriend' in my own mind – but I was still disappointed that he wasn't in the garden as usual. Another boy, named Roger, told me he'd gone on holiday. He must have realised I was sad and bought me a glass of wine.

Roger had finished school that year. He was sixteen and had started work as an apprentice engineer at a factory in Chatham. We talked for ages. He said I looked fab in hot pants, but it wasn't like being with Harry when he said that sort of thing. Roger made me laugh and did amazing imitations of the different teachers at school. There was a programme on television then called *Please Sir!* which I had seen a few times, and Roger could quote all the funny things that happened in the fictional school where it was set.

When he suggested we went back to his pad, I didn't hesitate. I thought it was going to be where his mum and dad lived, but turned out to be a flat he shared with his older brother. Roger put his arm around me as we walked along and, after two glasses of wine, I felt like I was floating. The flat was in an old industrial building that had been converted. We climbed a metal stairway and entered a big room with paisley material over the sofa and orange light bulbs that made everything look hazy and cool. There was a poster with an Indian God with a blue face and eight arms, and a grinning Chinese Buddha made of plastic with a green light inside. Roger introduced me to Del, his brother, who was in his twenties.

'Hey, a cool chick,' he said, and held up a clenched fist. 'Keep the faith.'

He was sitting cross-legged on the floor with an album cover balanced between his knees. He had long hair wound up on top of his head like the Buddha and wore white puja pants and a leather waistcoat without a shirt. He was the hippest person I'd ever met and as handsome as a pop star. He suddenly smiled.

'Hey, you wanna smoke a joint?' he asked, and I nodded.

'Yes, please,' I said.

I knew he was talking about drugs, it was the hot topic among the boys at school, and I was both nervous and excited about trying it for myself. I watched as Del stuck three cigarette papers together on the flat surface of the record cover. He broke open a regular cigarette and tipped the tobacco onto the papers. Then, with his lighter, he heated a dark green ball of resin.

'Moroccan hash,' he said. 'It'll make you high and take you higher.'

I leaned forward with big eyes as he broke off tiny crumbs from the green ball and sprinkled it onto the tobacco. He made a filter by tearing off a piece of card from the Rizla packet, curled the papers into a tube, then licked the gum to hold it all together. He turned the open end of the joint into a tight spiral like the fuse on a firework and gave it to me.

'My lady,' he said, and lit his lighter.

I sucked hard on the spliff and felt a complete idiot coughing my heart out. The boys laughed and said it was normal. They took long drags, showing me how to do it, and the second time

I didn't cough quite as much. The smoke drifted down to my lungs and up into my brain. I instantly felt silly and giggly and was conscious I should try and act like a grown-up.

Music was playing, Pink Floyd or Deep Purple, something mystical and dreamy. There were cans of beer, ash spilling out of the ashtray and my legs looked oddly long in the orange light. My throat was scratchy from the smoke and I sipped beer from a can. Del asked me how old I was and I said nearly fifteen.

'That's cool,' he said, and I just grinned.

Del left the room and was gone for several minutes. I stayed on the couch with Roger and felt content with his arm around me just staring into space. When Del came back, he was carrying a guitar. He turned the music low, and sat cross-legged again on the floor playing a folk song. He was really good, like a professional, and I was mesmerised watching his fingers moving over the neck of the guitar in the same dextrous way that he had rolled the joint.

He stopped playing when we heard footsteps on the metal stairway and three more men arrived. Two of them were in their twenties like Del; the third looked older with a pointy beard and staring eyes. At our school, there were two Pakistani girls who always wore headscarves and I thought the older man was probably their dad. His name was Ali. Mo had terrible pockmarks on his face and scary, close-together eyes. The last one had a name that sounded like Adam and wore a suit and tie. They said their names as they shook my hand. They were very formal and I couldn't work out what they were doing there in that flat.

Del made a fresh joint and passed it around. Ali waved it away when it was his turn and I noticed his eyes were on me all the time. I sipped beer. I took puffs on the spliff. Maybe it was another spliff. I wasn't sure. My head was spinning. The music was loud again and had a pulse like a hammer striking against my temple. The air was thick with smoke and it was hard to focus. Roger kissed me. He pushed his tongue into my mouth and ran it over my gums. It felt funny and I wanted to giggle but that would have been childish.

As we broke away from that strange kiss, two hands rose over the arm of the couch and started lifting my top over my head. I was vaguely aware of the zip on my hot pants being lowered and, as another pair of hands started pulling them down, I had this weird idea that the blue God with lots of arms was undressing me. I thought it was just a joke.

'Don't do that. Don't do that,' I said.

I tried to move away, but there were hands everywhere, white hands, brown hands, blue hands, orange hands, all these hands unsnapping my bra, pulling my panties down.

'No, no, don't.'

I wriggled and hit out but I didn't have a chance. Del loomed over me.

'Stop that. Stop it,' he said, and slapped my cheek.

I froze. My voice had gone dead, it was lost inside me somewhere, and I needed all my energy to try to speak.

'Please don't. Please.'

Del's long hair was hanging down now. He looked completely different. His eyes were orange and as he stared at me I was totally petrified. It was like looking into the eyes of a wild animal. One of the men was holding my shoulders and stretching back my arms. Del wedged his knees between my legs and it felt as if I'd been split in two as he pushed up inside me.

'Please, please . . .'

I heard or felt a snap, a sudden pain, and bit down on my lips. I wasn't a virgin any more. I would feel ashamed and dirty and disgusted, but not at that moment. My brain was scrambled. It seemed unreal, like a terrible nightmare, like the shadow that had been chasing me through the years had finally vanished up into my body, tearing and breaking everything on its way.

I thought about the dogs in the park as Del pushed on, pumping away and I felt a warm gush as he cried out and suddenly stopped. I thought for a second it was over, but it wasn't. As Del moved off, Adam climbed between my legs and did the same thing, but now something even more horrible happened. My head was over the edge of the sofa and Del pushed his cock tasting of my blood into my mouth and my stomach churned as I sucked it.

Adam finished what he was doing and it was Roger's turn.

'Please don't, Roger, please stop,' I pleaded.

His eyes were glazed. He couldn't see me. Tears washed over my face. Roger wasn't a funny boy from school any more. He was part of the pack and I was dimly aware that the others were urging him on as he lowered his jeans and pressed down between my legs.

'Please, please . . .'

I tried to get away. You keep trying, even when it's hopeless, it's impossible. There were five of them. There was nothing I could do. They held me down and passed me around like a bag of sweets, from the couch to the floor and finally into another room where I was forced down on a single bed. Mo slapped my backside and called me a bitch. 'You bitch, you little bitch, you fucking bitch.' He hoisted me up so I was on all fours like a dog, and I didn't know I was lucky it was only my vagina he raped and nothing more.

When he was done, Del came back for more and Adam as well.

I must have passed out because the next thing I remember is opening my eyes and seeing Ali on top of me. I was on my back. He was balancing on one hand and held my throat with the other. He was wearing a blue shirt and had a fat tummy.

'Look at me. Look.'

I stared back into his eyes.

'Good. Good. You good girl. I like.' He smiled then and that smile made me even more frightened. 'Good girl. Good. Lift your knees. OK?'

I did exactly as he asked. He rested his palms either side of my head. His eyes were piercing like sharp points as he gazed down at me. He wasn't rough. He moved slowly at first and gradually faster. He started gasping for air. I could see beads of sweat standing out on his forehead. They ran down his face and dripped on my bare skin.

He sighed and pushed up a little harder as he climaxed. He remained there with his palms next to my head. He was nodding in that way people have when they've reached a decision, his pointed beard like a knife wavering above me.

'Is good. You sexy girl. You like?'

I think it was a question, I wasn't sure.

'I want to go home,' I said.

'I take. No problem. You good girl.'

He slid off the bed, hoisted up his trousers, and left the room. There was an excruciating pain between my legs. My hand when I checked was slicked with blood and semen and the smell on my fingers would stay in my head for the rest of my life. There was no music now. I could hear voices, laughter. I lay there like a broken toy drifting in and out of consciousness, more dead than alive.

Being gang-raped is worse than being thrashed with a rhino-whip and the scars remain so fresh and vivid it could have happened yesterday. I have tried to cast my mind back to tell what happened that night without exaggerations or distortions. I was thirteen years and two months old. Four men and a boy of sixteen raped me over and over again. They laughed. They spilled beer on me. They treated me like nothing, like I didn't matter, like I was a dog, worse than a dog.

I passed out again and it was Del who woke me. He was gentle, coaxing.

'Come on, time to go. Come on, let's go.'

I struggled to my feet and he led me down a long corridor to a bathroom where there was hot water waiting in the bath with lots of soap bubbles floating on the top.

'In you get,' he said, and I did.

I washed away the blood and sperm mechanically and it felt as if I were washing one of the younger children at the holding bay. The staff didn't care. No one cared. If I didn't help them wash, they went dirty. My head was throbbing with the mixture of wine and beer and hashish. My hands were shaking. I knew the word rape. It was a word teenagers used a lot. He's a rapist. He's going to rape her. She got raped. It was a word like fuck and wank and cunt, words you learn at thirteen and feel grown up as they slip from your tongue. Now I had been raped for real, five times, more. Del came back and pulled the plug. He showered the soap bubbles off me and held up a towel. It didn't even occur to me to feel embarrassed that I was naked. When shame takes over embarrassment disappears. While I dried myself, he went and got my clothes. I dressed in my sexed-up costume. The sexualisation of children that's in the news now had started then, the grooming and gang-raping of girls from broken homes and in council care that's happening today was happening in a quiet little Medway village in 1969.

We returned to the bedroom and Del told me to sit on the bed. A couple of minutes later, Ali came in. He moved the chair beside the bed and sat facing me. I was trembling and the way he reassuringly patted me on the leg didn't help.

'You have good time, plenty of fun, yes?'

I didn't know what to say. I was afraid to say no and I wasn't going to say yes. I shrugged.

'You sexy girl. Men, they like,' he continued. 'You like being sexy girl?'

I shrugged again. 'I want to go home,' I said.

'Yes, yes. No problem.' He leaned forward. 'When you want to come again, you go to the pub, you see Roger. He's a good boy. You understand?'

I shrugged again. I didn't understand. He spoke softly. He was trying to sound kind but I knew he was pretending.

He nodded his head as he spoke. 'I look after you. I protect you. You need money, no problem. You want new things. You tell, and I get. I like you. I am your friend.' He paused and smiled. 'What you say?'

'Yes, I understand.'

'Good, good. Next time, is better. No problem, OK?'

He was quiet for a moment and his hand on my bare leg squeezed a little tighter.

'What are you going to say when you get home?'

'Nothing. Nothing. I won't say anything.'

He spoke slowly now, in a low voice. 'You good girl. You learn. I teach. You say something, anything, and I tell you what I do . . .'

He didn't tell me. What he did was push out his mauve tongue, he made scissors with his fingers and showed me how he would cut my tongue off.

CHAPTER 14

Someone Else

Ali drove back to the Reception Centre without asking me where I lived. He knew. The pimps and groomers are watching. They know where to look. It was summer. If I wasn't with my family, it meant I didn't belong to anybody.

He turned off the engine and rolled to a stop a good distance from the building. I went to get out of the car.

'You wait,' he said.

I froze in the seat as the car door swung open and the light came on. My hands were shaking and my teeth hurt I was pressing down so hard. I watched from the corner of my eye as he reached into his pocket. There was a flash of silver and for a terrible moment I thought he had pulled out a pair of scissors. I was paralysed with fear, the breath caught in my throat and I gasped as I realised it wasn't scissors he was holding, it was a money clip. He peeled off two twenties and pressed them into my hand.

'You good girl. You want, I give. Anything. I look after you now.'

He kept hold of my hand. I was staring back into his face and in the pale glow of the light he could have been the devil with that sharp beard and piercing eyes that seemed to be looking into me, into my mind. His breath smelled of sour eggs. It made me feel sick. I wanted to turn away but couldn't. Again, he did that thing with his tongue, cutting it with his fingers, only this time he smiled like it was our private joke. He patted my leg to show affection, then leaned closer and kissed my cheek.

'You good girl. I like. You come to pub. OK?' he said, and I nodded my head.

I got out of the car and watched as he slowly reversed, turned and drove away. The lights disappeared. Then it was silent. I remained there in my little clothes under the big sky, my mind spinning. I sniffled and took deep breaths.

They raped me. I'm not a virgin any more. Nobody loves me. No one will ever love me now.

There was a pain in my throat and chest, a pain between my legs and up inside me. I had been stretched. I was still growing and those big men had forced themselves deep into my body. They had left their mess inside me. I could feel it, swishing around like slops in a bucket. My stomach hurt and bile rose into my throat. Tears gushed from my eyes, a lake of tears, enough tears to float a small boat and let it drift off into oblivion.

Why did it happen? Why?

I asked myself that question, but I knew why. I had painted my face to look pretty. I had been so full of myself in my hot pants. Showing off. I should never have gone back to the flat with Roger. I shouldn't have drunk the beer and wine. I shouldn't have smoked their joints. Mum was right. She was always right. I was my own worst enemy. I burned down the school to please Bobby. Now I'm not a virgin any more.

I suddenly thought about Alan pushing his cock in my mouth and Harry running his hands down my knickers. Would it have been worse being violated by those five men had those things never happened? No. Nothing could have been worse. But at least I had learned that if I were ever alone with a man who wanted to molest me, hurt me, abuse me in any way, then he would and I wouldn't be able to stop him. Men are strong. Girls are weak. You can't fight them.

It was dark but I could see the trees, a black fringe against the horizon. It was cold now. I felt tiny, irrelevant, empty, hollow, unloved, a piece of dirt. I didn't want to be dead. I wished I'd never been born. Why did my real mother discard me? Why did Mum hate me? Because she did. I knew she did. The first time she beat me she set off a chain reaction that had led to me standing there in the middle of the night with £40 pressed in my hand.

The banknotes were hot in my palm. I unrolled them and tore them into tiny pieces that drifted away on the wind. I shivered and limped along the road between the grey fields to the holding bay. The back door was unlocked. The staff must have known I went out every night. Out of sight, out of mind. There is little care in care homes, no attention, no love. Children are hidden away and the care workers employed to watch over them are mostly untrained, underpaid and often have their own social and psychological problems.

I put on my pyjamas and lay in bed staring out at the night. Every part of my body throbbed with pain and what went through my mind wasn't those men raping me, but Ali pushing out his tongue to show how my tongue would be cut off if I ever told anyone what they had done. Not that I would. I was too ashamed and no one would have believed me anyway.

The days of summer were coming to an end. I never went into the garden any more. Just the sight of Harry made my stomach clench, and every time he saw me in the distance he winked to remind me of our little secret.

I looked after Jeanie and Diane, the two little girls left behind at the holding bay. Jeanie suffered from some minor mental disorder, although all she really needed was some attention. Just as my sister had tried to teach Annie to read, I did the same with Jeanie, her stubby fingers running earnestly over the words. When I was with the little ones, I joined in their games, reverting to childhood. We built camps out of cushions and played with dolls and teddies; there are always masses of toys in care homes, endless boxes of donations from parents with children who have outgrown them.

Playing with Jeanie and Diane got me through the days, but at night I lay in my bed squeezing my hands together and trembling. The shadows moving over the windows and the flash of lights every time a car approached made me think Ali was coming to get me. I saw his face form in the cracks on the ceiling and the smell of food drifting up the stairs reminded me of the smell of eggs on his breath.

I was squinting again. I was afraid all the time, and it was almost comforting to accept that being raped was inevitable, as inescapable as gravity. After what had happened with Alan and Harry, I should have been more careful. But I wasn't. I had gone out that night in a skimpy top with bare legs. I had dressed as if I wanted sex and those men couldn't help themselves. You sexy girl. You like. I didn't like, but they didn't know that.

I was badly bruised and there were small rips around the upper part of my vagina. It stung when I went to the toilet, but the hot water when I took a bath was soothing. Young bodies damage easily and heal quickly. The stinging gradually went away, but not the pain, not entirely. You learn to tolerate cold, heat, hunger, discomfort, but the memory of being raped leaves a dull ache that stays with you, and when you can't feel it, you see it in your face.

After Mum beat me the first time, I didn't recognise my own reflection in the mirror. I had that feeling again. I would step from the bath, clear the steam from the glass, and the eyes squinting back at me looked haunted, cloudy, alien, like they belonged to someone else. I felt like a little mouse in a world of giant cats all out to get me. When I closed my eyes, I kept seeing the same scene over and over again, me naked beneath the orange glow of the light bulbs with those men ramming into me one after the other.

Sometimes, those mental images seemed unreal and I wanted to believe it was all in my imagination. I pretended when I was playing with the little girls that I was just having bad dreams. But the bruises were still there changing from blue to pale green to yellow. I remembered Del slapping me when I became hysterical, his eyes shiny like a wolf. I kept seeing myself on my knees, Mo's brown hands gripping my hipbones as he stabbed into me from behind. He held my hips so tightly there were blue marks like fingerprints on me the next day.

It was difficult to get to sleep and, when I did sleep, I had horrible nightmares. I saw myself on that couch being raped, and sometimes it was Alan Briggs looming over me and sometimes it was Ali with eight arms and his pointed beard as he pressed down towards my face.

Neither Mrs McCann nor Mrs Tucker seemed aware that I had been out every night all summer and now I never went out at all. They didn't notice that I spent hours in the bathroom and long afternoons playing with dolls with two girls aged six and seven. It never struck them that I had stopped parading around half naked in miniskirts and a push-up bra, and now kept myself covered in jeans and a big shirt.

I wrote cards to Amy and waited every day while Mrs McCann sorted the post.

'Don't know what you're hanging about for, there's nothing for you.'

I got it fixed in my muddled mind that Amy knew I had been raped and was ashamed. It was a long time before I learned that those pale blue cards when they arrived on the Briggs doormat were scooped up by Mum and dropped in the bin.

It was a relief when Doug Mortlock returned from staying with his aunt. The new term had started and I stayed close by his side when we walked to school. I wanted to tell him what had happened. He was my only friend. But Doug was just a boy, he wouldn't have understood, and I was afraid he'd only hate me for being a slag if I told him.

I was still terrified Ali was going to grab me. I had given up running and hadn't dared go into the village again. Like the pain that never quite goes away, I had the constant sense that they were out there, watching, waiting for me, that in the old coach inn across the village girls like me were being stalked and groomed for any and every type of exploitation. This wasn't my imagination. One day when we were coming home from school, I saw Ali and he saw me. Our eyes met and a shooting pain shot across my chest. I gasped and grabbed on to Doug as I stumbled.

'You all right?'

'Yes, I've just got a tummy ache,' I replied, and held on tightly to his arm.

Ali was in his car watching the girls leave school. His eyes were like X-rays and, as I stumbled, he did that thing with his tongue. I was afraid of him and he knew it. He wanted me to be afraid. Like a moth to the flame, fear often draws you to the very thing that frightens you. Ali knew if I wanted money, as girls in care usually do, I could go to him and he would give it to me. He would protect me. I would be in his debt and I would end up doing everything he wanted. You sexy girl. I had been raped by five men. Would five more make any difference?

The rips and bruises inside me healed, but about a month later, a couple of days after I'd seen Ali outside the school, I woke feeling nauseous and rushed to the bathroom. When I threw up, I thought the bile that came out of my throat was the stuff the men had left in my body, that all those weeks it had been churning through my intestines turning everything inside me to poison.

I was relieved to spit it out. But it happened again the following morning and every morning, the vile stuff tasting of acid flowing out of me as I kneeled over the toilet bowl retching and weeping. I stopped eating, everything made me feel sick, and just drank cups of hot sweet tea.

'See, I told you you'd get to like my tea,' Mrs McCann said, and refilled my enamel mug.

'I want more tea!' Jeanie yelled.

'All right, all right, keep your hair on, I'm coming.'

Jeanie and Diane giggled at that. It's easy to make little girls happy. You just have to be nice to them.

Mrs McCann lurched around the table with her giant teapot. Doug ate about eight slices of toast and no one noticed that I didn't eat anything at all. My suntan had vanished. I was getting paler by the day, and my school uniform that had been tight in July was hanging off me by the end of October. One time walking home from school I stumbled again. Doug put his arm around my shoulder, but it reminded me of how Roger had wrapped his arm around me going back to the flat that night, and the sweetness of the moment turned sour. Rape is like an echo that hums through every relationship and making love carries its memory.

We didn't play hockey at my new school, just netball and rounders. One day, when I was charging around the rounders' pitch, I must have fainted and woke up in the back of an ambulance. At the hospital, I was examined by a nursing sister in a dark-blue uniform. She then took me down a corridor and into a cubicle that smelled of chemicals.

'Undress and put this on,' she said, giving me a gown.

'Do I have to?'

'Yes, you do. You can't be examined properly otherwise.'

'But I'm all right now.'

She stared at me and I did as I was told, but kept my underwear on.

'Everything, please.'

I didn't want anyone to see my body. I was sure just by looking at my ribs and hips she would know I'd had sex with five men. I closed my eyes and did as I was told. I sat on the narrow bed and the sister filled up a form asking my name, age, school, address. When I asked her if she wanted my home address or the address of the holding bay, her expression changed and the ripples that ran across her brow seemed to show that she now knew a good deal more about me than she had when I arrived in the ambulance.

She had just about finished when a doctor entered, an older man with reddish hair and blue eyes. He looked at the forms the nurse had filled in, then spoke to me in a broad Scottish accent.

'Emily MacKenzie? I'm Dr MacDonald,' he said. 'If we go back far enough, lassie, we're probably related.'

I had no idea what he was talking about. He started his examination by pulling back my eyelids to look into my eyes. He gazed down my throat and made me say 'ah'. He took my temperature and, listening through his stethoscope, made sure my heart was beating, which it was, really fast. He then rubbed his palms together.

'You'll have to excuse my cold hands,' he said, and peeled back my gown.

The sister stood to one side, watching, the sun through the window shining off the face of her upside-down watch. My jaw tightened as Dr MacDonald felt my throat, then ran his palms over my tummy. I was thin with bones sticking out all over the place, but my stomach was distended like the people you see on the news when there's a famine in Africa. He paused and took out his handkerchief to clean his glasses. Then he leaned down closer as he ran his fingertip over the fine patch of hair that had begun to grow on my pubic bone. I closed my eyes and shrank into myself. I had never been more embarrassed.

'Hold tight, Emily. I'm not going to hurt you.' I opened my eyes and his tone changed. 'But someone certainly has,' he added.

I didn't answer. I was shaking. He knew. He knew what they'd done to me. He looked closely at my hips. The bruises pressed into my skin by Mo had gone except for a few faint yellow marks. He examined my stomach again. Then he covered me up and took my hand.

'You know, I think you're pregnant, lassie,' he said.

I burst into tears. I couldn't stop myself reaching for the doctor and it was nice the way he took me into his arms and hugged me. I wept over his tweed jacket. I wept and wept as if the tears would never stop.

'I'm not,' I cried. 'Please. I'm not.'

'What happened, Emily?'

'Nothing. Nothing. I didn't do anything.'

'You can tell me, lassie. I'm only here to help. I'm not going to hurt you.'

'I don't know,' I said.

'Tell me now, have you got a boyfriend?'

'No, it's nothing like that.'

'You've been assaulted, haven't you?'

I didn't answer. He used his handkerchief to dry my tears.

'I didn't do anything, honestly.'

'I know you didn't.' He sat down, pulling the chair close to me. 'Tell me, can you remember, when did you last have a period?'

The question woke me as if I had been in a deep sleep. I swallowed hard. Since I'd started having my periods I'd been as regular as Big Ben.

'In the summer.'

'Three months ago?'

I nodded. I bit my lips and had to summon up all my courage to ask the next question.

'Am I going to have a baby?'

He cupped his chin and turned his head to one side. 'It's too early to say for definite, lassie. We'll have to do some tests to make sure.'

I didn't need the tests. I suddenly knew. I think I'd known all along. I'd sensed something shifting and growing inside me. I'd thought the wiring inside my head must have changed after smoking hash, that once you lost your virginity you crossed a bridge that crumbled behind you and you became a different person when you arrived at the other side. I had been playing with dolls with Jeanie and Diane. Now, I was going to have a real baby to play with. I felt stunned, overwhelmed, and an odd sort of relief. Ever since that night, I had been living in a fog of anxiety and dread. It was over. I was going to be a mum. I intended to be a real mum. I would never give my baby away, and I would never smack my little girl as she grew up.

They kept me in hospital overnight and I had a blood test, pap test and tests for chlamydia, gonorrhoea and hepatitis, things I'd never heard of. I got A stars in them all. I didn't have any infections. I was a healthy, if slightly anorexic thirteen-year-old and, just as Dr MacDonald had established from feeling my tummy, I was carrying a baby.

CHAPTER 15

Cops and Doctors

The wheels of the care system move slowly. Weeks and months can go by without you even noticing. But, when something major happens, the wheels spin so fast you are carried along in a whirlwind of confusion.

Mrs McCann came to collect me from hospital in the mini-van and I was taken straight to the police station where she remained, my responsible adult, while I was interviewed by two detectives, Inspector Whitley and his sergeant, who sat beside each other behind a desk that was empty except for one closed file. Dr MacDonald had reported that I had been assaulted and the police had begun an investigation.

I sat in front of the desk, knees locked together, that prickly feeling under my arms. Mrs McCann was off to one side, her plump hands in her big lap. She was wearing a hat with a feather and a double-breasted coat with a furry collar. I looked back at Inspector Whitley with his thin black tie, black suit and hair swept back with Brylcreem. The sergeant was young and was writing in a notebook even before I said anything.

'Now then, in your own words, take your time,' the inspector began, and I sat there staring back at him as if I had lost my tongue.

I had already had three brushes with the police, after the fight with Barbs, the row caused by my exchange of love letters with Richard Symons, and the time I jumped out of the window in Woolworths into the river. Each time the police had made me feel as if I were one of the Great Train Robbers, a master criminal finally brought to book. I was convinced that whatever I said, they would twist around until it became clear that I had been raped because I had gone underage into the pub dressed like a little tart and broken the law drinking alcohol. It was what I believed about myself, so it was obvious they were going to reach the same conclusion.

While these thoughts were spinning through my mind, I had another thought: aside from having little faith in the police, I was afraid Ali would still be able to get at me wherever I was, a feeling that lingered for years.

The inspector lit a cigarette and tried again. 'Would you like a drink, water, a Coke?'

'No, thank you.'

'So, then, from the beginning?'

'I was walking home from the village and a gang of men just jumped out of the bushes.'

'How many men were there?'

'I don't know. About five.'

'Five?'

'Yes.'

'Were they boys of your age?'

'I'm not sure.'

'Or older?'

'Older, I think.'

'Local boys?'

'I don't know.'

'Have you seen any of them before, or since?'

'No.'

'So they weren't local, then?'

'I don't know. Honestly. It was getting dark. It all just happened.'

'What time was it, approximately?'

'I don't know.'

He glanced at Mrs McCann, then back at me. 'Don't you have a time when you have to be back, a curfew or anything?'

'Yes,' I answered, not telling the truth. 'But I was a bit late.'

'What time's the curfew?'

Mrs McCann piped up. 'Eight o'clock,' she said.

'May I remind you, you will remain silent. Do not speak again,' the inspector told her.

He paused, lit another cigarette, and leaned back.

'Five men in what was still daylight jumped out of the bushes while you were walking home and assaulted you?'

'Yes.'

'And now you are pregnant?'

'It's not my fault. I didn't do it to myself,' I replied, as angry as I dared.

'No one presumes it is your fault. I need the facts if we are going to apprehend these men, and you are the only witness.'

He leaned forward. 'Now, think carefully,' he said. 'Were they all white, you know, English, or were any of them dark-skinned?'

He knew something and he knew I was holding back. We held each other's gaze. This was my chance. I could have told him their names, even described where the flat was. I knew what kind of car Ali drove: a pale-blue Ford estate with a roof rack, the only car like that in the area. For just a second, a heartbeat, I was tempted to tell Inspector Whitley everything, but I swallowed my words. He had a shifty look in his eyes and I had a feeling that the more I revealed the more trouble I'd be in.

'You haven't answered my question?' he continued.

'I don't know. I don't know anything. I didn't do anything.'

'You can't describe any of those men?'

Mrs McCann butted in again. 'I think she's had enough for one day,' she said, and the policeman stared back at her with an angry expression.

'I've told you once, madam, be quiet. I'll decide when it's enough. If a crime has been committed, it's my job to get to the bottom of it.'

We started again, same questions, same evasions. The sergeant scribbled in his notebook. Smoke filled the room as Inspector Whitley lit one cigarette after another and I started to cough. He did his job and I, without knowing it, did what girls who have been raped, abused and beaten do. I protected the rapists. I made certain by saying nothing that they were free to carry on grooming young girls, perpetuating without knowing it a culture of abuse and cover-up that was rampant in churches, care homes, mental hospitals, prisons, even, we now know, in the back rooms at the BBC.

When we left the police station, Mrs McCann held my arm and opened the van door for me.

'There, that's done and dusted,' she said. 'You did very well, Emily. I'm proud of you.'

I wasn't sure what I had done, but Mrs McCann was pleased and that made a nice change. At supper, she gave me the lean cuts of meat and the biggest portion of pudding. From then on, she made a point of locking the back door at night and sent me to bed early with a glass of milk. If Jeanie was running around screaming, she told her to be quiet 'because Emily's feeling delicate'.

Mrs McCann couldn't resist telling Mrs Tucker and the part-time staff I was 'in the family way', and they kept flashing me little half-smiles and sideways looks. They could probably see a bit of themselves in me. They were women who had married young, lost their figures and looked after other people's problem children to try to make ends meet. Misfortune brings people together and it's always a relief when it's someone else's misfortune.

One night when I was tucked up early, Doug came in and closed the door behind him. He sat on the bed looking nervous.

'Is it true?' he asked, and I nodded.

'It wasn't my fault.'

Doug was like a man already, tall and broad. He was never pushy and I knew he'd always liked me.

'We could run away again,' he said.

'Where would we go?'

'I don't know, maybe Gretna Green.'

'What's that?'

'It's a place where people get married, you know, when they run away.'

'We could.'

'I'll look after you, Emily.'

Tears trickled down my cheeks, the first happy tears for a long time. We had both grown up that summer. We knew we couldn't run away, but Doug suggesting it was more loving than I realised at the time and I would remember it again often in the future.

Mrs McCann drove me back to the hospital for more tests a few days later. It was raining and she kept clearing the mist from the inside of the window with sweeps of her red woolly gloves. After being in a daze all those weeks and months, my mind was sharp again. I looked at Mrs McCann across the cab and she smiled.

'So, what have you got your heart set on, a boy or a girl?' she asked.

'A girl, definitely. I hate boys.'

She made a harrumphing noise. 'Hate boys! You didn't get a bun in the oven on your own, dear,' she said, and we laughed.

It only struck me then that she didn't believe my story about men jumping out of the bushes. It was, after all, unlikely, and assumed a girl who went out half-dressed was just the sort who gets knocked up. Mrs McCann was Catholic, originally from

Ireland. She thought children should be modest and obedient, and girls who ended up in care were being punished for their wicked ways, the very trait that should have prevented her being employed in a care home in the first place. She had never taken much notice of me, but now that I was pregnant, she was kind and compassionate. I was carrying one of God's creatures and all babies are innocent.

'Have you thought of any names?' she now asked, and it was something that had gone through my mind.

'Tracy,' I replied.

'Tracy?'

'Or Roberta.'

'I've always been fond of Maria, or Angela,' she said, and grinned suddenly. 'Or Gloria. That's my name.'

'That's quite nice,' I said, and she seemed content.

She parked and we wound our way through the corridors to the department of obstetrics where four other women with bumps under their maternity dresses were flicking through magazines in the waiting room. We exchanged smiles. There's a real feeling of solidarity when you're expecting, and it was amusing watching them try to work out who exactly was pregnant, Mrs McCann, who had a fat tummy, but was clearly too old, or me, thin as a rake, and clearly too young. I had a feeling Mrs McCann was thinking the same as me and we enjoyed this silent intrigue.

When it came to my turn, a lady doctor named Rahni Patel asked Mrs McCann to remain in the waiting room. Mrs McCann bristled for a moment, but Dr Patel had a powerful presence and the warden was one of those women who believed a word from a doctor was only one step less in importance than the word of the Lord. Dr Patel wore a sari, she was tall, young and pretty with jet-black hair and spoke like the mums of girls who went to my boarding school.

In the examination room there was a desk with a single file on top, the same as when I was in the police station. I took off my clothes from the waist down and the doctor ran her hands over my tummy. 'Thirteen years old and thirteen weeks gone,' she said. 'We've only just caught you in time.' She paused.

'In time for what?'

'A termination, dear.'

I didn't know the word but I feared the meaning by the way she'd said it.

'What's that?' I asked.

'You are here to have an abortion, a small procedure to end the pregnancy.'

'End it?'

Big tears rolled down my cheeks. I suppose I had known all along they wouldn't let me have my baby, but it was still heart-breaking to know that a little person was growing inside me and they were going to take it away.

'But why? Why? Why would you do that?'

'You are not equipped to have a baby,' she explained. 'For one thing, it can be dangerous, for a girl of your age. There are no facilities for girls with babies in care.'

'But, but why?'

'There just aren't.'

We sat quietly for a moment.

'I'll look after it,' I said. 'I promise. I really, really promise.'

'Do you know who the father is?'

I shook my head and as I looked back into her brown face, I was suddenly shaken by something that had not occurred to me before.

'If the father's, you know, brown . . .'

'Like me?' she said, and I nodded. 'Then the baby would be brown. Is the father Asian?'

'I don't know,' I said.

'It is for the best, I promise you.'

'It's not, it's really not. I don't want you to take my baby away.'

'Emily, it's not a baby, not yet. It is still a foetus. It is growing into a baby, but it doesn't have any senses or feelings yet. Do you understand?'

'It feels like a baby.'

'That's called maternal instincts. You will feel the loss, you must be prepared for it, but it will pass.'

'What if it doesn't?'

She dried my tears with paper from a blue roll.

'It will. Trust me, it is for the best, you have your whole life in front of you.'

I went to speak, but nothing I could have said would have made any difference. The decision had been made. It was Dr Patel's job to inform me, not discuss it with me. I was thirteen, a child, but had all the emotional fear and excitement normal in any pregnant woman. Since I'd found out I was having a baby, I'd felt more comfortable in my own skin. I had been eating for two, ten in fact, and lay in my bed at night stroking my bump whispering. 'Hello, baby, what are you doing inside me? Do you want to come out and play?' My breasts had filled and the injuries from being raped had gone away.

Dr Patel left me alone for a moment and went out to speak to Mrs McCann. I had no idea what she said, but Mrs McCann came over all huffy, her face turned red and she stormed off, slamming the door behind her.

A nurse took me to a single ward on the second floor to be readied for what she called 'the procedure'. She made me dress in a gown and told me she was going to shave my pubic hair.

'Why?'

'It's more hygienic,' she said.

I did think about struggling, but when you fight with adults you always lose. I pressed my head into the pillow and closed my eyes. It wasn't fair. I was never allowed to make decisions for myself. Mum had put me into care. Ali and his gang had decided to rape me. Now the hospital had chosen to take away my baby. No one ever asked me what I wanted. The nurse put cream on my pubes and as I sat up to watch it was like watching Alan when he left the bathroom door open shaving his chin.

'Lift your knees,' she said.

I did, and her words reminded me of Ali saying that: *Good girl. Lift your knees.* He had rested his hands either side of my head and entered me. He had moved slowly, staring into my eyes, and patiently planted his semen inside me. Ali was the father of my baby. My foetus. I knew it. It was a little Pakistani baby. They were going to take it away and suddenly I didn't care.

The nurse finished, wiped me dry and pushed a tablet into my vagina. This was to soften my cervix and widen the entrance to my womb. I didn't really understand when she explained, but she was being kind and it wasn't her fault that I was having an abortion. It was my fault.

Different nurses kept popping in and out, to make sure I wasn't going to try to kill myself, I suppose. One of them brought me a copy of *Country Life*, then went out and came back again with two comics, the *Dandy* and *Beano*. It was rare in 1969 to be preparing a girl of thirteen for a termination and the nursing staff weren't sure how to behave. I was starving, but they told me I couldn't eat anything until after the procedure. They did give me something to drink, a cloudy liquid like bad milk, and I dozed off.

When I opened my eyes, I felt heavy and I thought I must be hallucinating. Something marvellous and unbelievable had happened. The door was open and Dad was standing there. I shook my head and rubbed my eyes.

'Daddy . . .'

'Hello, Poppet,' he said, and the tears gushed from me again. He hugged me.

'You came, Daddy, you came.'

'Course I did, Poppet.'

Dr Patel was hovering around behind him.

'We're going to start in about five minutes,' she said. 'One of the nurses will show you the way to the waiting room.'

She closed the door and I stared back at Dad as he approached the bed and took my hands. He bent to kiss me, then stood back shaking his head. His face was ashen, like a dead person.

'This isn't good enough, is it, girl?' he said. 'You're going to have to pull your socks up.'

'I'm sorry, Dad. I didn't do anything.'

'I've spoken to the police. I know what happened. We don't ever have to talk about it again.'

'But I don't want them to take away my baby, Dad,' I said.

'It's for the best, Poppet.'

I still wasn't sure, but Dad saying it made it seem better. I knew I couldn't have a baby at thirteen. It wouldn't be fair to the baby for one thing. But I could feel that little life breathing inside me and taking it away didn't seem right. It was right. It was right for me. Right for my baby. But it didn't seem right lying there in that bed with the light turning dark through the blinds on the window.

'Can I come home, Dad?' I said. 'Please can I?'

He shook his head again. He looked exhausted, lined, beaten down. 'My hands are tied. I've spoken to my solicitor about this a hundred times. Your mother is your guardian. I can't change that. I've come here to sign the forms for the termination, but it was only with her permission.'

'Why does she hate me?'

'I don't know. There's something wrong with her, not you.'

He had never said anything like that before and it made me feel better.

'I didn't, you know, just sleep around, Dad . . .'

'I believe you, Emily, really I do.'

Two nurses and Dr Patel trooped in and Dad was directed to the waiting room. It was November. The dark falls quickly and the nurses hurried about closing the blinds and turning on the lights. I was given a local anaesthetic. The nurse who had shaved my hair again told me to open my legs and pushed a long rubber tube up into me. It was connected to a pump. The pump started pumping and it felt like a vacuum cleaner sucking at me.

'Are you all right?'

'Not really.'

'Are you in any pain?'

'No,' I said.

The vacuum kept pulling at my womb and it was quickly over. The baby had gone, sucked out, terminated.

It had been painless, but as the anaesthetic wore off I started to have severe cramps, like period pains. There was a lot of blood and Dad, who had come back into the ward, went rushing off, limping on his bad leg, and returned with the nurse. She jabbed a needle in my bottom, but I was still in pain. It was like my guts had been sucked out and my insides had been battered and crushed.

Dad stayed at my bedside. The injection put me to sleep. I had terrible dreams, Ali, Harry, Alan all chasing me, spreading my legs, filling me. I felt as if I were swimming against the tide, that I was being pulled down beneath the surface of the water. As I took my last breath, I coughed and woke up. There were little echoes reverberating inside me, but it passed and the pain went away.

Dad had come by train to Rochester, where he had checked in to a suite in one of the good hotels. We spent the night there. We had dinner. We talked about Amy and Aunt Alice, our holiday the previous year in Broadstairs. He drank a lot of wine and I really fancied a glass myself but I was too young.

I slept in the bed in the annexe to his suite and next day a taxi took us back to the holding bay. I was still bleeding and distressed after the abortion. I pleaded with him to take me home, but Dad was not a man who broke the law. He paid his taxes. He did the right thing, even if at the time it seemed to me to be the wrong thing.

He handed me over to Mrs McCann, who was grumpy and reluctant to shake his hand. My suitcase had already been packed and waited at the entrance for me to load into the minivan. The tall silent woman who had brought me to the holding bay was at the wheel, ready to drive me on to the next place. I had been at the halfway stage long enough and a place more appropriate for a thirteen-year-old girl who gets raped had been found for me.

Dad left. The meter on the taxi we had taken from Rochester was running and he waved out the window as it pulled away. I put my case in the back of the van and turned to Mrs McCann.

'Goodbye,' I said. 'Thank you.'

She bristled and threw back her shoulders. 'Don't speak to me,' she said. 'You killed your baby.'

CHAPTER 16

The Bin

Sometimes a tune and a few lines from a song get stuck in your head. What was stuck in my head, and it stayed there, was Mrs McCann's parting words: *You killed your baby.*

I tried to tell myself this wasn't true, but it was true, and it is truth not lies that hurts and leaves scars on your mind. I remembered Dr Patel saying it wasn't a baby they aborted, but a foetus. But that's just playing with words. It felt like a baby to me and I felt the loss, mentally and physically. My breasts tingled and I bled for two weeks. It was my fault for getting raped and my fault they took my baby away. I am a bad seed. I deserve everything I get.

I sat beside the tall social services lady on the journey back along the A2. Last time I had been on this road, everything was bright with sunshine. Now, the trees were stripped bare and pale mist hung over the fields and houses. I shivered and sat on my hands to keep them warm.

'Where are we going?' I asked.

'You'll find out soon enough.'

I was a child who had lost my child and lost my childhood. I was at my most vulnerable, anxious and damaged, yet this tall silent woman who worked in the care system provided no care, but rather the opposite – she was uncaring. I wasn't able to articulate these thoughts, but they were inside my head, even then. I turned back to the view. I wanted to shrink into myself and disappear like a puff of smoke. I stared out at the black clouds crossing the grey sky. I had been raped and now I was being punished. Tears welled into my eyes as I suddenly pictured myself being locked in a dungeon, and the only good thing was that Ali wouldn't be able to get me now.

We arrived in late afternoon on a bleak November day at a nondescript two-storey building with a flat roof on the edge of some small town. Across the narrow road, dominating the landscape, was a huge Victorian asylum like a castle in a horror film. There was still light in the sky, but the building cast everything about it in shadow.

'What's that place?' I asked, pointing, and the woman paused as if considering whether or not to answer.

'They call it The Bin,' she said. 'That's where you end up when you outgrow this place.'

The building rose up eight floors with towers and turrets at different levels. We were embraced by the shadow spilling across the road and I shivered as the cold rain that had been threatening all day began to fall. The woman's few words made it seem so terrifying and permanent. The asylum had black walls, dim lights, and my knees trembled as I imagined gruesome things going on behind those high arched doors.

Those last six months at the Reception Centre I had been monitored. Reports on my attitude, behaviour and psychological state would have been submitted by Mrs McCann and others. As a baby killer, I must have had a big black mark against me and my new placement was at a secure unit for under-eighteens, a mini-prison for children who had never been sentenced in any court.

This was like being sectioned. You are only sent to a secure place if your mental state is so precarious that it is deemed necessary for reasons of health and safety – your own and everyone else's. It is where you are assessed and treatments, like purges and magic potions, are designed to wash out the demon seeds planted in your mind. I was too young to be asked whether this was the right place for me, and I had no right of appeal. Only my guardian had that right and she had finally got me where she wanted me: locked up, out of sight, out of mind.

The first thing that struck me when we entered the new building was the stench of ammonia, a smell like Ali's breath. It hung in the air tainting everything you ate and every breath you breathed. That air of institutional apathy and neglect was just the same as at the holding bay but worse, with nerve-wracking screams echoing along the corridors. It was like entering someone else's nightmare.

I was handed over to the chief warden, Mr Blackmore, who took the file the tall woman gave him and placed it on his desk. He never once looked at me. He kept glancing down and running his fingertips over the file without opening it. That file contained a composite of who I was supposed to be and I felt at that moment as if I was merely the blue binder, an empty shell storing these irrefutable facts. Once you are in the system, who you are and who those files say you are can be completely different, even misleading, and there is no way to correct errors if they appear. Like a tattoo, it marks you for life.

After the silent journey, I had the sudden urge to tell Mr Blackmore that it had all been a big mistake. I had never wanted to burn down my school. I loved my school. I was only copying Bobby. At the holding bay, I had often tried to explain what happened to Mrs McCann, but she didn't see it as part of her job to listen. No one ever listened, and because they never listen, speaking out when bad things happen, like Harry molesting me in the tool shed, becomes impossible. You feel ashamed, you doubt that anyone is going to believe you, and you know before you start that they don't want to listen anyway – have an investigation, call the police – that's too much like hard work.

I looked at Mr Blackmore. He had a thin face like a skull and a tic throbbed in his temple. He wore a three-piece suit with stains on the waistcoat and the collar of his striped shirt turned up like wings. He had fine grey hair combed to disguise his baldness and dead-fish eyes that I tried to catch.

'Is that my file?' I asked, and the air turned icy.

Mr Blackmore remained stock still for a moment, then summoned up enough energy to lean out of the door and call one of the male nurses.

'Bob. Bob. Hope you're not busy, Bob. Hope I'm not disturbing you or anything? We have a new arrival,' he said.

'It's what I'm paid for,' the man replied.

As Bob strolled up, we were shuffled out of the office. The woman left without a goodbye and I was given the 'tour'. Bob Drake was about thirty with darting eyes, jerky movements and yellow irregular teeth too big for his small mouth. He was dressed in a grey uniform with patch pockets on the shirt and a wide leather belt containing a bunch of keys on a chain that rattled as he went.

We began on the ground floor. The central area contained admin offices, the staffroom, a playroom and a 'quiet' room, which was never quiet. Along the corridor there were classrooms, the kitchens and dining hall, the laundry room, a clinic with drugs on shelves from floor to ceiling, and 'solitary' rooms with padded walls, where we paused to have a closer look. Bob unlocked a cupboard to reveal the torture chamber it contained.

'Restraints, ball-gags, straightjackets, we've got the lot,' he said proudly. 'This is where you get sorted out if there's a problem.'

The blood drained from my face and he sensed my terror.

'That's not going to happen to you though, is it?' he added.

I swallowed hard and shook my head. 'No,' I whispered.

We climbed the stairs to the first floor, which was divided in two wings, boys one side, girls the other. I followed him down the long corridor with children lurching by with flat, expressionless faces and the sound of metal doors slamming with the sonic boom of car crashes. As I was about to discover, most of the children had mental disorders of various types and at varying stages including Down's syndrome, autism, bipolar and mood disorder, obsessive-compulsive disorder (OCD), which we all suffered from to some extent, and borderline personality disorder, under whose umbrella I fell (as well as psychological problems and other things written in that blue dossier).

'Why are these children here?' I asked, and Bob didn't mind answering at all.

'Them or you?'

I shrugged. 'Both, I suppose.'

He studied me more closely. After being pregnant, I still had a glow, and the way Bob Drake was checking me out sent a chill up my spine. My hands trembled I was holding my fists so tightly and I tried to keep them still behind my back. His features softened.

'What's your name, then?' he asked.

'Emily. Emily MacKenzie,' I said, hanging on to who I was.

'You're here, Emily, because the wires are crossed in your brain box,' he said, tapping the side of his head, 'and they can't find a place for you anywhere else.'

'But I'm not, you know, ill or anything.'

'That's up to the powers that be. I'm just here to clear up the mess,' he said, and took a long sniff. 'Most of 'em in here are freaks put out with the rubbish. They'll be here till Doomsday.'

'Really?'

He laid his hand on my shoulder. 'Now you have to decide. You one of them, or one of us?'

It was hard to know what to say. I was in a secure unit. I was suffering the postpartum blues of an abortion after multiple-rape and this man, Bob Drake, was being friendly in the way Harry the gardener had started out being friendly.

'It should only be temporary. My dad wants me to go home,' I said, and he grinned.

'Well, while you're here, I hope I can make your stay with us as comfortable as possible.'

He was being funny, friendly. He wanted me to like him, and I obliged with a smile.

'Don't you worry your pretty little head about nothing. Anything you need, just come to me.'

'Thank you.'

At the end of the corridor, we entered a dorm where a girl sat in the corner pulling out her hair and moaning in a slow drone like a plane coming in to land. Several girls lay under the covers in iron cots with flaking paint, and two girls sat close together like Siamese twins, leaning against the wall and holding hands as they stared into space. Why with their mental illnesses they were in that place and why I should have been sent there was a mystery I never solved.

The stink of ammonia was just as powerful in the dorm as it was in the corridors. It was accompanied by the reek of stale pee, a smell I was familiar with from sharing the bunks at the Briggs house, a period of my life I had hated, although now when memories of that time slipped by I had a certain nostalgia. Even the occasional thrashing from Alan was preferable to where I had landed.

'Here we are, then, home sweet home.' Someone had brought my case from reception. Bob pointed at a locker. 'Put your junk in there. And remember what I said, anything you need, I'm here for you.'

He left and I gazed about me. The walls were wet with damp. The light was dead. This was hell. I was being punished and the only way I was going to get through this was to accept it. I had killed my baby. I had to pay. That's how it works. If you are good at school you get a gold star. If you are bad, you have to be disciplined to make you better. I stood there looking lost, and was shaken from this reverie by the arrival of another girl who marched up with a smile on her wide face.

'Hi, I'm Kate, I heard someone else was coming today.'

'Emily,' I said.

She smiled. I smiled. It was like finding your own shadow.

Kate Conway was shorter than me, a little tough girl like Barbs with dimpled arms and a shapeless dress. There was so much I wanted to ask her, but all the questions were jumbled together and I just felt a relief that she was there at all. I remembered a history class, Stanley finding Dr Livingstone, and I would have liked to have been back in that classroom again.

We slept in adjoining beds. Well, not slept. I didn't sleep properly again for several weeks and then it was after a syringe had been jabbed in my backside. That first night, I snatched moments of rest between girls waking from nightmares screaming, weeping, crying for their mothers. It was like an asylum. It was an asylum, and I was aware as I pulled the covers under my chin that hanging on to my sanity in this place was going to need more strength than I felt I had. In a room full of people with flu you catch the flu. In the midst of children with mental disorders, you develop mental disorders. You lose you. You feel your inner self crushed to dust and you watch the dust scoot away under the locked doors.

We were roused from bed by a clanging bell. I used the bathroom and combed my hair, the glass lit by a shiny slither of winter light. My hair was silky with natural shades of russet and amber threaded through the chestnut brown. I had diligently trimmed the split ends and it was healthy from fresh air and good conditioner. After washing, I just had to brush it back and it rose from my crown in two waves that fell to the pit of my back. First thing that morning, someone came for me and they cut it off. I hadn't noticed that all the girls had short hair and, twelve hours after arriving, I was identical to all the rest.

Kate was waiting for me and we filed into breakfast. We sat at tables of twelve, about a hundred children all groaning and moaning, screaming because they were mentally ill and needed help, love, care. I sat close to Kate and we literally kept our heads down, eating anonymous cereal from plastic bowls as missiles sailed through the air, plates, cups, clothes. If the children weren't screaming, the staff were.

'Oi, you, shut your cakehole. Do as you're bloody well told. What's wrong now?'

If there was a plus side, with so many disturbed children, you could hide in plain sight, which is what we did. After breakfast, we were marched in bunches, boys and girls together, to the boys' bathroom.

'This is the worst part of the day,' Kate said.

'Why?'

She cringed. 'You'll see.'

The bathrooms were at the top of the stairs, one on each side. They were huge with pipes circling the green walls, showers without doors and each contained four oversized baths that stood in the middle of the room like it was Roman times. Bob Drake and another nurse named Dean Ricks got hold of a boy of about fourteen with Down's syndrome and undressed him. He happened to have abnormally large genitals and his penis was erect because of the attention he was getting. He was grinning and his limbs were wobbly like jelly.

Bob wore rubber gloves. He held the poor boy's penis and looked around the room.

'Does anyone wanna touch it?' he asked, his eyes settling on me. 'Now's your chance.'

I looked away and was astonished to see the two female nurses present were giggling. I couldn't understand why they should think it was funny when I thought it was cruel and horrid. Why we had been taken to the boys' bathroom I had no idea and I knew, too, that instant, that there was no question of the children being helped or rehabilitated or repaired, that once you were in The Bin, or the 'mini-bin', as they called it, the best you could hope for was to stay sane and endure. The men washed the boy, hosing him down like a car. He was roughly dried. The women dressed him, first in a giant nappy, I assumed the reason for their presence, and the boy giggled, happy to be the centre of attention. I saw this show repeated many times.

Although the boy, I seem to recall his name was Benedict, was humiliated in this crude way every day, most of the children only got to take a bath once a week. Again, this was a public display and I could hardly believe it when Kate and I and two other girls were forced to strip naked with Bob Drake and Dean Ricks watching. The two female nurses, Lynne and Beverley, were in charge, but did nothing to stop the two men ogling us from the doorway. I was still bleeding from the abortion and when the bathwater turned red with blood I had never felt more embarrassed in my life.

The following week, when I asked if I could take a bath on my own, Beverley said it was too dangerous.

'But why?'

'You kill yourself on my watch and I'm out on my ear.'

'But I'm not going to do that.'

'That's what they all say. We've had nine suicides in three years,' she said. 'And that's not counting the ones taking overdoses, the self-harmers and what not.'

'But why do the men watch while we're washing?'

'They're here for my protection.' It was clear by my expression that I didn't know what she meant. 'You could have a knife or something, it happens.'

Bob and Dean had gone about their chores and I was standing there with a towel around me. Beverley watched while I dressed.

'So, you had a kid then?' she said.

'No. No, I didn't,' I replied, and she shrugged as if she didn't believe me.

CHAPTER 17

Playing by the Rules

The unit was a dumping ground for what Bob Drake had called freaks. I had left the holding bay and landed like a time traveller in the nineteenth century. The asylum across the road held the unit in its shadow and was the only view through the steel-wired windows of the dorm. The metal fence marking the perimeter was lit at night by halogen arc lights that gave off a pale eerie glow and made me feel as if I were in a concentration camp. The patients confined to The Bin wore striped pyjamas at all times and wandered around after shock therapy like zombies.

I was living in a nether world, a madhouse. Any remnants of that girl who had dressed in hot pants and flitted like a butterfly around the pub garden had gone. I had kept a firm grip on my individuality in the holding bay. At the mini-bin, I was becoming a nervous wreck, squinting, biting my nails, crying because crying is something to do and you feel a bit better when you stop.

As part of my treatment, I was prescribed an antipsychotic 'to calm me down'. The problem is, if you are not psychotic, antipsychotic drugs make you psychotic. I kept seeing Amy wandering along the top corridor and when I ran to her, it would turn out to be just another girl from the unit. I thought Dad was coming to take me home and waited for his old Humber to appear on the narrow road between the two buildings. My dreams were insane, swirling images of Alan, giant pairs of scissors, Ali – 'you good girl,' he's saying – and there was a naked baby running away and I was always trying to catch her. Tracy, Tracy, Tracy, I called, but she got smaller and smaller and smaller and then vanished.

One day, I caught myself sitting on the bed rocking mindlessly back and forth and needed all my determination to stop doing it. It was the drugs. I knew if I refused to take them, they would pin me down, inject me and drip-feed me with something even worse. I had seen it happen. I saw it happen every day. I had been so traumatised since I arrived at the mini-bin I had survived by being compliant, helpful and friendly. I continued to be so. When it was drug time, I willingly put out my palm, threw the sunshine yellow pill into my mouth and took the plastic cup of water I was given. I swallowed the water down and said thank you. This time, as soon as the nurse moved on, I hooked the pill from where I held it locked against my bottom teeth and flushed it down the lavatory as soon as I had the chance.

Christmas came and Christmas went. It made the ordeal of being imprisoned worse. The walls and halls were strewn with home-made decorations, the paper chains hanging in mismatched loops, the giant tree in the playroom shedding needles that were still there three months later. On Christmas Eve, the local mayor and his wife came with boxes of toys, most things too young for eleven- to eighteen-year-olds, and the Chief Warden hovered around them like a nervous fly. Mr Blackmore was afraid of the staff and afraid of the children; his fear of doing the wrong thing leading him to do nothing at all. He wasn't a bad man. He was simply the wrong man in the wrong job.

In my experience, nine out of ten people working in care should not be there, from probation officers and psychothera-pists to wardens and nurses. Any initial desire to be of service is soon crushed by the system, the repetition, the brutality, that sense of trying to build a sandcastle to hold back the tide. Good people leave and those who remain often have emotional and personality problems, low self-worth, a superiority-inferiority complex and a lack of education. The care system also attracts paedophiles, bullies and lost souls like Andrew Blackmore who had nowhere else to go.

I received cards and postal orders from Dad, Aunt Alice and Amy. I tried to picture them in my mind, but they were becom-ing hazy like old photographs. With my pale cheeks and cropped hair, it didn't look like me in the mirror. I looked like everyone else, a rubber doll pressed out on a moulding machine. My brown eyes had turned to mud and my wide mouth was pinched and colourless. In care, it's hard to even care for yourself. Vanity, like privacy, like individuality, all vanish.

I rarely left the unit, except for my weekly visits across the road to have an IQ test and an EEG, an electroencephalogra-phy, a terrifying experience, although you get used to it. The first time I entered the asylum, the people in striped pyjamas emerged out of the gloom moaning and talking gibberish.

'I didn't do it, I didn't do it!' one man was shouting, and Bob Drake, who always accompanied me, leaned over to whisper.

'Oh yes he did. Killed his wife and cut her into six pieces in the bath,' he said. 'They've been giving him electric shock therapy for two years. Don't make a blind bit of difference.'

'Then why do they do it?'

'Makes people more, you know, receptive,' he said.

I didn't know there was a difference between shock therapy and EEG and, that moment, my heart stopped.

'That's not what they are going to do to me, is it?'

'Nah. Not this time.' He grinned. 'I told you, I'm looking after you.'

We filed into an office with an oak desk and loads of books on polished shelves. Bob sat in the corner and I sat opposite Dr Wolfe, a thin young psychiatrist with a beard, a black polo-necked sweater and horn-rimmed glasses. He began by asking me my name and age, all that sort of thing, then gave me an IQ test consisting of pictures of cubes, spheres and other figures in diverse combinations. I had to select shapes that didn't fit in the various patterns, number things in order of volume and so on. Dr Wolfe told me that each age group has a mean average of 100 and that most people scored between 70 and 130.

'Don't worry if it's below, it doesn't mean anything,' he said, and of course I knew as he said it that, on the contrary, it meant everything.

'If I have a high score, will that help me to be sent home to my father?'

He had not been expecting the question and looked back at me as if he were seeing me for the first time, that I was a person, not just a list of data in the blue file.

'Is that what you want?'

'Yes, ever so much,' I blurted out. It was the first time anyone had ever asked me.

'Your parents are divorced?'

'Yes.'

'And you don't want to go home to your mother?'

'She hates me, I don't know why.'

'Why do you think she hates you?'

'Because I'm a bad seed, that's what she said, and, when I was little, I never won any talent competitions when she wanted me to.'

'Is that what you wanted?'

'It's what she wanted, and she always had to have everything she wanted.'

'You said your mother hated you. Perhaps it is you who hates your mother?'

'I didn't then. I do now.'

'That's something you must think about and we shall discuss again.'

He glanced down at the test paper and I asked the same question again. 'Will they let me go home if I do well?'

'Well, let's see how you get on first, shall we.'

I had thirty minutes. Bob lit a cigarette and Dr Wolfe smoked a pipe, tamping down the tobacco every few seconds and relighting it in a way that reminded me of Grandpa MacKenzie. When I had finished, I turned the sheet around and slid it across the desk. He glanced through my answers, looked up at me, then looked down at my answers again. I had surprised him in some way and didn't know which way.

'How did I do?' I asked.

He took off his glasses. 'I'll have to mark it up properly before I can say.'

We left the office through an adjoining door where I came face to face with a weird-looking device with wires coming out in every direction like mad hair.

I gasped. 'Oh my God, what's that?' I said.

'It's an EEG machine, it's perfectly harmless,' a nurse in a white uniform replied. 'Come along now, sit down. I haven't got all day.'

'Will it hurt?'

'No, no, no, just sit down and behave; it'll be over before you know it.'

'Do I have to?'

The nurse leaned forward with an angry expression. 'Yes, young lady, you do.'

I took a deep breath and sat in the chair next to the machine. I was tired of fighting. Bob Drake grinned at me across the surgery and raised his thumb in a supportive gesture.

The nurse then stuck literally dozens of electrodes to my scalp with a glue that I was still picking out of my hair when it was time to return the following week. The EEG records the brain's spontaneous electrical activity over a period of thirty minutes and this data, I assumed, would be added to the file. Electroencephalography is useful to diagnose epilepsy, tumours, encephalitis, brain death and sleep disorders. What they were trying to measure in me I did not know and it would be a long time before I found out.

When the process was over, Bob was about to take me back to the unit when Dr Wolfe's head appeared around his office door and he stopped us in the corridor.

'Have you done this test before?' he asked.

'No, never,' I replied. 'Why?'

'No matter, you can do another one next time.'

The tests continued on a regular basis and I could see Dr Wolfe was becoming more and more frustrated because my IQ scores did not match what was in my file and those files were sacred like the Ten Commandments. Finally, he leaned across the desk after I'd done the most recent test, took off his glasses and stared into my eyes.

'Emily, tell me the truth, are you cheating?'

'Cheating? Of course not. How could I?'

'How could you indeed.'

'You have never told me how I've done,' I then said.

He took a long breath and steepled his fingers. 'You have a mean average of 138.'

'That's good, isn't it?'

'Yes, it is, which makes it all the more curious why you have gone through bouts of kleptomania, arson and early psychological assessment, not to mention more recent activities.'

Recent activities meant getting pregnant. As no one was ever brought to justice, the file would have reflected my having had an abortion, not being gang-raped. As for my other misdeeds, they were the result of low self-esteem created and perpetuated by my mother.

'I don't think I should be here, Dr Wolfe. It's just been a sequence of mistakes,' I said, and he looked reflective.

'Burning down a school, hundreds of thousands of pounds' worth of damage. It doesn't sound like a mistake to me.'

'I didn't want to do it, not really. I just wanted to be in with the other girls,' I said.

'And you needed to burn down a school to make friends?'

'It's not like that. It's hard to explain.'

'That's why you are here, to find out.' He paused. 'That's all for today – we will discuss this again in the fullness of time.'

During these excursions Bob Drake always regaled me with macabre stories of lobotomies and electric shock treatments that turned patients into 'head bangers'. On the way back that day, we stood and watched through the wire fence as the inmates wandered in circles arguing with themselves, walking in weird ways, or just standing still and staring at something only they could see. The man who had cut his wife into six pieces was clinging to the fence.

'I didn't do it. I didn't do it.'

'Oh yes you did!' Bob shouted back, and the man's mouth dropped open in surprise. Tears ran down his cheeks.

Bob turned to me. 'Once you earn your pair of pyjamas, you never get out of them,' he said, and we paused before crossing the road back to the unit. 'So, you're a bit of a clever clogs, then?'

'That's what the tests say.'

'Did you cheat?'

'No. You can't cheat.'

He considered me for a few minutes. 'I like you, Emily,' he said. 'I'm going to make it my business to look after you.'

It wasn't what he said but the way that he said it that was terrifying. He took my hand and we ran between the cars.

'See you later, alligator,' he said as we entered the unit.

I smiled and ran upstairs back to the dorm where Kate was waiting and I told her everything that had happened across the road. Our lives were narrow so each little thing took on greater significance than it warranted. Kate Conway was my lifeline, the light in the darkness, and surviving in that despicable place would have been much harder without her. No one discussed why they were in the unit. Most of the children didn't even know, but that day it just came up naturally in conversation. I told her I had burned down my school with some other girls and she thought that was really daring.

'I beat a boy to death with a hammer,' she said matter-of-factly.

'But why?' I blurted out.

'He was trying to pin me down in the garage at the back of his house and, you know, do it. I reached for a hammer and just hit him.' She broke off. 'After I'd hit him once, something sort of took over and I just kept on doing it.' She gave a little shrug that made me feel sad. 'I suppose I'll be here for the rest of my life.'

My throat had gone dry. For the first time since I'd arrived at the unit I realised that Kate's problems were worse than my own.

A teacher came in every weekday for the handful of children who could sit still long enough in a classroom to concentrate. The levels and ages varied, but this was one of the few quiet moments in those long noisy days and I tried to get something out of it. The rest of the time it was bedlam. Children were always fighting and howling. Some child was always being rushed along the corridor to 'solitary', where they were tranquillised with God knows what and would return to the regular dorms like robots from *Doctor Who*.

In the playroom they played table tennis as if it were badminton. There were games like Monopoly where each person taking part played by their own rules. The quiet room was the place where children went to cry and was always full. There were books, but most had missing pages, these incomplete stories a metaphor for the entire system.

With the staff occupied stuffing pills into the inmates, Kate and I killed time folding clothes on the table in the laundry, a large steamy room lined with machines that drummed and clanged like an out-of-tune orchestra. We cleaned the floors, spreading the acrid-smelling ammonia over the surface with big ragged mops, and helped the nursing staff to a point where I ended up being the main carer for two little boys, one whose urine had to be tested every day for diabetes, the other who required special pills and was on a diet that had to be monitored. I learned how to take temperatures, give injections, and read the fragmented storybooks to the little ones when they went to bed at night, making up the scenes that had vanished with the missing pages.

The staff were happy to be relieved of these responsibilities. They all had their own lives, their own children, their own troubles. Working at the unit was just a job and, like most people in low-paid work, they did the minimum and got away with as much as they could.

It was different for Kate and me. The staff were there for eight hours a day. We were locked under that roof 24/7 and as long as I was working, particularly with the female staff, I could avoid the bantering and innuendo from Bob and Dean, which was ever-present, like the slow release of gas, waiting to explode.

One afternoon, I was on my own in the laundry room folding clothes. The door closed and Bob Drake was standing there, back against the door, his intentions written all over his face.

'Please don't, Bob, please.'

He stopped in his tracks. He had been planning this and my words had put him off his stride.

'Please,' I said. 'Please.'

He shook himself out of his trance and swaggered towards me, the keys on his belt ringing, his crooked teeth revealed by a sudden smile. 'Come on, stop all that. You know you love it.'

'I don't, Bob, please.'

'You're just a little prick teaser,' he said.

As he edged around the long table, I circled away from him. I made a dash for the door. I managed to pull it open, but someone pulled it closed from the outside. Bob pinned my arms against the wall and I jerked my knee up into his groin. He winced with pain. Last time I was raped, I had been drugged and passive. I was going to be raped again. But not without a fight. Not this time.

He grinned. 'Like a bit of rough, do you?'

He grabbed me and carried me wriggling and kicking to the table. He laid me down. I tried to roll off and landed one blow after another as he pulled off my shirt. He gripped me around the waist and I punched his back and kicked out. He hoisted me up from the middle, lowered the zip on my jeans and pulled them down. The same with my knickers.

'There, that's better. Now you're dressed for it,' he said, taking a breath.

I rolled off the table to the floor and crawled away, but there was nowhere to go, nowhere to hide. This was England in 1970. I had been sent for safety to an institution and it was the most unsafe place in the world. There was nothing, absolutely nothing I could do to stop Bob Drake stripping me of my clothes and doing whatever he wanted to do. I was a toy, a plaything. He caught up with me, pulled at my feet and rolled me onto my back.

'Don't do it, Bob, don't do it. I'll report you.'

He wasn't listening. He had that glazed look that comes to rapists and, in that Jekyll and Hyde moment, they stop being human and become animals. He had been waiting to do this since the day I arrived with colour in my cheeks. I was, at thirteen, the paedophiles' pin-up with pert little breasts and a faint frosting of hair on my pubic bone. I looked like what I was, a child, and terrified.

Bob pinned me down, his hand like a dead weight on one shoulder. He spat on his palm, wet his cock, and pushed up inside me with one lunge. It was painful like a knife cut and quickly over. He rammed in and out, and withdrew, spurting his semen over my stomach. He tried to kiss me and I moved my head away.

'There, that's better. That's what you needed. You'll be all right now.'

He scrambled to his feet, zipped himself up and jerked his way to the door. My stomach was sticky with semen and there was blood on my thighs. My period had started.

Bob tapped from the inside, the door opened and Dean entered.

'All yours, mate,' he said.

Dean must have been guarding the door from the outside. It was his turn. They had planned this, probably down the pub after a few drinks. They had chosen the time carefully. Two of the female staff were away sick and, late afternoon when half the children were drugged out of their minds, it was unlikely they would be disturbed. The other thing that struck me, then or later, it doesn't matter which, is that rapists feel more comfortable when they are not alone. If you're molesting a child, it doesn't seem quite as monstrous if your mate's at it as well.

'Please don't do anything, Dean,' I begged, and he looked down at the blood and mess on my body.

'Don't worry, I'm not going where he's been. You can suck on this,' he said, and pulled out his cock.

Bob may have had some shred of humanity about him somewhere. Dean had none at all. He was a lean, silent man with gaunt cheeks and psychopath eyes. He did the job for the perks. I was one of the perks. I was on the floor still, my back hurting from taking Bob's weight on top of me, but I wasn't going to do anything without a fight.

'I'm thirteen. I'm going to report you!' I shouted, one last attempt to save myself, and he just grinned.

'Your word against ours, sweetheart. Who do you think they're going to believe?' He pulled me up by my cropped hair. 'Come on, it's not the first time. You know you want it.'

'I don't. I don't. Please, please, Dean, I'm thirteen, I'm not old enough.'

'You know what they say, if they bleed, they're old enough.'

I moved my head from side to side. He used both hands to get a grip on my cheekbones and I kicked him as hard as I could.

'Feisty little bitch, ain't we,' he said, and slapped me across both cheeks. They like that slap, hard but not too hard, self-controlled, a taster of what to expect if you continue to struggle.

He was grinning. Holding me still. They don't mind you fighting. They like it. If you hurt them, and I tried to hurt them, they like it even more. It justifies their own violence. You are a wild child. You have to be tamed. Taught a lesson. Broken. He kept trying to push his cock in my mouth and I wouldn't let him. In the end, he was so excited, he shot his load in a long spurt across my face. He rubbed the mess over my lips and I stared back at him with sheer loathing.

'You're disgusting, you know that.'

'Yeah,' he said. 'And you're in a place for nutters.'

I was on my knees. He pulled me up under my chin and leaned so close our noses were almost touching. 'Listen, girl, you're just a wet hole, you're nothing. You're less than nothing.'

'I'm here to be cared for,' I spat.

'You having a laugh? You like fucking and you're in the right place – you're here to get fucked.'

I assumed Bob and Dean had read my file. They had all read my file – Dr Wolfe, Beverley, Mr Blackmore.

He made his way back around the table. I was terrified of this man. I was naked, down on my knees, but I was shaking with rage and wouldn't let it go.

'I'm reporting you!' I screamed. 'I'll tell the nurses what you've done. I'll tell Mr Blackmore.'

He stopped, paused for a second, then came back. He grabbed my arms. He wasn't angry. He was sneering.

'Do that, and we'll have you killed.' He leaned in. 'Or we'll have you kill yourself. You'll do whatever we make you do.' He pushed me away. 'Now, you little cunt, get yourself cleaned up.'

He bowled off, a spring in his step. I washed my face and body in the sink and dressed.

That made seven.

I ran the tips of my fingers under my eyes. There were no tears. The girl who had cried because sadistic things had been done to her had gone. I was someone else. My emotions had closed down, died like cut flowers. I was locked behind metal doors and unbreakable windows. There was no one I could tell. No one who would listen. No one cared. I was not deranged when I arrived at the unit, but I felt suddenly as if my sanity was hanging by a thread. I was becoming what the file said I was, what they wanted me to be. I had been loved and cherished. Now I was rubbish, a wet hole for any pervert to take advantage of.

How did this happen?

The male nurses and carers were employed to protect me and they hadn't, they had violated me. My vagina hurt. My back hurt. The only thing left in me now was anger, hatred and misery.

Early that evening, I stopped outside Andrew Blackmore's office, but was unable to summon up the right words to tell him what they had done to me. The door was half open. Before he looked away, our eyes met and I realised in that split second that he knew what was happening in the unit. He knew, but was too weak or afraid or lazy to do anything about it.

Bob and Dean came for me again two weeks later. Once paedophiles get a taste for it, they can't stop. They are normally loners, but recognise the craving in others. They find each other, they pass girls on to each other. They get jobs in schools, hospitals and children's homes. They volunteer at youth clubs and churches. They are clever and manipulative, often charismatic, at least to children, and the moment they sense that someone is on to them, they move on, taking their references to the next place.

There is a season for everything. This was the rape season. Bob and Dean raped Kate, a virgin, and it needed all my care and comfort to help her get through it. They raped another girl of twelve, who went into a state of deep shock and never spoke another word again. There was a pale beautiful girl of fifteen who had fits; after they raped her, the fits got worse and she started scratching the skin on her arms until she bled. How many others were abused and violated I have no idea. It was something no one ever mentioned, but you could guess when a girl became more withdrawn and shaky than usual.

Another thing that happens – a survival mechanism switches in your brain. You start to justify what's happening. In my case, I was being punished, and however strange and misguided it appears, when other girls are being raped it doesn't seem quite so bad being raped yourself. It becomes the norm, a way of life. In that unit for psychologically damaged children, there were two male nurses who wanted sex with teenaged girls and there was no system of safety or complaint, nothing within the organisation to stop them. The abuse was out of control, Andrew Blackmore was ineffectual, and I found it hard to believe that the female staff had no idea that girls in their care were being brutalised and violated. If they did have any suspicions, it is beyond belief that they said and did nothing about it. They were mums. They had children themselves. Did they see us girls in care as a different species – society's rubbish, little slags to be used and abused by the men they worked with? I thought about smuggling out a letter, or writing to Dad, but, had I done so, I would have been thought of as a liar and a fantasist, proof that I was in the right place.

I spent every waking hour trying to keep away from Bob and Dean, but when the urge took them, they always found me. Each time, I fought harder. I bit and scratched. I cut Dean Ricks's face so deeply, he stopped ripping off my clothes and punched me with his fist. I blacked out.

Bob must have appeared. They picked me up, raced me down the corridor to the padded cells and stuck a needle in my bottom. I slept like the dead for many hours, woke with my jaw aching, and went back to sleep again.

For several weeks they kept me sedated. If I didn't take the drugs passively, they forced my mouth open and washed them down my throat. When I had the energy to fight back, they tranquillised me again. My memories are patchy, but I recall, hazily, as if in a dream, lying catatonic in the padded cell, hands and feet strapped down, my nightdress around my waist and Dean Ricks rubbing his finger between my legs. He grinned at Bob.

'Can you believe it, little bitch is sopping wet?'

Bob grinned back at Dean. My body was immobile. My eyes flicked from one to the other. Why did they allow men to look after little girls in the care system? Who made the rules? The unit was like a cage and we were treated like rats. There was no humanity. Friendship was more about shared suffering than affection. We were all alone. I felt it like a needle.

The drugs put me to sleep. My days blurred like the view of a racing train and my nightmares were a surreal version of my past life, everything exaggerated, Mum a giant and Dad a tiny little man with a big pipe; Harry and Ali chasing me around the field at my last school; Alan Briggs flexing his rhino-whip. I know a thing or two about children, he said. I heard in my dreams 'Für Elise' but it wasn't Richard Symons playing the piano, it was Beethoven with a cloud of snowy white hair like the Father Christmas in the store where Mum worked.

When I returned to the dorm, I felt hollow, confused, dis-orientated. I kept saying my name, Emily MacKenzie, forcing my identity back in my mind. My memory was raw and disjointed. My head ached, my muscles ached. I staggered around in a trance and spent whole days staring through the windows watching as the spring turned slowly to summer.

CHAPTER 18

In Solitary

Days drift by like sand in an hourglass, one day like the next and the same as the last. I discovered it was my birthday when cards appeared from Dad and Amy. I was fourteen. June had arrived, the sun high, the shadow from The Bin relinquishing its grip on the dorm windows and allowing the daylight to warm my face.

When I was first placed in the unit, I did not have a mental illness. In those long months of sporadic pill-popping, confinement and abuse, I now had low self-esteem and a loss of confidence; I suffered anxiety attacks and found it hard to concentrate. My IQ results went down, pleasing Dr Wolfe.

Children in that care unit were broken, their minds and personalities destroyed. When they crossed the road to the asylum, their brains were scrambled, any hopes of normality removed for good. Others would be released with minimal support into futures of petty crime and prison, lives blighted by violence and addiction – glue, heroin, booze, self-harm. Not all, but a wide majority would end up on the streets begging. Most homeless people have psychological problems and most grow up in children's homes or are ex-soldiers, or both, a shameful way for a wealthy nation to treat children and men who serve in the armed forces.

I watched the cars racing by on the road outside. The people in those cars were going somewhere. They had started at one place and would end up at another. They had a plan, a purpose, a direction. I didn't look for Dad any more. I just wanted to be out there in one of those cars. Again I stopped taking the yellow pills, using my old technique. The fog slowly lifted from my eyes and I began to make a study of the unit.

Over the coming days, I checked every door and window. Only the dorms and bathrooms were left unlocked at night and wardens circled to make sure all the little children were safely in their beds. Between their rounds, I hid at the top of the stairs to see if the main entry door was ever left unlocked, but it was only opened and relocked when the staff went home.

When I went across the road to the madhouse for my EEG and IQ test, I looked for opportunities to break away from Bob Drake. Dr Wolfe said once I was clever without being smart. His words stayed with me; they stay with me still. There was never an occasion when I could have escaped and I took no chances. I started long-distance walking up and down the top corridor to get fit again, this activity I'm sure noted by the staff as a sign of my progressive mental illness, although the exercise, in fact, made me think more clearly.

At the end of the corridor, at the boys' end, there was an iron ladder leading up to a hatch workmen used to check the flat roof. Summer was the time when repairs were made and the hatch was often open. One day, when no one was looking, I climbed the ladder and poked my head over the top. I watched the workmen laying tarpaper on the opposite end of the roof. It felt good breathing the air, even tainted with hot tar. I was tempted to try to abscond, but again thought better of it.

What I did do, was keep a constant watch on the workmen coming and going, and finally told Kate my plan.

'I'm going to break out of this place. I'll go mad if I don't.'

'I already am mad,' Kate replied, and I pretended she hadn't said that.

'Will you come with me?'

'You don't think I'm going to let you go on your own.'

I gave her a hug and she froze. Kate didn't like being touched. Not any more.

'I'm waiting till they leave the hatch open, then we have to go immediately.'

'What are we going to take?' she asked, unusually practical.

'Just money, if you have any.'

'I haven't got very much.'

'Don't worry. I have.'

I'm not sure why I decided to take Kate with me. I knew I would have a better chance on my own. But there was a part of me that needed an accomplice, the same as when I ran away with Doug Mortlock, and another part that wanted to give Kate a glimpse of the world and a taste of the air beyond the unit. Kate had become institutionalised. After the rape, her emotions had closed down completely. She tried to be cheerful, but I knew not far below the surface was a girl who would take her own life just as calmly as she had killed the boy assaulting her in the garage.

I kept watch for several more days. Then, one afternoon, they unscrewed the hatch from its hinges to cover the top and sides with a fresh layer of tarpaper. When the workmen went home, the sky was looking in. This was our chance. I had to get out of there, and my only concern was abandoning the small children, especially the two little boys I had been caring for. But they had survived my time in the padded cell and I kept my fingers crossed that they would survive again.

I told Kate to remain dressed that night and be ready. I lay in bed and listened as the wardens patrolled. They changed over at 9.00 p.m. and stood about together downstairs in the hall chatting. This was the moment. I pushed my pillow under the bedclothes and woke Kate. I dragged her from her bed, did the same with her pillow, and she followed me on tiptoes along the corridor, straight up the ladder and on to the roof. Kate was unfit and began to breathe noisily. I held my finger to her lips.

'Shush,' I said.

We lay flat. I waited until the two night staff climbed into their cars and watched until the cones of their headlamps disappeared. It was silent as I searched for a way to climb down, a task made easy by the halogen blaze of the lights around The Bin. The only option was to use the drainpipes. I tested them to make sure they weren't coming out of the walls and chose the wide pipe at the side of the building.

'We're going to have to climb down,' I said.

'I wish I could fly,' Kate replied.

'Can you do it?'

'What, fly?' She grinned and shrugged her plump shoulders. 'I can if you can.'

I went first. I lay on my tummy, eased my legs over the edge of the roof and took a grip on the wide bowl at the top of the pipe. I stared back at Kate.

'Go slowly, and don't fall.'

I kept a grip with my legs and eased myself down a few inches at a time. When I reached the bottom, I looked up and Kate was staring over the edge, her eyes like neon in the ghostly light. My life, I suddenly thought, hangs in the balance. If Kate falls, I will be a murderer as well as a baby killer and I will remain here at The Bin being raped and beaten for the rest of my life.

Kate's strong legs emerged over the edge of the roof, her body appeared, and she clung on to the downpipe with both hands. She moved slowly at first, but then seemed to lose control and started to slither faster and faster. She landed with a bump and I caught her as she fell backwards. She was grinning.

'That was great,' she said, and I sighed with relief.

We set off at a trot. I tried to go slow and Kate tried to keep up. It was late summer. The night was warm. Beyond the ugly lights, I could see the stars and a slip of moon. I had no idea which way we were going, or how far we were from the nearest town. It wasn't that late, but the road was quiet and we must have gone a mile or so when I noticed lights approaching from behind. I stuck out my thumb and the car screeched to a halt. I couldn't believe it was so easy.

I climbed in the front seat and Kate got in the back. The driver wore a flat cap and flicked ash out the window as we went.

'Where you off to, then?'

'Just into town,' I answered.

'Going somewhere nice?'

'That's the plan.'

His hand brushed my leg as he changed gear.

'I suppose you're meeting your boyfriends?'

'Yes, as it happens,' I said, 'they're waiting for us.'

After two turns and ten minutes, the lights of the town appeared, the buildings growing more defined as we drew closer. We were almost there, when the man pulled over and turned off the engine. He cupped my knee with his big work-man's hands.

'So, where do you want me to drop you?'

'In the centre would be great.'

His hand pushed up my thigh.

'So, what do I get for the lift, then?'

I gritted my teeth as I tried to pull his hand off me.

'Don't you dare do that!' I shouted, and he suddenly screamed out and lurched forward against the steering wheel.

'Ouch. Ouch. Jesus Christ,' he cried, and started rubbing the back of his head.

'Touch her and I'll kill you,' Kate hissed.

I glanced round. Kate had found a hammer from somewhere and had bashed him on the head with it.

'Fucking little bitch – it was only a joke.'

'Not a very funny joke,' I told him, and climbed out of the car. I opened the back door for Kate, the engine roared back to life and he sped off.

'Where did you find the hammer?'

'On the roof. I thought it might come in useful.'

'It certainly did,' I said. She grinned and I became serious. 'Throw it away now, Kate – you don't want to get caught with it.'

She chucked the hammer over a hedge. As we continued, the buildings getting closer, I started to feel more confident. If we could get a train to London and then home, Dad would hide us and I would try to explain why we had to escape. We turned another bend and I could see a spire rising over a church. Then we crossed a bridge and two policemen were sitting in a patrol car with their elbows resting on the open windows. My heart sank.

'Come on, run,' I said.

We set off, back the way we had come. The police crossed the bridge by car, quickly reached us, then gave chase on foot. They caught up with Kate and I took off like a rocket, running like I had run every day the previous summer, my legs strong and firm, doing what they were meant to be doing. There were no drugs inside me. I was clean, for a moment, euphoric. The policeman chasing me couldn't keep up, but the other one must have put Kate in the car. He passed me, the blue lights flashing from the roof, and pulled over, blocking the path.

I was trapped in a pincer movement. I knew I was going to get caught, and I didn't want Kate to be taken away on her own, but that short sprint made the escape seem worth it. The policeman who had been chasing me caught up. He bent over double.

'Where'd you learn to run like that?' he gasped.

'From running away,' I said.

★   ★   ★

We were taken to the police station and questioned separately for about two hours. I told them it was my idea to abscond from the unit, not Kate's, and I had done so 'because the wardens and staff are unkind'.

'They do their best,' the runner said.

'That's not true. They don't do their best. Bad things happen in the unit, really bad things.'

'Well, come on, tell me, what kind of things?'

The policeman was young with blond hair and blue eyes. He was good-looking with an honest face and I didn't get any sense that he was judging me or thought I must be a loony.

'There are children with mental disorders who are not getting the treatment they need,' I said. 'There is a lot of unkindness and bullying, and there are worse things I can't even begin to describe. What education they provide is poor and there is little opportunity to get fresh air and exercise. There's lots more.' I shrugged. 'It's hard to explain.'

'You seemed to have explained yourself very well.'

'My father wants me to go home. He has been to court many times, but my mother's my guardian and she is stopping it,' I went on. 'I ran away because that place is dangerous . . .'

'Dangerous? What do you mean by that?'

I took a breath and stared back at the constable.

'Nine children have killed themselves in three years. Lots more have been rushed to hospital trying,' I replied. 'What makes them do that? Are they being pushed into it? Are they being helped? It is dangerous. I'm afraid to go back.'

The policeman didn't seem to know what to say. In my outburst, I had told him everything, well, not everything, but I was certain he had believed me. His colleague brought tea and Bourbon biscuits, the taste of childhood. The policeman I had been speaking to gave me a long stare and left the room. I listened as heavy boots marched up and down the corridors and people talked into telephones.

My future was being decided.

I finished the tea and ate all the biscuits. Two cars arrived. Kate and I were being taken away separately. We had the chance for a wave, no more, and the young policeman accompanied me down the steps.

'Good luck,' he said. 'Try and keep up your running.'

'I intend to,' I replied, and he smiled.

I was taken to another asylum two hours away, another Victorian monstrosity with rows of windows like dead staring eyes and a tall tower with a domed roof. The building was soulless and menacing. I was sure the architect who had built it had emotional problems.

'Come along, young lady, here we are,' the driver said.

He was an older man in a black suit like an undertaker. I could have run away. But I was being smart. Anywhere was better than the secure unit and I had a feeling that young policeman had said or done something to prevent me from being sent back – to protect me, to protect them, it was hard to know, and something I would think about in the coming months.

The driver took me by the arm and I was led up a flight of stairs into a marble lobby with a mosaic pattern. Across the lobby was a wide, curving staircase with a broad handrail that gleamed with polish. Everything was tidy with a smell of pine freshener. I felt as if I had wandered into a costume drama on the BBC.

The woman who greeted me wore a nurse's uniform from the era of the Crimean War with an intricate white hat and a white apron over a dark-blue dress. She signed the form the undertaker held out to her and he bowed his head in an old-fashioned way that reminded me of Grandpa MacKenzie.

'So, here were are, Emily. It's very late, you know,' the nurse said, glancing at her watch. 'I'm going to take you straight to your room. Is that all right?'

I nodded. 'Yes,' I said. 'Is Kate here?'

'I really don't know. Everything will become clear in the light of day.'

She told me as we walked along the corridor that I was to call her Nurse Blake or Miss Blake.

'Are you related to the writer?' I asked her.

'Writer?' she said.

'William Blake.'

'No, I shouldn't think so, dear.'

After thinking about Grandpa with his nice manners and bronzed moustache, I remembered Grandma sitting in her favourite chair, her fingers knitted together in her lap, her eyes glowing in the pastel light. The book she kept on the table beside her was an illustrated collection of poems by William Blake, a red silk ribbon marking her page. In the coming months, I would rack my brain trying to remember the verses Grandma had read to Amy and me on those calm Sundays a lifetime ago.

At the end of the corridor, I was accompanied to the bathroom. We then set out to climb the staircase spiralling up inside the tower like a skeleton inside a body. We walked round and round. The stairs seemed to go on forever like in a bad dream or a painting. We arrived finally at the very top where there were three doors and Miss Blake took a big breath. She opened the door on the left.

'Here we are, dear, this is your room.'

The room was white, stark, clean with the smell of roses and had one window too high to see out of unless you stood on the chair. There was a nice bed in the corner and a chest of drawers with wooden handles, nothing sharp or dangerous.

'You will sleep here tonight,' Miss Blake said. 'You will be locked in, but don't worry, someone will be close by.' She smiled. 'Good night, then, dear.'

She left. I listened to the lock snap and lay on the bed looking at the stars through the high window. I could hear trees rustling and shadows crossed the ceiling. I wasn't sure how to feel. I was relieved to be away from the mini-bin, out of reach of Bob and Dean, but where I'd landed seemed totally weird.

When I woke in the morning, I thought everything had been a dream and was content that it wasn't. Almost immediately, the door opened and another nurse in the same sort of uniform came in. Her name, she told me, was Nurse Pettifer.

'Hello, did you sleep well? Are you hungry?'

'Where's Kate, Kate Conway?' I asked her.

'Kate's next door.'

'Can I see her?'

'No, I'm sorry, Emily, that's not allowed.'

I thought about getting angry, but controlled myself.

'Where are we?' I asked instead.

'This is a women's mental hospital.'

'No men?'

'No.'

'But where are the other women?'

'They are in another part of the building. You are too young to mix with them, and you are perfectly safe here.'

I paused. 'Have you seen my file?'

'Your file?' she repeated.

'Yes, it follows me everywhere.'

'Well, I don't know anything about that, I'm afraid.' She smiled. 'Are you hungry?'

'Starving.'

Nurse Pettifer left, the lock bit automatically and she returned again carrying a tray with scrambled egg, toast, orange juice and tea. I ate every scrap. She brought me a bowl of water for me to wash and a commode on wheels was pushed in so I could relieve myself. The tower was ancient and there were no loos.

I started to have that hourglass feeling again almost immediately. The days frittered away. They provided reading books and drawing books. My clothes were laundered and new clothes that appeared to be from another century were placed pressed and folded on the chest of drawers. Everyone was kind, but distant, and I felt like a goldfish in a bowl, a specimen they were studying. There were drugs, of course, always the drugs, but I was adept at not taking them.

When I asked if there were letters from my dad, Nurse Blake and Nurse Pettifer both said they didn't know 'anything about that sort of thing'. At least in the other place the letters had kept coming. Dad was doing well in his business; instead of competing with the new supermarkets, he was supplying them with local fruit and veg. He had another van and a new driver. Amy had passed her eleven-plus and, at Mum's suggestion, would be starting at the grammar school in town in September.

I asked if I could at least write to my father. They provided the material, but I would discover one day that those letters were never sent. I continued to ask if I could see Kate, but, again, that was not part of my 'treatment', which seemed to consist of kindness and solitary confinement. The nurses were always pleasant. They brought bowls of water to wash my hair and I measured time as it grew longer.

There were many dead hours for me to look back at the past. Seven men had raped me, two of them my carers. It was hard to comprehend, and it was hard to believe those two men were still there at the mini-bin abusing helpless children. How could such a thing ever have been allowed to happen and, in modern times, why was there no system to keep the children safe?

It occurred to me that, having told the young policeman the unit was dangerous, his superiors had made sure I was moved to this silent, solitary place where my voice went unheard. That way, there would be no investigation and the status quo would continue unchanged. Care home managers, councillors and police chiefs all know each other, they are Rotarians and Masons and members of the same golf clubs. Children in care are there because someone else had been careless. Best let sleeping dogs lie.

The highlight of my days was the regular visits by Dr Hermione Grant, the psychotherapist, a tall, slender woman with shoulder-length blonde hair. She wore tight-fitting clothes, A-line dresses with bare arms like a model, neat suits with short skirts, and very high heels that must have made the climb up the spiral staircase a nightmare.

I had been through all this stuff before with Doctors Lewis and Wolfe. We talked about my childhood, growing up, my sister, parents, divorce, stealing things from school friends, burning down my school and landing up in a secure unit. I told her how I had been whipped and sexually assaulted by my stepfather, abused by the gardener at the holding bay and skirted the truth when we talked about the mini-bin. She wrote everything down, crossed and re-crossed her silky legs, and asked the same questions again and again. I was never sure if this was a technique to make me delve deeper into my memory, or whether she was trying to catch me out.

'You were raped at thirteen?'

'Yes. By five men.'

'What do you think about that now?'

'Dr Grant, I don't think about it. It was more terrible than I can describe.'

'You lost a child?'

'I didn't lose a child, it was taken away from me.'

'How did you feel about that?'

'These are feelings you can't put into words and can't imagine unless it has happened to you. It's like being crucified.'

'Strong words,' she said.

'Yes, but it's really like that.'

She paused for a moment. I knew what was coming. Psychotherapy seems to be about establishing patterns, then repeating them until the patient confesses or is driven stark raving mad. She tapped her pencil.

'Do you feel safe here?'

'Yes, I suppose so.'

'Did you feel safe at the secure unit?'

'You've asked me that before.'

'Just answer the question.'

'The unit has male nurses caring for young girls. That doesn't seem right.'

'You still haven't answered the question.'

'The things that go on behind those doors are not how they seem from the outside,' I said, choosing my words. 'If the carers are unkind or violent or abusive, there is no one to stop them and no one who will listen if the children try to explain.'

'There is a chief warden.'

'That doesn't mean he's going to listen, or care.'

'Were you abused in that unit, Emily?'

She had been building up to this for weeks. This was my chance to tell someone who was ready to listen, but doubt ran through me like a charge of electricity. What was her function? Why was Dr Grant giving me so much time and attention? I felt a visceral need to tell her what Bob Drake and Dean Ricks had done, but I had an intuition that it would come back and bite me.

'No, Dr Grant,' I said.

She looked up from her notepad and our eyes met. She was beautiful, except for one thing, the flaw that always exists in perfection. She had a squint, like my own, although mine for some reason had gone. Her lips were full and pink, her teeth as white as a row of pearls. I hated the questions – it all seemed such an incredible waste of time – but Hermione Grant brought the outside world into my cocoon and I liked studying her different costumes and looking at her beautiful face.

She came to her feet and so did I. She had always been distant – it is the role of the therapist – but that day she did something strange. She leaned down from her great height and kissed my cheeks.

'Good luck, Emily,' she said.

She left, clacking on her heels. I heard the metallic rasp of the lock, and her perfume lingered the rest of the afternoon. I knew by the length of my hair that four months had gone by and I was beginning to suffer from what I would one day learn is called cleisiophobia, the fear of being locked in. We are, the literature says, social creatures who need to share our feelings and thoughts with others. When this basic contact is removed, mental illnesses such as depression and personality disorders often result.

There was one plus side to being isolated at the top of the tower. When I had first arrived, my arms and legs were speckled with bruises in endless shades of blue and green. They had gone, wiped from my body as I tried to wipe Bob and Dean from my mind. I started doing sit-ups to keep strong. I read voraciously, one book after another, but always in the back of my head was the feeling that I could disappear forever and no one would ever know.

One day, out of the blue, Nurse Blake came in with a smile.

'I have a visitor for you,' she announced, and my heart thumped so hard it nearly jumped out of my chest. I thought it was going to be Dad, but it wasn't. It was Kate. I went to hug her, then remembered she didn't like that.

We chatted non-stop for ten minutes, about what I can't recall. Then she was gone and I never saw Kate Conway again.

Kate had been in the next room to me for four months, even through Christmas, but the 'treatment' made it necessary to keep us apart. I have never been sure what our isolation was expected to achieve, although what does happen when you are left alone with your own mind for long periods is that past events take on a hallucinatory quality. A man tearing off your clothes, wetting his cock with his spit and ramming it up into your body is so horrific, the brain starts to air-brush the memory, mitigate each assault, smooth off the rough edges, the slap with an open palm, the clenched fist, the hot sperm like scalding acid splashed across your flesh.

Sexually and psychologically abused children habitually blame themselves. They acquire 'learned helplessness', becoming passive, taking gifts when given, like dogs with a biscuit, and accepting the abuse as normal. This survival technique works for a while, but it is just a thin veneer, a plaster over the psyche that peels off sooner or later and ends in mental breakdown, self-harm and suicide.

During those months of isolation, I had learned to stop blaming myself for what those men had done to me. I was stronger and, by avoiding the drugs they had tried to give me, more alert. When I was told that same day that a place had been found for me at an open care home for normal children, I knew Dr Grant was in some way behind this decision. I was also aware that sufficient time had gone by for the police to look into what was going on at the secure unit and, in time-honoured fashion, to move the perpetrators on and cover it up.

CHAPTER 19

Secret History

1971. Another year. Another placement. Flowers are coming into bud and the leaves on the big elm trees in the garden are silvery green. I must have sprung up a couple of inches and my flares flap about my ankles. The muscles in my legs are as hard as rocks now I'm running again. I learned somewhere that because of the curve of the earth, the horizon is always about three miles away and sometimes I feel like jogging to that invisible line to check, and then to keep going until I find myself back where I started. I'll do it one day.

The radio in the kitchen always seems to be playing the same two songs: 'Chirpy Chirpy Cheep Cheep', by Middle of the Road, and 'Knock Three Times' by Dawn. Mixed in with the music are news items and I hear them describe the Education Secretary as 'Thatcher the Milk Snatcher' because she's taken the free school milk away from all the children over seven. Mrs Thatcher probably doesn't know that there are poor people whose children rely on that milk to get them through the day. Petrol has gone up to 33p a gallon and the average price of a house is £5,600, so I don't suppose Alan Briggs will be moving out of his council house any day soon.

I wonder what happened to Christmas? And where was Kate? I missed her, her sad optimism, her ready smile, her being there. How was Dad's bad leg? Was Amy happy at her new school? Had Aunt Alice taken the plunge and coloured her hair? She'd asked my opinion once and I'd told her to go for it. I had missed all that stuff and, as the letters started to come again, catching up was a lifeline. I felt as if I had been held under water and had come up for air at last.

Finally, I spoke to Dad on the telephone. He had been duped into believing that I had suffered a mental breakdown as a result of the abortion. The fact that in all that time, a year of my life, Mum had prevented him from seeing me revealed a hatred that was unhinged. With her mood swings, alcohol dependence and a self-image that relied on the admiration of men, it was my mother, not me, who had borderline personality disorder and I, like a puppet, or a mirror image, reflected her emotional instability.

I would learn later that my father had contributed financially towards my care. It would have killed him if he had known he was paying to keep me locked in a prison where I was raped, neglected and brutalised. Until the day he died, I never told him. This is typical. The abused unwittingly conspire with the abusers to maintain the silence and the police, probation officers and social workers prefer it that way. Better let the little children suffer than cause a fuss.

When officials and journalists do report on the abuse of children in care homes, churches, schools and troubled families, the generic term 'abuse' is used to protect the delicate ears of listeners and readers. It is a euphemism that could imply that children are being forced to sleep in damp rooms, or endure an unwanted hug or tap on the bottom. It is not that at all. 'Abuse' when it reaches the evening news means rape. The vaginal and anal rape of girls, the anal rape of boys, and oral sex and sadism in all the combinations paedophile rings and evil men conjure up in their vivid imaginations. Abuse means someone's life has been ruined. It means normal friendships and relationships will be tainted forever by doubt, fear and suspicion. It means making love will always be painful. Women try to be strong. They put the rape or rapes in a box and close the lid. They carry on. They make the most of life. But being raped is like a third-degree burn. It leaves a scar that never goes away.

The place I had come to was an experimental children's home set up in a rambling country house across the Medway not far from London. The grounds were unkempt, weeds grew through the cracks in the driveway and the wooden gates were never locked. It was run like a family with twenty children under the care of a married couple, Caroline and Michael Flood. As a newcomer, I had my own room and would later share with two other girls. The rules were 'lite' and we only used first names.

Michael liked to be called Mikey. He had a curly ginger beard, pale watery eyes and nodded continually, screwing up his nose like a little mouse. He wore collarless shirts, bell-bottoms and sandals. Caroline had a liking for long cheesecloth dresses, her lips were set in a perpetual look of grace and she always wore a leather thong with a photograph of Bhagwan Shree Rajneesh. They were vegetarians, kind and creepy.

I returned to school. Now I knew I had a high IQ, I made the classic mistake of assuming I was clever and daydreamed through classes without concentrating. I didn't study, I picked things up like a magnet with iron filings, everything jumbled and disorderly with missing parts like the children's books with missing pages at the mini-bin. The school had a good gym and I was picked for the hockey team because I was fast more than adept with a hockey stick. The children at the home were normal, as normal as me, at least. I fitted in, made friends and everything would have been great except for one thing. Caroline and Mikey took me to the doctors 'for a check-up' and only when I got there did I discover that I was to be put on the contraceptive pill.

'No way,' I said. 'I don't like taking pills and I'm not going to take them.'

Caroline turned her head to one side and smiled like a saint. 'But it's for your own good,' she said, and glanced at the doctor, a no-nonsense sort of man in shirtsleeves and a knitted tie.

'They won't do you any harm,' he assured me.

'But I don't need them.'

Now Mikey chipped in.

'It's for the best, given your record, Emily,' he said.

It was that blue file again. I carried it like Christian's burden in *The Pilgrim's Progress*, an invisible thing that defined me. I had read Bunyan's book in that silent tower and thought it much like my life, a baleful journey to somewhere that may not exist.

I stared back at Mikey, at his pale eyes and twitching nose. Like Caroline, he wanted to give everyone the impression that he was on first-name terms with God, but it was all just an act.

'I do not need pills!' I screamed. 'I don't want them, I don't need them and I am not going to take them.'

That shut them all up for a moment. But only a moment.

Caroline took my hands in hers. 'But it's for your own good,' she said.

'No it's not. You're thinking of yourself, not me.'

She tilted her head to one side. She was skirting the subject, the real reason for my being there. Rape and abortion are like swear words, vulgar and taboo. It was something I didn't like to talk about, and the doctor, who had my records, had the good sense to know that. He had a wise look and people outside in his waiting room were flicking through old copies of *Punch*. He couldn't waste any more time.

'Try them for a month and see how you get on,' he suggested. He had thick eyebrows supporting a brow that was deeply furrowed and there was a twinkle in his eyes I took for complicity.

Be smart, Emily.

'All right,' I said. 'I'll try them for a month.'

Caroline and Mikey were terribly pleased and took me to a coffee bar while the prescription was being filled.

The pills were small, pale blue and came in a tinfoil packet. Every day, I pushed one out of its plastic bubble, crushed it into dust and flushed the dust down the loo. This was a successful enterprise until Caroline walked into my room one morning without knocking and caught me in the act.

'Oh, Emily, you are so naughty,' she said. 'I put my trust in you and you've let me down.'

'But I don't want to take pills.'

'You have to be more adult about these things.'

'But I'm not an adult, Caroline, I'm fourteen.'

Her lips were pressed tightly together and she held her hands clasped under her large breasts.

'Emily, while you are here, I am like your mummy and you must do as you are told. You will use contraception, or you will have to be punished . . .'

'Are you going to beat me?'

A tremor ran through her body. 'Dear God, no . . .'

'My mother did.'

She carried on shaking. 'Well we don't do things like that here. You will be confined to your room for the weekend and at breakfast you will take the pill with me watching. Is that clear?'

'Yes, Caroline.'

This test of wills continued for months. Sometimes I swallowed the pill, but most days I was able to keep it lodged behind my teeth and spat it out in the lavatory.

In her campaign to stop me getting pregnant, Caroline came up with another strategy that was completely barmy and highly suspect. At a parents' evening, she met Mr and Mrs Colette, whose daughter, Annabel, was in my class, and decided to encourage a friendship between us. Caroline loomed over Mrs Colette with her angelic smile and I could scarcely believe my ears as she invited Annabel to tea that weekend. The poor girl grew pallid and Mrs Colette's jaw was quivering as she said what a lovely idea it was.

Annabel was chocolate-box pretty, young for her age and had a fondness for gingham dresses with Peter Pan collars and dancing shoes of the type I'd worn as a little girl. I had given up all that girlie stuff, burned my push-up bra in a moment of feminist solidarity and become a tomboy with Levi jeans and T-shirts.

When Mr Colette dropped Annabel off that Saturday, I was waiting on the steps with Mikey and Caroline, who was dressed in white like a Madonna with flowers in her hair. Mr Colette pulled out of the drive and Annabel, all in pink, wore one of those glued-on smiles that show the teeth while the lips remain dead still.

We filed into the kitchen for spiced tea and burfi, Indian sweets made from condensed milk, sugar and pistachios, a recipe Caroline had 'picked up in the East'. She had prepared the confectionery and smoky-flavoured tea without taking into account that children rarely like to eat things they are not familiar with, or that Annabel was clearly a fizzy orange and Jaffa Cakes sort of girl. She made a brave attempt nibbling at the sticky squares of burfi. Her smile was stuck in place, her nose twitched and she looked a bit like Mikey, who sat across the long pine table nodding in incessant agreement with something. We were then sent off to the lounge 'to enjoy ourselves'. There was a big collection of records and you could always judge what people were like by the records they liked.

'Ooo, look, you've got Cliff Richard,' Annabel said.

'You wouldn't rather hear Pink Floyd?'

'Oh, no, that's horrible.'

I was invited back to Annabel's house the following week and felt embarrassed that Caroline was clearly harassing this family. Annabel was like a china doll normally kept in its box. I felt sorry for her, although I rather liked her dad, who reminded me of my own dad with his moustache and kind eyes. That Saturday he took us to see Rochester Castle, a twelfth-century fortress with a Norman tower overlooking the Medway. Annabel shivered in the shadows of the rag-stone walls and hated the museum of swords and pikes.

We went to have hamburgers at the Wimpy Bar in the old town. When we left, I had a flash of déjà vu as I came face to face with the hotel on the opposite corner. It was where I had spent the night with Dad after the abortion. I was a girl with a secret history. Annabel was a glass of clear water. Caroline was dedicated to doing good but didn't have what it takes to make a success of it.

I visited the Colette family several times, although Annabel never came again to eat Indian food at the children's home. Like her mother, Annabel was highly strung, and I got the feeling that Mr Colette saw the upside of his daughter spending time with a robust sporty girl interested in most things and, given the chance, able to talk about anything.

The county schools cross-country race was scheduled for June and, all through those warm months of spring and early summer, I went into serious training. I was lucky to fall into the under-fifteens category, which improved my chances of doing well.

On the big day, Caroline and Mikey were joined by Annabel and Mr Colette; rain had been forecast and Annabel turned up like Little Red Riding Hood in a red cape and matching hat. They were at the starting line when I set off, then drove to the finishing line to watch the end of the race.

There were about 400 children taking part, boys and girls in equal numbers. We set off, girls first, boys three minutes behind. The course was five miles and started out straight for the first half-mile before winding through woodlands, up and down hills, over ditches and across fields. I didn't have a plan. Five miles for me wasn't at all difficult. I sprinted from the start to get ahead of the crowd, then ran at a steady jog to get my breath back. Some of the competitors had trained together and were running in groups to encourage each other and push their best athletes at the end of the race. I was on my own and preferred it that way.

After the first mile, the field spread out and I was with the lead group of girls, about twenty of us trying to keep up with a tall runner from Rochester Grammar School. 'Sandra Lee,' a girl whispered in admiration as she ran along beside me, 'the county champion.'

It wasn't long before the older boys caught up and overtook us. There was a boy from my school, Roy, who I'd run with before. I latched on to him and made him my pacemaker as he went past the other girls. Sandra Lee had kept up a gruelling pace, but I didn't feel tired. I felt as if I were floating. Running for me was a release, a meditation, the one activity when I could stop thinking, worrying, calculating, and just let my body go.

I had not been lucky in my life; I had a great big blue dossier that spelled it all out. But that day, bad luck must have been looking the other way. I stayed close to Sandra Lee, knowing instinctively that she was saving herself for a sprint finish. We went across a field that was deep in mud from the recent rains. There was a gate on the far side that opened onto a cattle grid that was wet and slippery. As Sandra leapt across the metal bars, she lost her footing and tumbled over.

She scrambled back onto her feet, but I had overtaken her and could see the finishing line ahead. The course narrowed into a funnel lined with flags. People all along the way were cheering and it seemed for a second as if they were cheering for me. It gave me energy. I wasn't tired. My legs felt like pistons on a machine and I didn't slow down, I started to sprint. The best among the boys and girls who were over fifteen had finished the race, but as I came into view, the officials held up a white tape and I ran through with it clinging to my chest. Sandra Lee was two seconds behind me.

I was so happy I cried. Mikey hugged me and swung me round in a circle. Mr Colette took us all to tea and the tall silver trophy I'd won was prominently displayed back at the children's home.

Winning that race was the best day of my life. I was truly happy and, a week later, I ran away.

CHAPTER 20

Up West

We had physics that afternoon at school and the idea popped into my head like the answer to a riddle, like Einstein suddenly scribbling his epic equation $E = mc^2$. As soon as I got home, I changed out of my uniform, took what money I had and said I was going for a walk.

I walked straight to the station and caught the train to London. I arrived at Victoria and got the tube to Piccadilly Circus. It was the place to go. I don't know how I knew, I just knew. I had grown up with Piccadilly Circus wired in my head like Shangri-La and Timbuktu, places that sound yummy in the mouth when you say them and you dream of going there without even realising it.

The Underground station at Piccadilly was huge. I walked in a circle looking at all the exits, then climbed the steps and gazed up at Eros, the God of Love, wondering for a second if anyone would ever love me. I had no idea what I was going to do, where I would sleep that night, what would become of me. But it felt good breathing the air of the big city and being anonymous among the crowds. Eros looked intense. He had fired his arrow and was wondering where it had landed. I felt like that myself.

From where I stood, I could see three wide thoroughfares: Piccadilly, Regent Street and Shaftesbury Avenue. I didn't know it at the time, but would learn when I began to make a living, that Piccadilly leads to Mayfair and Knightsbridge, where the rich people live. Regent Street goes north to Oxford Street and the big departmental stores, or south to Trafalgar Square and the National Gallery. Shaftesbury Avenue leads to the West End theatres, Chinatown, Soho and the red light district. That's the direction fate took me.

I was a stranger in a strange land feeling as if I had arrived home. As I walked past the theatres I felt a rush of fear and adrenalin. I could smell hot bagels, coffee, Chinese food. At the end of Shaftesbury Avenue, I turned left and entered the maze of Soho, bookshops selling dirty books, underwear shops selling underwear of the sort I had never seen before, market stalls with exotic fruit that was nothing like the apples, pears, plums and cherries Dad bought from the farmers and sold to the shops.

The people, too, were exotic; some posh in evening clothes dining early before the curtains rose at the theatres. I saw girls with the shortest skirts and boys with the longest hair, tramps in rags, girls standing in doorways in killer heels, and men dressed in leather clothes with chains hanging from their trousers. Everyone was going somewhere and I was going nowhere, just taking it all in.

I ambled up Wardour Street, turned one corner after another and found myself in Carnaby Street where a man in a green suit was throwing coins out of a window and hundreds of people were scrambling around on the ground picking them up. On the 15th of February that year, the country had gone decimal and I managed to get my hands on two shiny new 50p pieces.

There was a sign across the road with the words *Carnaby Street Welcomes the World*, and it felt like that, warm and welcoming as I window-shopped my way past brightly lit boutiques with the latest fashions. Everything is normally designed for old people, but in Carnaby Street it was the reverse. Everyone was young and everything was mod, hip, swinging. People wore psychedelic clothes and psychedelic rock poured out of hidden speakers, The Doors, Cream, The Grateful Dead.

I was just catching my breath when the street erupted with the sound of drums and cymbals. Then, a snaking line of dancers dressed in saffron robes with shaved heads wound their way through the crowds chanting *Hare Krishna, Hare Krishna, Krishna Krishna, Hare Hare*. People stopped to clap. They joined in the chant and a man in a fur coat joined the dance. I had never seen anything like it in my life. It was magical. It was like a bubble and I had found my way inside.

On the corner, there was a life-sized poster of Twiggy wearing red stockings, a blue dress with white hoop stripes and a red leather jacket. I looked at her face and I thought, wow, that could be me. What do you have to do to become a model? An actress? A dancer? Who do you speak to? I knew you had to know somebody to get to know somebody, but how do you start?

It was probably illegal to walk up Carnaby Street without buying something and when I saw a red leather jacket in the window of Lord John it felt as if a message had reached me from heaven. I wandered in as if hypnotised. The music was loud. Girls were dressed like boys and the boys were dressed like girls. The changing room was unisex and the assistant who brought me the red jacket to try on reminded me of me long ago in hot pants and a skimpy top. I zipped the jacket up. It was snug to the waist and had a big collar the girl turned up before guiding me to the mirror.

'That looks cool,' she said.

'I'll take it.'

'Far out.'

The jacket cost £35 and I had just enough. I bowled out of Lord John feeling fab and wandered back the way I had come. It was getting dark. As the shops began to close the bars began to open. The smell of food was in the air. I was starving. I didn't want to spend my lucky 50ps and had a feeling that Soho would provide as God had sent manna to the Israelites when they were wandering in the wilderness.

I turned out to be right for a change. As I made my way back down Wardour Street, on the left, just before I reached Shaftesbury Avenue, there was a tall iron fence around a garden and, from inside, the smell of food drifted through the open gates. I sidled up among the crowd and discovered that here in the gardens of St Anne's Church was a soup kitchen and night shelter. I didn't know if you had to pay and stood in the queue waiting to find out.

A man with a clipboard appeared, they always have clipboards, and moved along the line asking everyone their name. I discovered that newcomers were allowed to eat and stay in the hostel for three nights. I was worried that I was too young to be helped, it's often the case, but that didn't seem to be a problem. The only criterion was whether you had been assisted with accommodation before and, if so, there was no longer a bed for you. That seemed weird, but everything about being on the street is weird.

My turn came. My name was added to the list. I was given a mug of tea, some stewed meat with vegetables, soup and the tastiest bread I had ever eaten in my life. The food was donated by Soho restaurants. I sat at a table and found myself next to a young Scottish boy of about twenty who told me his name was Robbie Gillan. Opposite was an older Scotsman named Jock, who had brilliant-blue eyes and a scruffy dog named Scratch, who was under the table scratching.

'You got a bed again, you jammy bugger,' Jock said to Robbie.

'They only give you a bed if you're good-looking and you, you're too ugly.'

'You wee bastard, I'll kick your arse.'

'Oh, aye, you and whose army?'

Jock stroked the dog and looked up at me. 'Who's the lassie – she your girlfriend?'

'No, she's my boyfriend.'

Jock stared back at me. 'You got a place, then?'

I nodded. 'Yes, I did.'

'That could have been mine, you jammy bugger.'

Robbie peeled out his Rothman's King Size. Jock took two, sticking one behind his ear, and I shook my head when Robbie offered the packet. Robbie and Jock lit up and sighed content-edly, the anger gone. I would discover that they always spoke angrily and never meant it.

It was getting chilly. I had no idea where Jock was going, but he limped off with Scratch on a length of rope, smoking another cigarette.

'Will he be all right?' I asked Robbie.

'Oh, aye, he's been down here for ten years. Jock's a survivor.'

'Does he have a gammy leg?'

'Not any more, they cut it off. His only worry is if he gets woodworm in his false one.' He smiled, but he must have seen it made me feel sad. 'Don't you worry about old Jock. We're all the master of our own ship,' he added.

He lit another fag and stood away from the table. Like me, Robbie had no bags, but carried a plastic case with a guitar. I followed him to the hostel and he grabbed a set of bunk beds.

'Top or bottom?'

'Top,' I said.

'If you've got any money, hide it. Keep your clothes on, specially that red jacket, and keep your shoes on. They always nick shoes.'

I did as he said and crawled under a blanket that smelled as if it had been used to clean the toilets. The hostel consisted of one enormous dormitory and there must have been about two hundred people, mostly men, stretched out in the half-light trying to get to sleep. The stench was overpowering, unwashed clothes, pee and poo, dirty feet. All night they coughed and belched and farted and cried. I covered my head with the manky blanket and was terrified that someone was going to climb up into the bunk and molest me – probably Robbie Gillan, who had been kind, and kindness was something I had learned not to trust.

I was tired out after the long day but it wasn't easy to get to sleep. The sound of footsteps reminded me of the secure unit, the night staff doing their rounds, the day staff coming to take you across the road to the asylum or down to the laundry room to be molested. I must have dozed off, then woke with a start, aware of a presence. A man was standing beside the bunk staring at me. I screamed like a girl in a horror movie and Robbie leapt out of bed.

'What do you think you're up to? Go on, fuck off,' he said, and the man wandered back between the rows of bunks like a ghost. Robbie squeezed my hand. 'Don't you worry yourself, he's just a mental case. He won't do nothing.'

I curled up like a foetus with the pillow over my head and remembered the man at The Bin who had cut his wife into six pieces, the poor Down's syndrome boy being stripped and humiliated, Mr Blackmore with his dead blind eyes. The night shelter in Soho was frightening, but safer than the unit.

They turfed us out at daybreak. Robbie showed me where we could get a cup of tea and a slice of toast from the Salvation Army. We sat in Soho Square and he pulled out his guitar, a battered old thing with a missing string. He watched his fingers as they moved over the neck of the instrument and his enthusiasm made up for his lack of polish.

'I've just got to learn three or four songs and I can busk on the Underground,' he explained. 'You have to find ways to make a crust or you'll starve to death.'

He hammered out 'Blowing in the Wind', the Dylan song everyone knew, and I joined in singing the chorus.

Robbie Gillan had slender features, corn-yellow hair and blue eyes magnified behind the thick lenses of his glasses. He was wiry, gentle, smiled easily and I felt safe with him, the first man I'd felt safe with for years. After his practice, we went to Berwick Street, where he bought twelve dozen sets of love beads from the Indian wholesaler and had to borrow one of my 50p pieces to make up the £4 they cost. Throughout the rest of the day, we hung about Leicester Square selling the beads to tourists for 20p a strand.

We had made almost £20 profit by the time the pubs opened and I could tell by six o'clock that he was ready for a drink. We went to the Coach & Horses, where he had a pint of Watneys Red Barrel and I had a lemonade and a bag of crisps. After one pint, he had another pint, bought two packets of cigarettes and we wandered back to St Anne's where we met Jock.

'Hope you got a good night's sleep, you wee bastards,' Jock said in greeting.

'I slept like a babe in arms,' Robbie replied.

'I didn't,' I said.

Jock focused on me for a second. 'What are you doing here, girlie?' he said. 'You should go home where you belong.'

'I wish I could.'

'Like that, is it? Fockin' bastards.' He looked at Robbie. 'Got any fags?'

Robbie held out an unopened packet. As Jock was about to grab it, Robbie pulled it away again. He did this about six times and Jock became furious. He lost balance swinging a fist at

Robbie, who just laughed until Jock ran out of energy and dropped down on a bench ready for his free meal and mug of tea. When Robbie gave him the packet of fags, I realised this was just a game they played. They both came from Glasgow, a tough city where you must never show weakness or affection, even when you feel it.

'I'm going to kick your arse, laddie, you wait and see,' Jock spat.

'You, you're all mouth and no trousers.'

They lit up and, smoking happily, Jock looked at me.

'There's a free doctor here if you need one, lassie,' he told me. 'Dentist, and all, from time to time.'

I shrugged. 'I'm all right . . .'

'Aye, I can see you are, but I'm telling you for when you're not all right,' he said impatiently. 'When you need new shoes, just speak to the lady at the Sally Army, she'll sort you out.'

'Thanks . . .'

He stabbed out his fag and looked deadly serious. 'Now listen, tell me, what's the difference between Bing Crosby and Walt Disney?'

I liked puns and puzzles, but before I could think, he leaned across the table to tell me the answer.

'Bing does and Walt disnae.'

It was years before I understood the joke.

Jock took off with Scratch and Robbie told me as we were going back to the night shelter that Jock was a heroin junkie. The volunteer doctor had prescribed diamorphine, pharmaceutical heroin, to wean him off the addiction, and Jock went every night to the twenty-four-hour chemist in Piccadilly with his script to collect another day's supply. I took all this in without really knowing what he was talking about.

The night passed, smelly and safely. The next day followed the same pattern. Robbie had just enough money to buy another gross of love beads and we set off for Leicester Square to sell them.

During the day another boy came bounding up; he was wearing a skinny-brim blue beat hat, black velvet trousers and a black leather jacket. He told me his name was 'Johnny Moss from Waltham Cross'. He inspected my jacket and nodded with approval. 'Cool,' he said, then touched his nose in that way people do when they are about to pass on a secret.

'If you need any free bus tickets, I'll sort you out.'

'Remember, Em, he said *free* tickets,' Robbie said, and Johnny leaned forward, lowering his voice.

'Listen, I can make a score on a deal, I just need a fiver. I can give it back to you tonight?'

Robbie immediately dug out the small change he had taken selling the beads. Johnny dropped the £5 in coins in his pocket, and left as quickly as he'd come.

Robbie and I ate fish and chips, went to the pub and Robbie downed his two pints. He told me he planned to go south for better weather, either to Margate, going east, or Newquay, going west.

'Go to Margate,' I said, 'it's great.'

'You know it?'

'I used to go to school near there.'

'Before you ran away.'

'Something like that.'

'I got out of Glasgae because it's a shithole,' he said. 'Soon as I've got enough, I'll hitch down to Margate and set up selling the jewellery.'

He quaffed his pint.

'If you kept more money you'd be able to buy more love beads and, you know, build up,' I said, and he laughed.

'Oh, aye, I've thought of that.' He lit up. 'Then, I might get hit by a bus tomorrow and all that saving up would be a waste.'

'Just be careful when you cross the road.'

'Aye, I will. But I reckon the future's God's little secret and we have to live for today.'

He smoked, blowing rings that curled into each other, and seemed totally content.

'Do you always give people money when they need it?' I asked, and he laughed.

'Not when I haven't got any,' he replied.

After three days, Robbie Gillan left and I always wondered if he went to Margate to sell beads and play his guitar on the beach. My time at the hostel was up and I was lucky that morning to run into Johnny Moss in Soho Square.

'Listen, you wanna job? You'll be able to earn a few quid.'

'Yes, please,' I said.

Now that Robbie had gone, I didn't know how I was going to survive on the streets but the magic of Soho had blessed me again. If I got hold of some money, I knew where to buy jewellery, and you could get a room for the night for £4. Eating was free and, if you were really stuck for somewhere to sleep, you could travel round and round on the Circle Line half the night.

The job was cleaning out the inside of a basement bar that had closed down and was reopening as a strip club. The new owner was a man from Malta with a big chest and a bristly moustache. He agreed to pay us £5, of which Johnny would take £3 because he had set it up.

The Maltese man provided me with a huge broom, I hung my red jacket on a hook and started sweeping from the back wall towards the stairs. The place was thick with dirt and dog-ends. A cloud of ash rose into the air and I almost coughed my heart out. Johnny saw himself in more of a managerial position and spent most of the time smoking and keeping a lookout in case the boss came back to check on us.

Sweeping dust is like that Greek myth where some unfortu-nate fellow is forever rolling a stone uphill, only for it to come rolling down on top of him just as he's about to reach the peak. When you sweep dust, it rises in the air and settles behind you, so you are always going back to start again. After collecting as much dust as I could in plastic bags, I washed the wall behind the small stage. Johnny emptied the dirty buckets of water in the street and brought clean ones. I was moving along one of the side walls whistling 'In the Summertime' when two policemen marched in and I was terrified they were looking for me.

We were told to empty our pockets, then they searched us. We were jostled up the stairs, shoved in the back of a Black Maria and, sirens wailing, raced through Soho to the West End Central police station in Savile Row, the street where all the rich men go to get their suits made.

Inside the station we were separated. I was questioned by a plain-clothes policewoman named Inspector Yeoman with a uniformed sergeant sitting in the corner operating a tape recorder. There were no windows in the room, the lights were dim and the woman sat opposite me across a small narrow table. She was quite young with piercing eyes and a tough look on her narrow face.

She must have worked out how old I was just by looking at me. I was obviously a runaway and, as she began firing questions at me, I decided to just tell the truth, the whole truth and nothing but the truth. My file would eventually be found and it would all come out. I told her my name, address, date of birth, the home where I'd run away from. I told her my mother had put me into voluntary care, that my dad wanted me to go home, and that I had been 'abused' when I was thirteen. I didn't mention what had happened in the secure unit, it was so terrible, so improbable, I was forcing the truth out of my own mind.

Inspector Yeoman finally paused, lit a cigarette and sat back, crossing her legs.

'Do you take drugs, Emily?' she asked in a casual way.

'No, I hate drugs. They try and make me take the pill at the home and I spit it out every day.'

'Does your friend take drugs?' I wasn't sure who she meant for a moment. 'John Moss,' she then added.

'I don't think so, I don't know. I've only met him twice and he offered me a job sweeping up.'

'Do you know who owns that club?'

'A big man with a moustache,' I replied.

'Have you met him before?'

'No, only today.'

'Did you see any drugs at that club?'

'No, just a lot of dust from sweeping up.'

She smiled.

'Does Johnny deal drugs?'

I shrugged. 'I don't know, I don't even know him,' I said.

I remembered Johnny Moss borrowing £5 from Robbie to do a deal and it only occurred to me at that second that it was probably to buy drugs, not that I was going to be a rat and say anything.

Inspector Yeoman asked me for the telephone number of the home and wrote it down in her notebook. While she went to call Caroline and Mikey, the sergeant told me to accompany him. We walked along the corridor and entered a large room with smaller rooms off to one side. We stopped in the doorway to one of these rooms and I saw Johnny lying scrunched up on the floor completely naked. Standing over him were two officers who had taken off their jackets and ties. As I watched, they began beating him with rolled-up towels. He cried out, but they didn't stop.

The sergeant turned me to face him, leaned down and stared into my eyes.

'Let this be a warning to you – watch and remember,' he said, and turned me back to face the room again.

He then took me upstairs to another room that was brighter. Inspector Yeoman was there with another woman, who was younger and in uniform. The questioning started again, but it was informal. They wanted me to tell them what I knew about drug deals and pimping.

'What's that?' I asked.

'Pimping?'

I nodded.

'Are you telling me you don't know what a pimp is?'

'No, I don't, honestly. Is it, like, someone who's really short?'

'That's a shrimp.'

'It sounds the same.'

The inspector sighed. 'When young girls come to Soho, there are men waiting for them. Clever men. Devious men. They give the girls presents and buy them clothes. They tell them they love them, they need them, then they ask them to do something for them. Do you know what that is, Emily?'

I shook my head. 'Not really,' I replied, although I had guessed by then.

'They turn them into prostitutes. The men are called pimps and the girls go with any man they can find, five a day, ten a day, any number. They are trapped into this life, often for years.'

'I'd never do anything like that,' I said. 'I hate men.'

'What do you know about drugs?'

'Nothing. I don't know anything. I only came here three days ago. I've been sleeping at the night shelter.'

'Emily, do me a favour, when you go back to the children's home, you stay there. I know you want to grow up quickly, that's normal. But it's not safe here on the street. The pimps will find you, they'll trick you, they'll get you, and if the pimps don't get you first, the drug dealers will.' She held up her hand. 'You may not want to take drugs, but the dealers and criminals use teenagers like you to move them about.'

My initial fear of being arrested had gone. The young woman in uniform left and Inspector Yeoman carried on asking questions and giving me advice. I had learned that it was always best to agree with everything and then do what you want.

The door opened and the policewoman returned with the older sergeant. He was carrying a tray with a pot of tea and four blue mugs. The woman held a plate with a sponge cake.

'Sorry there's no candles,' she said, and my mouth fell open.

'Happy birthday,' added Inspector Yeoman.

I'd lost track of the days. It was my birthday. I was fifteen.

CHAPTER 21

Beastly and Boring

If being arrested wasn't bad enough, I lost my red leather jacket that day. I'd left it hanging in that club and, by the time I remembered, it was too late to go back and get it. I didn't usually have attachments to things, in care you lose everything, but I really loved that jacket. It defined me. When I was wearing it, I felt as if I belonged, that I was inside the bubble instead of outside forever looking in.

I was off to yet another placement, my fifth in three years. Normally, the wheels of the care system need a squirt of oil to get going, but for once they had moved at lightning speed and I got the sense that Inspector Yeoman was a woman who knew how to get things done. In her striped trouser suit and laced-up shoes, she looked like one of those women trying to prove herself in a man's world, but my initial impression had been wrong. When she wasn't acting tough, she was sensitive with intelligent green eyes that didn't miss a thing.

A man from social services arrived at the station. He had thick sideburns and a moustache like Frank Zappa. The sergeant, an older man with a military look and medal ribbons, looked him up and down for a moment, blew out his cheeks, then gave him a slice of cake and a mug of tea.

'All you social workers got long hair now, have you?' he asked.

'Only the good-looking ones, sergeant.'

'The folly of youth, if you ask me. Not that anyone is.'

The sergeant offered me the last piece of cake. I shook my head, my tummy was full of butterflies, and he perched on the edge of the table and ate it himself. When he'd cleared away the last crumb, we came to our feet. Inspector Yeoman then did something totally unexpected – she took me to one side and gave me a hug.

'Emily, you are too smart to end up on the streets. Be sensible,' she said. 'You're fifteen now, by the time you're sixteen, everything will be different. You'll see.'

'You don't know what it's like in those homes.'

The inspector had her thinking face on. 'How long have you been in care?' she asked.

'Care,' I repeated. 'It's not like what you think. It's been three years and it seems like a life sentence.'

She was nodding slowly and there was a deep line between her eyebrows. 'It's not the first time I've heard that. It's something we need to look into.'

'Care isn't care. It's a punishment.' I crossed my heart. 'I'm telling the truth.'

'I believe you. As I said, when you're sixteen, you'll be more grown up and you'll have more rights.'

'What kind of rights?'

'You'll have more of a say in the decisions that are made on your behalf.'

I filed this away in my head like an equation, or a date in history.

She had her hands resting on my shoulders and, for some reason, I welled up in tears. I was afraid of going back into council care. Each institution is damaging in its own way, different but damaging. I suddenly yearned for the impossible. I wanted Inspector Yeoman to take me home to live with her. The sergeant joined us and the mood changed.

'You think about everything that's happened today, young lady, and don't you forget it,' he said, and I remembered Johnny Moss lying on the floor being beaten with rolled-up towels.

The sergeant put the mugs back on the tray. It was time to go.

The social services man who had come to collect me was named Terry. He was still doing his training and was full of passion and energy. He didn't know that the normal way to deal with distraught, broken children is with harshness, sarcasm and silence. He pulled out of the police station car park, threaded through the West End traffic and headed for Westminster Bridge.

'Where are you taking me?' I asked, testing him.

'They've found a place for you at a remand home near Maidstone.'

'Isn't a remand home for kids who have broken the law?'

'Yes, generally speaking—'

'But I haven't done anything. I only ran away.'

'That doesn't sound fair.'

'No, it doesn't.'

'Well, I don't know, Emily, we'll have to tell someone,' he said, and I smiled.

It was funny being with a trainee. I knew more about the system than he did. There is no question of 'telling' the authorities that you are in the wrong place, that you are 'innocent' until proven guilty. Each decision is logged in the file with indelible ink and there's nothing you can do to erase or change it.

A child in care is a number, a case, a product. Chief wardens run care homes like tyrants in walled cities. They have firm views on how children should be treated, and their own ideas about what's right and wrong. Most wardens in the 1970s were middle-aged. They would have been brought up by parents born in the Victorian era and it was Victorian ideals and methods that remained in their minds. Like colonial governors in the Empire who considered it perfectly acceptable to beat, torture and murder 'the natives', a lot of wardens believed if you spared the rod you spoiled the child, that, like the natives, children in care needed to be beaten down and civilised.

Inspections and reviews were largely ignored because wardens assumed they knew best and government recommendations applied to other care homes, not their own. At the holding bay I had been free to roam the pubs at night until I was raped. At the secure unit I was violated repeatedly by male members of the staff, fed antipsychotic drugs and subjected to EEGs and psychological testing. I had been locked in solitary confinement in a tower like a lunatic in some Gothic nightmare, a creepy experience I have never been able to figure out, and with Mikey and Caroline I had felt as if I were being watched constantly for my dormant promiscuity to raise its dirty little head. I didn't run away because they were bad people. I ran away to find myself.

I looked at Terry with his lush moustache and velvet jacket. He was a new breed of social worker, and I wondered how long it was going to be before he left the profession, disillusioned, or changed and became like the rest.

We turned off the motorway at Maidstone and I lowered the window. The smell of the countryside was ripe with things growing and changing. The road narrowed as we curved between apple orchards and fields sparkling with crops. They call Kent the Garden of England and I thought one day, when I grew up, if I ever made it that far, I would live in Kent and have a big garden with flowers and lots of dogs.

We slowed to a stop in Headcorn, a medieval village with storybook cottages and shops with dimpled windows. In front of us was a line of girls on horses, tack shiny with polish, backs straight, the tails of their jackets dancing over their tight jodh-purs. It was a scene that reminded me of a past so distant now it felt as if it belonged to someone else. As we passed, I thought, those girls with their bright faces and bright futures could have been me, that we don't know what's going to happen in our lives; nothing is spelled out and one slip, one stumble, one wrong turn can lead you into a deep ditch that you can never dig yourself out of.

Outside the village Terry accelerated. We went through a larger town filled with bustle and children coming out of school.

On the outskirts, he swished through an open gate and pulled up outside a gloomy building with rows of windows shiny in the afternoon sun. A broad woman with big shoulders, a tweed skirt and polished brogues marched out the moment I opened the car door.

'Hello, Emily,' she said with the sort of smile normally reserved for people who know each other. 'We have been waiting for you for a long time. I'm Mrs Beasley – how do you do?'

'Very well, thank you.'

'I knew you'd be coming to stay with us eventually. It was just a matter of time,' she added ominously. 'Come along now.'

Terry had stepped out of the car and stood to one side looking lost. Mrs Beasley gave her hand a little flutter.

'Thank you, everything's in hand. I'll take over from here,' she told him.

'Right you are,' he said, and glanced at me. 'Bye, Emily, good luck.'

'Thanks, Terry, you too . . .'

Mrs Beasley hurried me up the steps and into her office.

'First-name terms, I see. Best not to get too familiar, especially with the men,' she advised, and we sat down, the blue file in front of her a bit thicker than last time I'd seen it. 'Now, my dear, it was decided a while back that a remand home would be ideal for your needs. It was only a matter of time before you came to me.'

'But I haven't broken any laws,' I said.

'You did burn down your school.'

'That was a long time ago.'

She leaned forward with her head cocked to one side. 'I'm sorry, what was that?'

'I said it was a long time ago.'

'That's exactly right. As I said, I have been waiting for you for a long time. Now you are here, I suggest you make the most of it.'

I looked back at Mrs Beasley. She had a face like a bulldog and wore around her neck a lanyard with a whistle on the end. Her job was to break me. I smiled sweetly and my heart deflated in my chest.

The remand home was for girls only. Except for the boiler man, the staff was made up of women and there was a general air of calm and efficiency. The doors were mainly left unlocked. Teachers came in for our schooling and we scuttled between rooms without running or talking too loud. The staff never shouted. If you did something wrong, you heard the piercing shriek of Mrs Beasley's whistle and it stopped you in your tracks like a bullet. If you were close to the whistle when it sounded, it reverberated for hours in your eardrums. In bed at night, eight to a dorm, the rooms sparse and grey, like the food, you couldn't hear your thoughts, you heard the echo of that whistle. It was the soundtrack of the remand home and it had made Mrs Beasley partially deaf.

The girls called Mrs Beasley Mrs Beastly. Her assistant was named Mrs Goring. They called her Mrs Boring. It summed up the place. It was beastly and boring. The days were long and dull and I kept thinking about the life I'd left behind, the crowds in Carnaby Street, my red leather jacket, Robbie practising 'Blowing in the Wind', Jock limping along with Scratch, the

Hare Krishna devotees parading through the streets beating drums and cymbals. There was a life going on and I was missing it.

At Christmas, I got a three-day pass. Dad collected me and we drove home in his new Rover. We talked about the past and avoided everything that had happened since the last time I'd seen him. Amy and Aunt Alice were waiting. Amy threw herself into my arms and we cried. She was twelve and looked grown up in jeans and a baggy sweater.

'I missed you.'

'I missed you.'

We rubbed our noses together. There was so much to say and it was hard to say anything at all. I wanted to warn Amy about Alan Briggs. I wanted to tell her all the things that had happened to me when I was twelve. But I gagged on the words that described the deeds. I had never told anyone. I was ashamed. It was horrible, dirty, perverted. What words could I use? All I could do was shed a tear and live in the land of pretence.

We drank tea from china cups and ate the ginger cake Aunt Alice had made because it had once been my favourite and she'd remembered. My family treated me as if I had just come out of hospital after a long illness, and those days at home were like stepping into someone else's life, everything familiar but glazed in dust. I felt like a soldier who had been away to war. I had seen things and done things I could never share with anyone except other soldiers who had fought the same battles.

The music on the stereo was Bizet's opera *Carmen* and, later, I heard Rodrigo's *Concierto de Aranjuez* for the first time. It was

Aunt Alice's Spanish period. She had finally darkened her hair, wore a ruffled skirt like a flamenco dancer and a waistcoat over a white blouse with big sleeves. Aunt Alice had never worked before and had always looked old. She had taken her first job teaching music at a private school and seemed twenty years younger.

I took a long bath. Amy told me about life at grammar school. She was happy. She liked a challenge and liked being with people who were smart.

'Like you,' she added.

'Me?' I shook my head. 'There's a difference between smart and intelligent,' I said.

'There, see, you would have to be smart to say something like that.'

We laughed and then I got serious. 'How do you put up with Alan and the kids?'

'I just do. It's not all bad, you know.'

'Alan's not a bully? He doesn't . . .?' I couldn't find the words. 'Just be careful.'

'I am, Emmy, I promise.'

We dressed in matching blue velvet dresses, a bit old-fashioned, pre-Christmas presents that recalled other times.

It was Christmas Eve and we sat down to dinner with carols on the radio. A tree with lights and presents below the branches stood in the corner, the fairy in pink on top the same fairy that had reigned over the Christmas trees when I was little. The table was set with a white cloth dotted with sprigs of holly. Dad lit two red candles. Shadows circled the walls and I caught my reflection in the silver spoon in front of me. My lips formed a half-smile but my eyes were far away and what came into my mind was my mother burning my arm with a teaspoon taken from a hot teapot.

The following morning, Dad made a phone call before driving us across town to the council estate. The moment we pulled up, Alan and Mum spilled into the yard with the rest of the brood. Billy was tall with long greasy hair, his mean face meaner than ever. Barbs had always been greedy and had gone from being a plump little girl to an obese teenager with an angry, piggy face. I was slender, hair to my shoulders, clothes well fitting, the sort of girl who might have teased Barbs at school, and she looked at me with all the hatred she had for all of them. Little Orphan Annie seemed frozen in time with the same glassy eyes and dead expression. Mum was as thin as Alan's whip in skin-tight red trousers that showed her good bum and long legs. Alan, like Dad, looked older, smaller, greyer. I realised someone was missing.

'Where's Patch?' I asked, and Billy glared at me.

'Died, didn't he,' he snarled.

'Cancer,' Alan added.

He seemed to be wiping away a tear as he strolled up the path to the gate. He was wearing a Father Christmas hat trimmed with mistletoe, which added an absurd pathos to his display of emotions. He went out into the street to admire Dad's new car. It was parked behind the Jaguar Alan had bought after selling Mum's Mini.

'What's it do to the gallon?' he asked.

'About twenty-five on a run.'

'Better than my beast,' he said.

I looked at Alan Briggs standing there in that silly hat and a donkey jacket. I felt like shouting out all the evil things he had done, but as I ran the words through my head, it sounded untrue, even to myself. The trauma of sexual abuse for a child can cause retrograde amnesia – selective memory loss – regarding those particular incidents. Shame and self-loathing are such powerful emotions, the mind deals with them by putting the events into a sort of fog that makes them distant and muddled. The memory of each incident is pushed to the back of the mind, but then something can happen randomly and they jerk back into sharp focus.

I stayed two hours in the Briggs house. It was a shambles. A place for nothing and nothing in its place. The neighbours' goats had gone, victims of new times, but the smell remained like a noxious memory. The kitchen table was awash in beer cans and fag ash. It reminded me of the secure unit. Every surface needed a paint or a polish. I could see by the look in Mum's eyes that she knew what I was thinking; she had always been good at reading me. Her lips were pursed, her cheeks drawn. She was riddled through with hatred and, I grasped for the first time, that it wasn't only me she hated. She hated herself. My mother had made a mistake when she left Dad. She was too stubborn to have admitted it, even to herself, and would pay the price in that slum of a house for the rest of her life.

Amy survived by sheer guts and character. When I was with her, I wanted to be like her. When I came under the spell of Roberta Raimondo I had wanted to be Bobby. I had lost the self-confidence to be myself and that's what beatings, parental neglect and care homes do.

When Dad came back to collect us, Alan Briggs made a show of giving me a hug. My mother never touched me. I didn't care any more. I carried a lot of hurt inside me and, as I closed the garden gate and climbed into Dad's new Rover, it really felt as if one of my cares had been left behind.

We went to a carol service and then home for lunch. Amy and I helped Aunt Alice peel vegetables. We listened to music and I tried to fight off the invasive sense that I was acting a role, that the girl I was that day wasn't really me but a visitor inside my head or, alternatively, it was me and I spent most of my life playing someone else. I still wanted to warn Amy to be careful of Alan Briggs, but to have warned her what might happen would have been an admission of what had happened to me. I couldn't do it.

Back at the remand home on New Year's Eve, all the girls dressed up in their finery – like little tarts, to be honest – and we were allowed to stay up until midnight to see in the New Year. The all-important Christmas No 1 in the charts was Benny Hill singing 'Ernie (The Fastest Milkman in the West)', a silly song, not a pop song. The 1960s were receding. It was 1972. It seemed to me that time was running out and I just couldn't bare the restrictions, the rules, the pettiness and that whistle one more day.

CHAPTER 22

Learning the Tricks

When I arrived back in Soho at the beginning of March, I found that every waking moment was taken up with trying to survive. After three nights at the shelter lying awake watching sleep-walkers and addicts with night terrors, I was on the street unsure what was worse: not sleeping from sheer fear or having nowhere to sleep at all. I soon ran out of cash using the public baths and fed myself on charity handouts.

I became part of an intricate subculture of runaways and rough sleepers living unseen like ghosts in the very heart of London. I learned on the street who I could trust and who you had to stay away from. I met thieves who would rob your blanket on a frosty night, conmen preying on the meek and vulnerable, and psychopaths who ought to be locked up, the key thrown away.

They were the exception.

Most of the people bedded down out there on park benches and back alleyways were damaged teenagers from broken homes, ex-soldiers, aimless men who ended up in prison for petty crimes, and women hiding from sadistic partners and fathers, who, as if by some cruel fate, found themselves on the game with sadistic pimps. A lot of bundles of humanity you see in shop doorways suffer from mental conditions that lead to addictions, depression and worsening mental health. They were doomed in infancy and inhabit mad fantasies and private hells.

Yet, in spite of their baggage and disappointments, perhaps because of them, the majority of homeless people I met were kind at heart and tried to help each other, even when they needed help themselves. Most would share a blanket, not steal it, the same as they shared fags and cups of tea. They had been stripped of everything and, when you have nothing, you lend a hand to the person you meet with less than nothing.

People from privileged backgrounds with private educations are often unable to recognise or identify with the needs of others. They see you on the street begging, or engulfed like a snail in a sleeping bag, and think you're scum, degenerate, a drug addict. They spit on you and kick you. They don't know, and usually don't want to know, that the life chances of children from dysfunctional backgrounds is diminished, sometimes to nothing. If you slip through the cracks and become homeless, it is close to impossible to get back on your feet again.

When my money ran out, I spent two nights going round and round on the Circle Line. Then I saw Jock and Scratch outside the gate at St Anne's.

'Hello, Jock, it's good to see you.'

He stared back with gritted teeth. 'Who are you? What do you want? I haven't got anything.'

'I'm Emily. We met before. Last year.'

'Last year.' He shook his head of stringy grey hair. 'You got a fag?'

'I don't smoke.'

'Don't smoke!' It was the craziest thing he'd ever heard.

Scratch was looking up at me with the same expression as Jock; dogs and their owners really do grow to look alike. Scratch was a golden retriever, friendly and harmless. I bent to stroke his head and he pushed himself into my hand, enjoying the affection.

'Mind you don't get fleas. It's a filthy beast,' Jock said, and I took my hand away. 'You got any money?'

'No, not a penny.'

'Go back when you came from, lassie; you shouldn't be here.'

'Better here than in a children's home,' I said, and he grunted.

'Aye, out of the mouths of bairns.' He looked at me more closely. 'Last year? What year was that then?'

'Nineteen seventy-one.'

'You got any fags?' he asked again.

'I don't smoke.'

We wandered down Wardour Street to Shaftesbury Avenue and on to the Circus. It was dark, cold, the misty rain in haloes around the street lights. People spilled out of the theatres speaking loudly as they told each other their views on the play they'd just seen. The restaurants were full. Nothing was said or planned, but I stayed with Jock as we threaded our way through to Jermyn Street and camped out behind the rubbish bins at the back of the Criterion Restaurant. Jock kept a couple of blankets in big plastic bags from Lillywhites, the sports store, and he gave one of them to me.

'Keep your wee head doon and don't answer back if somebody speaks.'

I wrapped the blanket about me and listened to Scratch panting, the heat of his body keeping me warm as he snuggled up between us. It was my first night under the stars, not that there were any stars that night. I had a dim recollection of being a Brownie and insisting that I sleep in the tent Dad had erected for me in the back garden. I must have been about six and was sitting there scared out of my wits when it started to rain and Mum came out to bring me in. She loved me then.

You lose track of time on the street but this would be my home for several days. Jock acted tough in that Glasgow way. But he was more the gentleman than the men in suits who mocked us and I felt safe with him. He never touched me or alluded to anything sexual. He was an old street person. I was a young street person. He was showing me the ropes. He went once a day to the chemist for his supply of diamorphine and complained bitterly that 'it eased the pain without the bite of horse', his word for heroin.

When Jock returned with his drugs, I took Scratch for a walk so he could jack up and chill out on his own. We crawled into our blankets never knowing what the night would bring. Sometimes drunks would 'put the boot in'. On more than one occasion I was pissed on, and I knew I had to make some changes in my life that night when the brief stream of urine provided a strange comfort and warmth.

We were awoken early by the bin men after a couple of hours of sleep and we'd shuffle off like zombies to get a mug of tea and a slice of toast from the Sally Army, good people who care and try to help. As you were lining up, you'd hear rumours that someone had frozen to death in the night, or overdosed, or committed suicide. It was sad, but it also gave you a feeling of accomplishment that you were still there blowing steam from your tea, the sun rising on another day. I was becoming drawn, tired, grubby, but never for a second did I think of returning to the remand home.

Later that day, and maybe it was the next day, I caught a glimpse of myself in a long mirror and my mouth literally fell open. I was hunched over like a grandma and there was a streak of dirt on my cheek that I rubbed away with a bit of spit. I took a deep breath and counted up to twenty.

Come on, Em, be positive. You're the girl who won the cross-country. You can do anything if you put your mind to it.

Slowly I let my breath out. Soho would answer the call and, to get ready for it, I just had to raise some money for the public baths. I started by going to the arcade and checking all the slots to see if anyone had left 10p behind. Then I did the phone boxes, one after the other, the length of Old Compton Street, up Greek Street, then down Frith Street, bashing the apparatus with the heel of my hand and checking the coin chutes.

I wasn't aware that I was being watched as I hit the phone boxes.

'Do you fancy a cup of coffee and a panini?'

I almost jumped out of my skin. The accent sounded familiar, like from my past, and as I spun round I saw the girl wasn't a street person. She looked like a model posing for a photograph with one hand on her hip and the other thrown out with a cigarette between two fingers. She was decked out in a short white dress, red stockings, white boots, a red woolly scarf and a short blue jacket with a fur collar. She had bubbles of blonde hair, a wide mouth with bow-shaped lips and a quizzical smile.

'Sorry?' I said.

'Never complain, never explain and never apologise. Are you hungry?'

'What?'

She spoke slowly. 'What . . . country . . . are . . . you . . . from?'

Finally I smiled back. 'Yes, I'm starving.'

She flicked ash. 'Thought so. Come on.'

We were outside the Bar Italia and the panini she had suggested turned out to be a roll made from crispy bread. They were stacked up inside a glass display case and I chose ham and cheese. The coffee was delicious and the girl peered at me over the rim of her cup as I was eating. She had small white teeth, a turned-up nose and the most remarkable eyes I had ever seen, the irises sapphire blue with flecks of silver. I stared back at her and she nodded as if she had reached a decision.

'Don't tell me, I read minds: you've run away from home?'

'No . . . well, yes, sort of.'

'I used to do that, look for coins. People are so mean the most I ever found was an umbrella and it wasn't even raining.' She gave herself a little shake and fluttered her eyelashes. 'What's your name, then?'

'Emily.'

'That's gorgeous.' She pointed at herself. 'Donna. That's my stage name.'

'You're an actress?'

'You could say that,' she said, and fluttered her eyelashes again.

She stubbed out her half-smoked cigarette, then offered her packet of Sobranie Black Russian, ciggies with gold filters that looked inviting, but I shook my head and watched Donna light up with a tiny revolver that shot out a feather of orange flame. She blew invisible smoke from the barrel like a gangster and real smoke in a long silvery stream over her shoulder.

Everything Donna said sounded like magic in my ears. I loved the movement of her hands, the way she stretched her long neck, the silver sequins floating in her strange blue eyes. It was like I had slipped through a crack in space and landed in the secret world I had peeked into from the rubbish bins and soup kitchens, the faraway planet of film directors and models, actresses, and people who step out of taxis on their way somewhere. The cafe was warm and a waiter in a striped apron was polishing the brass bits around the counter. I had gone by the cafe many times and was amazed that I had passed through the invisible barrier and arrived on the inside like I was supposed to be there.

Donna was saying she hated smoking but had to smoke because everyone else smoked and it was something to do with your hands when you were bored. As she was talking, I recognised her accent.

'Are you from Manchester?' I asked, and she threw up her shoulders dismissively.

'Darling, everyone's from somewhere,' she said. She took another puff on the golden filter and released a fresh cloud of smoke. 'Am I right, you've run away from home?'

'From a children's home,' I said, and she nodded sympathetically.

'Don't know what's worse, home or homes. Better off on your own,' she said, and we laughed.

She had given away something, a bit of herself. She knew things that I knew. She wriggled in her seat.

'It's hard at first, but it gets easier.'

'It's easy for you to say that, I haven't got any money.'

'Oh, getting money's as easy as pie, it's everywhere. It's like the sea to the fish. You just put your hand out and it comes dropping in.'

'That hasn't happened to me.'

'Then you're not trying hard enough.'

'I am, honestly.'

'You can't be serious?'

'Dead serious. I haven't got 10p for the bathhouse.'

She pinched her nose. 'So I noticed,' she said.

'I don't . . .'

'No, it's a joke, silly.' She stabbed out her cigarette, cupped her chin with her small hand, looked into my eyes and sighed despondently. 'I suppose you're a virgin?'

I had not been expecting the question and it made my armpits tingle. I gritted my teeth.

'No, not really . . .'

'Well, you either are or you aren't. You can't be a half-virgin, can you?' she said, and I giggled nervously. 'Now, here's the thing, darling, if you've already done it, you may just as well get paid for it.'

'You mean . . .' I didn't finish my sentence.

'What do you think it's for, peeing?'

My cheeks turned red. 'But, but isn't it horrible?'

'Sometimes.' She curled up her tiny nose. 'It's just a job.'

'But I thought you were an actress?'

'I am. I pretend the johns are handsome and act as if I like it.'

I could hardly believe what I was hearing. Donna had a gravity pull about her that had drawn me in. She was . . . poised, convincing. Her lashes flashed and she lowered her voice.

'And sometimes, I do.'

'Do what?'

'Sometimes I like it.'

'I never will.'

'Everyone says that. But it's, like, normal, it's what men and women do.'

'Have you done it a lot?'

She burst out laughing. 'Hundreds of times,' she replied. 'I've had more pricks in me than a second-hand dartboard.'

I laughed. I heard myself laughing. I hadn't actually laughed for ages.

'But doesn't it hurt?' I said, getting serious again.

'It only hurts when you don't want them to. You know, if you're forced.'

'Has that happened to you, Donna?'

She gave her thin shoulders a little shake. 'Course,' she replied. 'The rest of the time, it's nothing. Sometimes good, sometimes bad, like the movies. I love movies. I love Jon Voight.'

She made it seem like fun. 'How much do you get?' I asked, not so much making a decision but letting the suggestion wrap itself around me. I was tasting it, testing it, putting myself in Donna's shoes.

'About ten quid a pop, depending . . .'

She waited for me to say something but continued anyway.

'Whether it's a quickie, a blow job, all night, a threesome.'

'Threesome?'

'Sometimes with two blokes, sometimes when a bloke wants two girls crawling all over him at the same time. I quite like that myself.'

My palms were sweaty. My eyes were wide. I must have looked shocked. Donna leaned forward and her sapphire eyes glimmered.

'It's the oldest profession. That's what they say. If you can't do anything else, you just open your legs and think of England. That's what Flash says.' She paused. 'He's my pimp.'

'Oh.' I knew what a pimp was.

'I've got my own room. Flash pays all the bills . . . with my money,' she said. She smiled but she wasn't joking. 'It makes life easier. I get loads of tips and I keep all that for spending money.'

'I don't think I'd like that,' I said. 'I mean . . .'

I wasn't sure what I meant. I made decisions quickly, rashly, often regretting them and repeating them. But I had spent more than a week sleeping behind the dustbins being kicked and pissed on. The idea of earning £10 was very appealing.

'I mean, do you have to have a pimp?' I added.

'Course not, everyone's a free human being, aren't they?' Donna replied. 'Some girls are freelance, some have a pimp to look out for them, you know, procure clients, that sort of thing. It's like having an agent, it's just business.'

'I like to do things on my own,' I said.

'Give it a try, see what happens.'

I grinned. I felt oddly proud. I was wearing stained Levi's and a denim jacket that must have reeked of dustbins and beery piss – when you wear the same thing every day, you get accustomed to the smell and can't smell it any more. Even so, I must have been a bit pongy and this amazing girl who made me laugh thought I could *give it a try*. I had asked the Gods of Soho to help and they'd sent a guardian angel.

'Do you think I could?'

Before she could answer, a friend of Donna's waltzed in on tottering heels and joined our table. Her name was Debs and she looked totally groovy in a short frilly pink skirt, a top with hundreds of buttons in a darker shade of pink, a short black coat and a pink hat with a high crown and narrow brim.

'Nice hat,' Donna said.

'Someone bought it for me.'

'Who?'

Debs touched the tip of her nose. Then glanced at me with a smile.

'Hello,' she said.

'Watch out, Debs, Emily's going to nick all your regulars.'

'I have no worries, there, darling. I know how to keep them satisfied.'

The waiter brought her a coffee. '*Bellissima, signorina, un espresso doppia*,' he said, and bowed.

'How old are you, then?' Donna asked.

'Sixteen,' I said, and shrugged, raising my shoulders with a little fluttter. 'Next birthday.'

'I was fourteen when I started turning tricks.'

'She's such a show-off,' Donna said. 'None of that stuff matters. A girl's gotta do what a girl's gotta do. Right?' She sat back and buttoned her coat. 'I'm going to take you back to my pad. You can have a bath and we'll find you some clothes.'

Debs finished her coffee and the three of us walked a short way up Frith Street and entered a narrow door that led straight on to a steep flight of stairs. Donna's room was in the attic. It had a slanted ceiling, pink lights, a large bed with a pink candle-wick bedspread, a wardrobe stuffed with clothes and a chest of drawers with the sort of sexy underwear I had seen in shop windows but had never imagined anyone wearing.

'There's a bathroom next door,' she said, giving me a towel. 'Don't be too long. Flash is seeing his probation officer and I want to be out by the time he gets back.'

After washing my hair and giving myself a good scrub, I returned to Donna's room and sat with a towel wrapped around me. The girls fussed over me like mother hens, putting on make-up, something I had not bothered with since I was thir-teen. As my face changed with foundation and eyeliner, mascara and lipstick, it felt as if I were seeing myself from outside myself, as if the girl on the chair was becoming what she was always meant to be, the girl in the mirror.

'Stand up, then, let's see what you've got?' I wasn't sure what Donna meant and turned crimson when she made a sign with her fingers. 'Come on, if you can't let your mates have an eyeful you're not going to get far with a bloke, now are you?'

The word 'mates' sounded like a tinkling bell in my ears. I let Donna pull the towel away and stood there naked.

'Slim hips, nice curves,' Donna said.

'Very gamine,' added Debs.

I crinkled my brow and raised my shoulders.

'She means boyish.'

'But with nice firm little boobs.'

'They like that,' Donna said. 'They like girls who look like boys and the poofters like boys who look like girls.'

'It's a mixed-up, muddled-up, fucked-up world except for us two,' said Debs, and she pointed at Donna. 'And I'm not even sure about her.'

They rolled about in hysterics. They were pretty, happy, they had nice clothes. It was weird being discussed like an item for sale, but it was amiable and I could see it was important to look right if you were turning tricks. I liked that phrase. It wasn't like they were prostitutes, hookers, whores, slags. They were tricksters tricking men out of money by opening their legs for England. They made it seem like a laugh.

Donna produced from the drawer of the dresser a black bra with underpadding that pushed up your breasts and hooked together at the front. It came with matching knickers, the set in a sheer material that was almost transparent, each piece decorated with black silk bows.

'You are not serious?' I said.

'Never been more serious in my life. They like all this kinky stuff.' Donna turned to Debs. 'What do you think, schoolgirl?'

'You got it.'

'You have to take your best attributes and use them,' Donna explained. 'Girls with huge boobs go out with them on show. Girls with long legs show their legs. You look like you're still a schoolgirl . . .'

At that, she produced a tartan kilt, a white blouse, black heels high enough to make me wobble and a red imitation fur jacket, which didn't go, but really stood out. I put them on and turned to the mirror. The skirt reminded me of my uniform at The Priory, but apart from that, it still looked like a stranger in the reflection.

'Thing is, all those dirty old men fantasise about schoolgirls. If you've got it, darling, flaunt it,' Donna said. 'You ready?'

My heart was thumping, 'I don't know . . .'

Donna smiled and turned to Debs. 'Isn't it romantic? It's her first time, you remember that?'

'Are you joking, it was, like, twenty million years ago.'

'She's such a slag,' said Donna, and wriggled when Debs slapped her bottom. 'Come on, before Flash comes and ruins everything.'

We went bowling down the stairs, giggling, clip-clopping on our heels, and stepped straight into a London taxicab – my first.

'The Ritz, please,' Donna said.

It was easy, like jumping into a swimming pool. I had been searching for coins so I could have a wash. Now I was on my way to the Ritz in the back of a black cab. It was daring. I was living the life. You have to learn how to make a crust. That's what Robbie Gillan had told me the first time I was in Soho. What was I going to do: go back to a remand home and turn deaf from that beastly whistle or earn my keep the only way I could? My heart was still thumping but it seemed right. It seemed natural and fun. I had watched people hailing cabs and stepping in the back. Now I was in a cab.

The vehicle sped along Piccadilly. Donna paid and a doorman dressed like the ringmaster at the circus opened the door for us to enter the Ritz.

'Evening, ladies.'

'This is Emily,' Donna said. 'Meet Albert.'

'My pleasure,' Albert said as he ran his eyes over me like an artist about to do a sketch.

We hurried off to the Ladies. 'You should tip him a fiver every now and then, just to grease the wheel,' Donna explained.

My armpits were sopping. I washed and patted myself dry with the free towels. Debs had an atomiser in her bag and sprayed us all in scent. We brushed our hair and stared at ourselves in the big mirrors.

'The Three Musketeers,' Donna said.

'All for one and everyone for themselves,' said Debs.

Donna looked at me in the reflection. 'Ready?'

I nodded.

'Always ask for the money first, and if they're satisfied, ask for a tip,' Donna instructed.

'But where do you, you know, where do you do it?'

'If you pick up a john at the Ritz, they're usually rich and take you back to their place or a hotel but, remember, the rich ones usually like doing kinky things.'

'Like what?'

'Dressing up in weird stuff . . . drinking champagne from your pussy. You'll find out soon enough.'

My back was wet but I suddenly had cold feet.

'I don't think I can do it.'

'Everyone feels like that the first time. Try it once and, if you don't like it, give it up.'

'But I don't, I don't like it.'

'Girls who work in factories ten hours a day stuffing giblets up chickens' arses don't like it – it's just a job.'

Donna was forceful in an unpushy sort of way. I was wearing her clothes and the last thing I wanted to do was let her down. I pressed my nails into my palms until it hurt. I had to do it. I had to. I took big breaths as we left the bathroom and stationed ourselves outside the entrance to the bar. Almost instantly, Debs said she was meeting someone in Mayfair and was already late, then Donna said she had to go or Flash would kill her.

'But what do I do?' I asked.

'Just wait. Someone will ask if you want a drink, and you say something like "Only a drink?". Just be natural.'

'What if nobody asks?'

'They will. Albert will make sure of that.'

I wasn't sure whether that made me feel better or not.

'See you at the Italia tomorrow.'

'What time?'

She crinkled her nose. 'In the morning. It's nice then.'

The girls skipped back to the entrance like two sixth-formers. People hurried in and out of the bar. Smart men. Women in gowns. I felt as if I were stuck to the spot like a statue. Time seemed suspended. I could see myself in a misty mirror across the hall. I half wanted someone to talk to me and half didn't. Then someone did.

'Hello, I haven't seen you before.'

'Er, no, I . . . just arrived.'

'First time at the Ritz?'

I nodded, biting my lips. 'Yes.'

'Would you like a drink?'

That was it. The man was about sixty, awfully posh with a black jacket and striped trousers, his white hair neatly parted, his pale eyes peering down at my breasts pushed up in the white blouse. My throat was dry. I couldn't speak.

'Is it your first time?'

I nodded.

'Then I will take care of you. Come along.'

He guided me back to the entrance. Albert saluted as he opened the door and in two minutes we were in a taxi riding the short distance to Lowndes Square. Another doorman opened another door and pressed the button to call the lift. We stepped in, the doorman backed away, and the lift doors closed. The lift had tinted mirrors on three sides and the two people standing there, the man and the girl, were strangers to each other and the girl was a stranger to herself. She was saying, it's only acting, it's fun, it's the oldest profession. Then she smiled.

The lift rose to the third floor, which had a door at either end of a short corridor. We turned left, my heart thumped like a drum and suddenly I was in a large room full of books and sculptures, vases with curly handles and photos in silver frames like a museum.

'What would you like to drink?'

I thought about the question and wasn't sure how to answer.

'Fanta? Some milk? Champagne?'

'Champagne, please.'

'Wonderful choice. Champagne for my real friends. Real pain for my sham friends.'

He went off. I heard a cork pop and he came back with champagne in a bucket of ice. He poured two glasses and I took my first sip of champagne; it was fizzy and bitter and it made me giggle as the bubbles went up my nose.

'How is it?'

'Lovely,' I replied.

'What do I call you?'

I shrugged. 'Emily.'

'You shall call me Claude.' Lines ran across his brow. 'Is it really your first time?'

'Yes.'

'First time at the Ritz or,' he shook his head, '*the* first time?'

'Both,' I answered.

'Wonderful. Now you wait here and make yourself comfortable.'

He left the room, his drink barely touched, and was gone for ages. I sat down, then stood up again. I'd only had two sips of champagne and my head was spinning. I looked at the photographs. Claude, if that was his name, must have been a judge or a barrister – at least there were several pictures of him in black robes and a wig. There were no family photographs, except for Claude as a young man with a stern woman in a long grey dress, probably his mother, and another with Claude in cricket whites and what must have been his father, a man in a naval uniform with lots of medals and braid.

When Claude tottered back into the room, I almost fainted.

'Hello, little one, it's me. Don't I look gorgeous?' he said in a high whiny voice.

He pursed his lips and gave a little wiggle. He was dressed in black fishnets and suspenders, black corsets that held in his waist and made his chest look like breasts, high heels, a blonde wig and a gash of violent red lipstick.

'Well, come on, you haven't answered?'

'Yes, yes, you do.'

'Now, this is what I want you to do. Go and sit on that chair over there.'

My tummy was churning and my knees trembled as I sat down. I held them still with my hands. He sat opposite, a coffee table with lacquer boxes and silver ornaments between us.

'You are still wearing your coat. Now, take it off, take your shirt off so I can see your little tits, then take your panties off and put your left leg over the arm of the chair.'

I hesitated. I suddenly remembered, you had to get paid first. But it was too late and too weird to start talking about money.

I did as I was told.

'Stretch your leg back,' he instructed, and I did. 'Good, good. What a pretty cunt you've got.' He sucked the index finger of his right hand. 'Now, suck your finger, and put it inside your crack like a good girl. In and out. I want you to squeeze your nipples with your free hand and I want to hear your squeals of pleasure.'

That's what I did. I sucked my finger, pushed it inside me and moaned like I was enjoying it, which I wasn't. I was acting. He was my john and I was performing my first trick. He removed the black satin panties he was wearing, put his right leg over the arm of the chair, mirroring my position, and started masturbating. He was staring at me, devouring me, his watery eyes running down from my face to my crotch.

'Little cunt. Little cunt,' he groaned. 'Faster, faster.'

As he went faster, I kept pace and, in about five minutes, it was over. He caught his discharge in a handkerchief, came to his feet and left the room.

'You just wait, I'll return in a jiffy,' he said in his high voice.

I stepped back into my black knickers, buttoned my blouse and straightened my skirt. He returned wearing a silk dressing gown and no wig. He took a sip from his champagne and I noticed the streak of lipstick on his teeth.

'You are a very nice girl, Emily, I can tell. I like you very much,' he said.

'Thank you.'

'With nice manners. You are the kind of girl who stirs the emotions. Lovely, quite lovely. I hope you don't change.' He dipped his finger in his champagne and ran it over my lips. 'Now, Emily, how much do I owe you?'

I shrugged. 'Is ten pounds all right?' I said.

'That's not very much, is it?'

He reached into his dressing-gown pocket and took out two £10 notes and two £1 notes. He placed the money on the coffee table.

'There's £20 and enough for a taxi.'

'Thank you.' My heart was banging away. I was rich.

'If you're in the bar next week, I'd like to see you again.'

'What day?'

'Same as today.'

'What day is it?'

He smiled. 'It's Thursday, all day.'

I'd lost track of time being on the street but now I had a regular everything would be different.

CHAPTER 23

The Highwire

When I met the girls at Bar Italia, I told them everything.

'Bloody hell, if I got twenty quid everything time I stuck a finger up my crack I'd become a wanking machine,' Debs said, and Donna brushed away the remark as if at a nasty smell.

'You are so crude, especially in front of a minor.'

Debs lit a fag. 'My dad was a miner. He used to climb into my bed after the night shift still covered in coal. He started when I was nine.'

'That's why you're always in the bath,' Donna observed, and Debs shrugged as she looked at me.

'Dirty old bugger. Don't know what's worse, judges or coppers.'

'Coppers have got bigger truncheons,' Donna said, and we all burst out laughing.

It was like having two sisters. I had thought when I was twelve and Alan Briggs started his fiddling that I was the only girl in the world this had happened to. But I wasn't. It's what a lot of men do if they get half the chance. Donna was right – you might just as well get paid for it. I was still wearing her clothes.

'What about your things?' I asked, and she waved away the smoke.

'They're all yours, darling. I can't bear second-hand clobber.'

'Listen to Lady Muck,' Debs said. 'She forgets coming round my pad with holes in her knickers asking for cast-offs.'

'I wouldn't wear your knickers if you paid me.'

'You'd suck the paint off a pillar box if someone paid you.'

Donna ran her tongue over her lips. 'That's different,' she said.

Debs stabbed out her fag and came to her feet. We squeezed out of the narrow space between the tables and I felt so proud paying for our espressos and *torta di meli*. Donna must have learned the tricks from Debs. I was learning from Donna. It was like we were all members of a special club.

We wandered our separate ways. I went and found Jock, treated him to a fry-up and bought him twenty Rothmans. His eyes only focused on me in my make-up when he'd wiped the grease from his plate with a slice of bread. He peeled the cellophane from his ciggies and his face was scrunched up like an old apple.

'Now, just look at you, all done up like a Christmas tree.'

I raised my shoulders and fluttered my lashes. 'Girl's gotta do what a girl's gotta do,' I said, and he gave me one of his growls.

'Just don't start with the drugs. They all do.' He fired up a king-sized and stared at me through the smoke. 'You've been hiding your light under a bushel.'

'Is that a compliment, Jock?'

'Nae, lassie, I don't go in for compliments.'

I paid the bill and we walked up Greek Street. Scratch marked every lamppost. 'Come on, you filthy beast,' Jock kept saying and, when the dog growled, I realised he made the same sound in the back of his throat as Jock. They were inseparable, a double act, and I couldn't imagine one without the other.

Soho was just waking up and those spring mornings with the sun climbing over the rooftops always felt as if there had been a party the night before. Empty bottles littered shop doorways. There were no tourists. Girls who had yet to learn the tricks of the night washed windows and mopped pavements, the sun making rainbows on the soapsuds running in the gutter.

We stopped to watch two old soldiers with caps and medals, one on the penny whistle, the other playing a metal washboard with thimbles on his fingers. Like the Hare Krishna people, they filled the air with music and I wondered where they slept at night.

'Hey, you, now you're rich you can get yer money oot,' Jock said, and I put 50p in the cloth bag the whistle player held out.

I left Jock at the entrance to St Patrick's Church, where the meths drinkers went to fight among themselves, and made my way to Carnaby Street. I forgot I was wearing Donna's shoes and glided along like a pro. The secret is to arch your back, hold your shoulders straight and roll the hips. Walking in high heels is like running cross-country, you just have to find the rhythm.

As I cut through the network of squares and passageways, I felt at ease in my own skin. I thought back over what had happened with Claude and in the light of day it didn't seem sordid and immoral at all. It was just a bit of fun, a bit weird and crazy. He wanted to watch a girl playing with herself while he played with himself. We weren't dropping bombs on Vietnam. It didn't do any harm. He could afford £20, and that was what I needed to stay out of reach of the bullies and the rules in the care homes.

I had never been without money, Dad was always generous, but it was different earning your own money. Money means freedom and freedom gives you confidence. I had changed from an ugly duckling in smelly denim to a swan in stilettos and a tartan skirt. The men in suits and ties weren't spitting at me. They were giving me the eye. They stopped me to ask for a light, a good trick to start chatting someone up, and I was pleased that no one knew I was walking through Soho with a secret.

By the end of the day, I had bought a dress that was on sale, new shoes, pink undies and booked a space in a hostel that smelled of piss and despair. With new clothes and new hopes, it was time to move on and, next day, I rented a room in Brewer Street. If you took a john to a room for an hour, it cost £5. If you slept the night on your own, it cost £4. I paid for the night and my purse was almost empty.

It was a long time before I was due to meet Claude and thought I'd be able to borrow some money from Donna to tide me over. I searched for her everywhere, but she wasn't in the Bar Italia and I didn't dare go knocking on the door to her room. I finally ran into her as the sun was going down and people were lining up outside the theatres. She was skint, like me, and had a bruise on her cheek.

'What's happened?'

'It's nothing, just him in one of his moods.'

'You mean he hit you?'

'Not really. And I hit him as well. I'm going to bugger off one of these days. That'll teach him.'

We were on the corner of Frith and Old Compton Street done up in our heels. My new dress was high above the knee with zigzagging red and white hoops, a cinch belt, long sleeves and a scooped neck that made the most of my new underpadded bra.

'Emily, you little tart, you look totally fab,' she said.

She stood back, puffed away on her Sobranie, a sort of shimmy ran through her thin shoulders and her blue eyes suddenly sparkled as if a light had been turned on behind them.

'Tell you what, I'm going to go and do a bit of freelance – that'll kill him,' she said, and put an elegant toe down on her dog-end. 'Want to come?'

'Yes, please,' I replied, and she gave me a hug.

My face broke out in one of those cat-that-got-the-cream sort of smirks as we clipped along Shaftesbury Avenue, but my heart was thumping, my armpits were wet and I suddenly had a tummy ache. After making twenty quid in ten minutes with Claude, I had thought of little else except turning tricks. But now it came to it, I felt guilty and afraid. Those two little questions *why?* and *why not?* were spinning around inside my head and, by the time we reached the Regent Palace in Piccadilly, my knees were shaking.

'I can't, Donna, I just can't,' I said, and she looked really concerned as she took a grip on my shoulders.

'You've gone pale, darling. Come on, take deep breaths. In and out. In and out,' she said, and I did as I was told. 'Come on, don't stop. You listen to Doctor Donna.'

My heart slowed, my pulse slowed, my knees slowly stopped shaking.

'Is that better?'

I snivelled. 'A bit,' I replied.

'You had me going there for a minute,' she said, and patted her chest in that way people do when they're relieved. 'Now, I want you to do something. But you have to do it properly, all right?'

'I will, I promise.'

'I want you to think about the worst thing that's ever happened with a man. You know what I'm talking about. Think on it hard and, I'll tell you, Emmy, it'll never be as bad as that.'

The slithers of silver in her blue pupils were shiny in the hotel lights. It was Amy, my sister, who called me Emmy. Now Donna was my sister. I wanted to be like her, strong and resolute. The way the girls talked about turning tricks made it seem as if it was the only way to pay everyone back for all the bad things that had happened. I thought about Alan Briggs, Bob Drake, Dean Ricks. They were terrible, terrible men. Men who should be in prison. I thought about being gang-raped. You try to bury these things, but the memories are always just below the surface. They had stolen my virginity and made me pregnant. I had killed my baby because of those men. The reel of abuse ran through my brain and it made me so angry the colour rose up my neck and cheeks. Donna was right. Nothing could ever be as bad as what they'd already done to me.

'Am I right?' Donna asked, and I nodded.

'More than you know,' I replied.

She kissed her finger and put it to my lips, then tapped the side of her head. 'They can't touch you up here, Emmy,' she said. 'It's just a fuck. It'll be over before you can say Engelbert Humperdinck.'

She made me smile.

'That's better – come on.'

I took a deep breath and put on a happy face as we swung through the doors into the foyer. There was a farmers' convention going on and we planted ourselves outside the bar. It was all very posh with plush chairs and a chandelier hanging from the ornate ceiling. Within two minutes two men in tweedy jackets and striped shirts were chatting us up. I think they both fancied Donna, at least she did all the talking.

'So, ladies, you must be delegates,' the thin one said.

'Course we are,' Donna answered. 'I breed rabbits – in my spare time.'

'Well, we all know the habits of rabbits. What do you do the rest of the time?'

'What do you think?'

He took her arm, they wandered away and I was left with the fat one.

'Shall we?'

'Shall we what?' I said in the same flirty way as Donna, and he grinned.

That was it. Easy peasy. I'd had my moment of doubt and Donna had talked me through it. My underarms were prickling again. I was dead nervous, more nervous than when I'd been with Claude for some reason, and applied that trick I used when I was running or swimming. I separated my mind from my body and flowed along like a leaf carried on the breeze.

We went up to the fifth floor and entered a large room with a large bed and, off to one side, a sofa and chairs around a coffee table. He paid the £10 I asked for and immediately told me to take off my clothes. He had droopy jowls and wasn't smiling. I stripped straight away. I knew if I didn't, he'd probably rip my new dress pulling it off, and, anyway, Donna had told me you should get into your birthday suit as fast as you can because then 'they come before they've arrived'.

'Not much meat on you,' the man remarked.

'I'm not a Jersey cow, you know,' I answered, trying to be funny, and he didn't laugh.

He pulled off his clothes. He had a chest as big as a dustbin and a fat tummy. He slapped his chest, hollered like Tarzan and, as he reached for me, my instinct was to run, which I did, like Jane in the jungle. He chased me around the sofa and chairs. I skipped across the bed, did another circuit and he finally caught me.

He pinned me down between his big thighs. He was all sweaty and I'm sure he must have kept goats because that was the smell rising off his pink skin. He shuffled forward and his cock looked like a dodgem car at the funfair as it barrelled towards my lips. 'Open sesame,' he said, and I could barely get the head in my mouth. I sucked away, pretending it was a boiled sweet, and he groaned and scratched my neck with his bristly pubes.

I kept going, drawing his cock into my mouth, trying to make him come, but he stopped himself and slid his bulk down my body. He levered my legs open and stuck his tongue inside me. My own jaw hurt and I listened as he slobbered between my legs like Scratch supping up water from a bowl. When he pushed up inside me, it suddenly occurred to me that this was the first time a man had entered me without force. Donna was right. It didn't hurt.

He banged away for a bit. Then he pushed up hard, his breath grated like a bus straining on a hill, he moaned, then I felt his hot semen splash around inside me. He kept pumping away like he was squeezing juice from a lemon, then rolled off me.

'Here, come on, girl, clean it up,' he said, and I wasn't sure what he meant.

He grabbed the back of my hair and directed my head between his legs. I licked away the discharge and he laid back, sighing like a fat baby in a cot. As he was getting his breath back, I slid away and started to dress. He pumped up the pillows and watched. I had only been in the room for about fifteen minutes. I could see by his cross look that he wasn't entirely satisfied and wasn't sure what to do about it.

'That was great, thank you,' I said, and smiled.

'You want to put a bit more effort into it next time, it was like fucking a plank of wood with a knot hole in it.'

'I'm just a beginner,' I said, and he managed a smile.

'How old are you?'

'Nearly sixteen,' I replied, and he whistled.

'I thought you were eighteen.'

'It's all right, I won't tell anyone.'

'You'd better not. You don't know who I am.'

They all think they're something special. They all act as if they're something special. But whatever the opposite of special is, that's what they are.

After fucking the farmer I was terrified I might be pregnant, so Donna took me to see her doctor, a Jamaican man named Dr Winston. He gave me a test and I welled up in tears when he told me it was negative. I paid £5 for the visit and £3 for the same sort of blue pills I'd refused to take under the prying eye of Caroline Flood. I didn't need a prescription with Dr Winston and would pay £3 every month for a fresh supply.

The money rolled in and the money rolled out. The more you've got the more you need. I only wore pink underwear and smoked Sobranie Pinks with a gold foil filter. I treated myself to a silver cigarette lighter with an art-deco naked lady on one side. Debs thought it was so gorgeous she bought one the same.

I did a sandwich fuck between two men, one in my vagina, the other in my bum, and went next day to the casualty department with rectal bleeding. I was tested for Crohn's disease, herpes, syphilis, chlamydia, and a whole bunch of other things. By the time the doctor had finished I think he knew exactly why I had anal fissures but was polite enough not to say so.

Claude (not his real name) was a High Court judge. I saw his photo in the *Evening News* one night and saw him dressed in fishnets the next.

Apart from Claude, I had another regular, an inspector from the local cop shop, who liked to take off my clothes slowly, bend me over his knee and spank my bottom. He would then fuck me, put me in the bath and piss over me. I had no idea what that was all about. Both were highly ritualised and rarely strayed from their routines.

Sometimes, you earned your £10 in less time than it takes to make a cup of tea. Other times, they kept you all night. Once I was tied to an iron bedstead and a man spent about four hours licking out my 'elixir' as, he said, it was the secret of eternal youth. I was fresh meat and that's what they liked. Those men wanted to have sex with a young girl, the younger the better, fourteen, thirteen, twelve, eleven, there is no lower limit. Being fifteen was a safety valve: they didn't want to get caught and get sent down for ten years, and it also turned them on sufficiently that most times it was quickly over and done with.

I had old men who couldn't get it up and who cried in my arms. They told me about their lives, like I cared, their regrets and disappointments, overlooked for promotion, wives that grumbled. A City gent in a bowler hat brought me his sixteen-year-old son, home on holiday from boarding school, to 'whip him into shape', a phrase that sent a chill down my spine. There were men who just wanted to watch me walking around the room naked. Some came with cameras and photographed me from every angle. There was a man with two monkey suits laid out on the bed in his hotel room. We dressed in fur and went at it gibbering like primates.

There were those who lay back demanding service and those who wanted to be in control. They wanted to spread their semen over your face, piss on you, degrade you. Every trick is a walk on the highwire. You have to do whatever they want so that you don't get hurt and, sometimes, you do it all and they still give you a slapping. You are wicked, a wild child, a temptress. It is your fault for enticing them into this sordid criminal act and you have to be punished.

It doesn't make any sense, but there are men who seek out pretty young girls and want to damage them because they are young and pretty. It's like trampling on flowers. Like bombing cities. Their own lives must be so ugly and wretched, they want to make everything about them ugly and wretched. They convince themselves that you crave their cock in your mouth, your bum, your crack, but what really turns you on is the flat of their hand on your bare skin, the fiery red splashes of stinging flesh, the taste of blood in your mouth as they split your lips, the blue bruises that take weeks to go away.

You could turn ten tricks and earn £100 a day at a time when male factory workers were lucky to be on fifty quid a week. I did like the money. I liked buying clothes. I loved having coffee with the girls, Donna and Debs, Ashley, Antoinette and Ruby Tuesday, a black girl who had taken her name from a Rolling Stones song and who used to get smashed up more than the rest of us.

You could rake in the cash for days on end, but there were times when you were so badly beaten you couldn't work for a week. I'd stay in bed with mates bringing grapes they sat and ate as they talked about bad johns and plans to go to America, or to live on a commune in India which, as far as I know, none of them ever did. They were the dreams of damaged girls and damaged girls' dreams rarely come true. I often swore I'd never go back on the streets again, but it was never as bad as being gang-raped and, beyond a certain point, there is no way back to where you started. Hooking was what I did, what Alan Briggs had predicted I would do, and I lost the ability or desire to imagine I could do anything else.

The first time I went to Lowndes Square with Claude, I was an innocent. Once my innocence had gone, I faked it. I was as fresh-faced as any fifth-former and had acquired that air of self-assurance you get being on the highwire. When you put yourself in danger and survive, you grow stronger. I learned how to be cheeky, ask for tips and escaped more beatings than I received. Being on the game was like being on stage. My sexy little outfits were my costume, my armour. In my disguises, it wasn't hard to deal with what I was doing on an emotional and psychological level. You build walls around the different parts of your life. The person you show on the outside is not the person you are inside. The outer person does the acting while the inner person just lies there thinking about movies and trying to remember the words to new pop songs.

Did I enjoy being fucked by those men? No. Never. Not once. Not for a second. It was like stuffing giblets up a chicken's arse, except I was the chicken and I had arse fissures more times than I can recall. The ointment that healed them felt like you were sitting in a field of stinging nettles.

Was it all bad? No. Quite the contrary.

Soho was like the sun with two planets spinning around on different orbits. On one, the gangsters, call girls, drug addicts and rough sleepers roamed about blindly like banshees wailing from Pink Floyd's *Dark Side of the Moon*. The other planet was populated by the media, models and musicians bathing in the optimism of George Harrison singing 'Here Comes the Sun'.

Sometimes, those worlds collided and girls like me got invited to fashion shoots, clubs where bands were trying out new songs, and private screenings of films before they went into the theatres. Four movies that came out that year had a profound impact and I saw them all. The girls loved Francis Ford Coppola's *The Godfather*, with all the violence, while I preferred foreign films like *The Discreet Charm of the Bourgeoisie*, by Luis Buñuel, Werner Herzog's *Aguirre, The Wrath of God,* and *Last Tango in Paris*, the Bernardo Bertolucci film that made Donna want to run away to live in Paris. And sleep with Marlon Brando, too, I suppose.

This was the beginning of our French period. We bought pencil skirts, tight blazers, berets and chiffon scarves, more chic than street. I was surprised how much French I remembered and tried out the name Amélie, but it never caught on.

They like pretty girls to decorate receptions, and one night we went to a party to celebrate the success of *The Boy Friend*, where I saw Twiggy, my hero, and even spoke to Ken Russell, the director.

'Hello. Are you in the business?' he asked me.

I blew smoke over my shoulder. 'What business is that?' I replied, and he laughed.

He was about to say something else, but was pulled away by a girl with white-blonde hair and a clipboard. 'Come along. Come along,' she said. 'There's someone here from the *Guardian*.'

I also starred in a movie with Donna. Flash set it up. We went up winding stairs to a studio in Mercer Street where a round bed covered in white fur stood in the centre of the large room. The back wall was painted sky blue with puffy clouds and there were two statues with peeling gold paint standing behind the bed. What they represented I had no idea.

We dressed as angels in tutus and wings borrowed from the Royal Ballet. A man with a French accent gave directions, then told us to 'go with the flow'. A camera was set up on a tripod facing the bed. We drifted into frame, Donna from one side, me from the other, and acted surprised to meet another angel. We explored each other, touching lips, tits, bottoms. Donna brandished a red apple she'd been holding behind her back and, as I took a bite, she began to dismantle my wings and bodice. Naked, I gave the apple to her, she took a bite and I did the same. It was biblical.

We dropped down in the white bed and did all the things you can do, snogging, licking, my tongue in her pussy, her tongue in my pussy, a sixty-niner. The director was saying *Très bon, très bon! Oo là là, oo là là!* His words were mesmerising and, it's strange, but things I would never normally have done came naturally in front of the camera.

I would remember that day for a long time. I had never fancied girls. But, then, I certainly didn't fancy men. With the johns, I did it for the money. With Donna, it was the first time I had felt anything; the first time I had 'made love' and it was ironic, even sad, that it was for a porno flick. The film found its way to the shelves in the dirty bookshops in Soho, as well as the snobby shops in Charing Cross Road where collectors went to seek out first editions of *Alice in Wonderland* on the ground floor before slipping down to the basement for a copy of *Angel Nymphs in Paradise*.

I never found out how much the film-makers paid for our performance because Flash kept the money. He claimed I owed

him for the room he had found for me in the same building as
Donna and said he'd pay me when I went to see it.

'You've got a career in front of you, darling, movies,
Hollywood, it's all happening. You need me and you know it,'
he said.

'I don't want a pimp . . .'

'I'm not a fucking pimp, you little slag. I'm a manager.'

He squeezed my arms until it hurt.

'Ouch.'

He kissed me on the lips. 'Sorry, little darling, I don't know
my own strength. I just want to look after you,' he said. He
stroked my hair, then stood back. 'I tell you something, girl,
you've fucking blossomed.'

That was typical, first the violence, then the charm. I was a
valuable commodity and he couldn't stomach the idea that I was
walking the streets not earning money for him. Flash was probably Maltese, although I never knew for sure. He had wavy dark
hair, swarthy skin, a chameleon accent and always wore an
apple-green leather coat. He had a fast walk, like my mum, and
showed the odd streak of generosity. He once gave me a red
dress and matching shoes that he'd *acquired* for one of his girls
and she'd run away before he could give them to her. Another
time, coming home late at night, he pulled me into a doorway,
held a knife to my throat and stole the money I'd just earned
with a punter. I wasn't going to go crowing to the cops, and he
was letting me know that I needed a pimp to protect me from
the pimps.

Flash was on at me so much that, in the end, I did go and see
the room, just to shut him up. There was a window with blinds

that made stripy patterns on the wall, a refrigerator and a bath-room down the hall. Flash had furnished the room with a pine bed that looked new and a cassette player with a dual-deck so you could record your own music. It was larger than Donna's room and I suspected that, if she were being sent ten blokes a day, Flash would send me twenty. Donna was seventeen. I was fifteen. A lot of men loitering about Soho had paedophile lean-ings and that's what I'd get, an endless stream of men like Bob Drake and Dean Ricks.

I promised I'd give Flash my answer the following day and hid out in Hyde Park so he couldn't find me. This cat and mouse game went on for weeks. Donna kept saying it would be so much fun being in the same building and, although I thought of her as my best friend, I did wonder sometimes whether she was in cahoots with Flash. It was Donna who had enticed me into the game with that first panini at the Bar Italia. It was Donna who got me through my second trick. I had wanted to be like her. Now I was like her.

There was a song I loved to dance to in the discos called 'I Heard It Through the Grapevine'. For the first time in my life, I was on the vine, a part of something. I knew how to get free tickets for movies and passes for clubs. I knew where to go at any time of day or night to find a john, and wasn't afraid to try new things without Donna and Debs.

I auditioned as a stripper at the club I'd once swept out, but lacked the rounded hips and bouncy breasts you need to make those tassels swirl. With a push-up bra and make-up, I could make myself appear older but, the moment I took my clothes off, my true assets were revealed: I was still a child. The Maltese man who owned the club looked me up and down for a long time.

'How old you are?'

'Nearly sixteen.'

'You fifteen?'

'Yes.'

'You want job, I give job. I look after you. Money. Everything.'

It sounded too good to be true and I was really excited that night when another girl a bit older than me showed me the ropes. There was a changing room with dresses and costumes on rails, and the mirrors had lights around them like in a theatre. The girls sat smoking and gossiping as they did their make-up. Some of them were really glamorous like models or film stars. They wore elegant clothes and moved among the men making them laugh and speaking in different languages.

There were back rooms with beds for taking johns, seedy but safe. Side shows consisted of male-on-male oral sex, girl-on-girl sex, and once in the film room I saw a porn flick where a woman was having sex with a pig! There were strippers on stage and the smell of male lust was so overpowering it lingers in my nose to this day. Group booking would sometimes turn into full-blown orgies, the doors locked, the Vice Squad paid off *and* joining in. The Vice Squad was full of sex maniacs. The Drug Squad sold drugs. Coppers in general were bullies, care wardens were rapists, and in that gentlemen's club below ground all manner of perversions came together like in those paintings of hell I'd seen once while sheltering from the rain in the National Gallery.

Emily MacKenzie

My job was to sit at the bar in a gold silk dress about the size of a handkerchief and let the punters buy me glasses of champagne. It was poured from bottles of Bollinger, but was only ginger beer they refilled out the back. The men drank whisky or vodka – they probably knew the champagne was fake – and I watched their moods change. They were mostly harried or apprehensive when they arrived. After two or three shots they'd be laughing and feeling randy with my bare legs scissoring away in front of them. The Maltese boss would then whisper in their ear, and the deal was done.

It was at that bar in that dress where I met an elegant, white-haired man who was a member of the House of Lords. He took me home to an enormous mansion with a swimming pool with green lights. He covered me in oil and we rolled about on a waterbed like two slippery eels. He told me I reminded him of a beautiful boy he had known in school and did to me all the things he had dreamed of doing to him. We then slid into the pool. He talked about the Common Market and said that the new act going through Parliament was the end of the world as we knew it.

One night, the man I met at the bar turned out to be a chauffeur. He spoke to the boss in a language I didn't understand, then drove me to a house in Mayfair with a red, white and green flag flapping on a pole outside. The man waiting for me was an Italian diplomat who covered his privates in strawberries and cream for me to eat while he supped at my elixir in search, I assumed, for his lost youth.

There was a banker named Sir something or other, a footballer always in the newspapers and a man they called the

Bishop, who said as he slipped my dress from my shoulders, 'For what we are about to receive, may the Lord make us truly thankful.'

I went home with famous people, dangerous people, the men who run things and own things. Money was never discussed. They were beyond money. I was paid by the club owner who had, without me realising it, become my pimp. The men I went with were a lot like Alan Briggs, but had the one thing he wanted and never had. Power. Real power. They were men with wives, children, with secretaries at their feet and between their sheets. But men with everything only crave the things that are out of reach, and there is nothing more desirable than the forbidden fruit of underage girls.

Powerful men have profound feelings of entitlement. There is a taboo when it comes to sex with children and breaking that taboo is something they convince themselves they deserve. It doesn't matter about your feelings, your future, your needs. You are there to service their needs as the doorman is there to open the door. Those men will shoot the last animal of an endangered species. They believe they are special, chosen; many go to church because they are chosen and their Maker has given them the privilege of taking anything and everything they want. They know they won't get caught and, if there is a whiff of scandal or suspicion, they can buy their way out and have the charisma and connections to hush it up.

My Maltese boss knew these things and had carved out an empire catering for them. I was one of the girls at the heart of his operation. I had grown into a good little actress, as Mum had dreamed I might one day become. I played the child discovering sex as if for the first time knowing that if anything went wrong and I disappeared, no one would ask questions. No one would know.

When I decided to quit the bar, I knew the owner would be furious. It took me days to pluck up the courage and I finally told him one afternoon.

'I'm going home to see my dad. I won't be around for a while,' I said.

He rocked back and forth, studying me and stroking his moustache.

'This is your home. I am your father.'

'But he's ill. I have to see him.'

'You no tell truth,' he said, and ran his finger across his throat. 'You pay. I find—'

'Honestly,' I said. 'Cross my heart.'

'You come back. You want money, clothes, anything. Is good. You good girl. I like.'

You good girl. I like.

I had a flash of déjà vu. It could have been Ali standing there saying those things and I knew vaguely then, and for certainty now, why girls who have been abused submit so readily to the groomers and pimps. Girls entering puberty are often confused about their sexuality, their role. They want to be told they are pretty. They crave affection. They feed on the kind word, the glittery gifts, and those girls from broken homes and children's homes give up the gift of their innocence. Girls from loving families seldom face these dangerous and bewildering situations. They may become doctors, probation officers, magistrates, psychologists, but they cannot begin to understand why the thirteen-year-old surrenders to these men and why, after the first time, there is no way back.

I smiled. 'Thank you,' I said.

While I'd been working in the club, I'd been safe from the clutches of Flash. Like him, the Maltese man would try to keep me in his orbit. Girls locked into that way of life are lured back, even when they try to escape, and the pimps play the long game certain they will get you in the end. I now had two shadows to look out for instead of one, but as I climbed the steps out of that dark basement, I felt like a bird released from a cage.

One night, I met a rock drummer at a party and went back to his house in Highgate. We drank red wine. He was young and handsome. I took a Quaalude and did two lines of coke. We danced. We stripped. We drummed away on his big bed till dawn and only when I was on the Tube heading back to the West End did it occur to me that I had actually gone to bed with someone without getting paid for it.

That gave me a lot to think about. First, it wasn't terrible – in fact, I quite liked it; and, second, I wondered if I'd liked it because I had been stoned out of my head or because the drummer was from a well-known band; or maybe both. The wheels of the train were thumping at the same rate as my heart and my head was going round and round like the Circle Line.

Jock had always warned me I'd end up on drugs. The old prostitutes in Soho were all junkies, 'turning tricks for the price of a fix', as they said. It reminded me, I hadn't seen Jock for weeks. I'd lost track of the people I used to know and went out later that day to nose around my old haunts.

The first person I ran into was Johnny Moss from Waltham Cross, who was standing outside the entrance to the Tube in Leicester Square hopping about like he had St Vitus Dance. He had drawn cheeks and sunken eyes. He was about twenty and could have passed for forty. I must have changed a lot, too, and he didn't recognise me. Last time I had seen him, I was a little girl in a red leather jacket. Now I was all grown up in my French garb, tight skirt, jacket, beret and poor-little-match-girl ankle boots, my favourite disguise.

'Johnny, hello,' I said, and he tried to stand still. 'Remember me? We were arrested together cleaning out that old strip club.'

'Yeah, yeah, I remember,' he said, although I don't think he did.

'They beat you up . . .'

'Fucking bastards.' He concentrated now. 'Hey listen, can you lend us a fiver – it's dead urgent?'

There was sweat on his brow. He looked desperate.

'Johnny, have you seen Jock?'

'Jock? Jock? Who's that?'

'The old Scotsman, the one with one leg.'

'With a dog?'

'That's him.'

His eyes focused. 'Got a kicking, I heard – they took him to hospital.'

'What?'

He'd started to shake again. 'You were going to lend me five quid . . .'

I took my purse out but didn't open it straight away. 'What hospital, do you know?'

'St Mary's. That's what I heard, over in Paddington.'

I gave him the money. He ran off and I went straight down the steps to the Tube. I asked directions from Paddington station and arrived at an enormous red-brick building that reminded me of the asylum where I'd lived in the silent tower. The reception was crowded with busy people racing in every direction. I bought a bunch of flowers from a kiosk and asked where I would find the men's wards.

After climbing two flights of stairs, I emerged in a long corridor lined with doors leading to big wards with thirty men and smaller rooms with four. People hurried by like I was invisible and I finally stopped a young nurse in a pink uniform.

'I'm looking for my Uncle Jock,' I said. 'I can't find him anywhere.'

'It's not visiting time, you know,' she told me.

I welled up in tears. I was good at that, but I meant it. They were real tears. I was coming down from the red wine and coke. I felt jittery and depressed.

'Please help me, please,' I moaned, and her expression changed.

'Don't cry now – it'll be all right. What's his full name?'

'I don't know, I just call him Uncle Jock . . .'

'Is he Scottish?' she asked, and I nodded.

'With one leg,' I said.

'Come, I'll show you. You can stay for five minutes, but no more.'

'Thank you, you're really kind.'

We walked the length of the corridor and turned a corner. There were four single wards.

'Here we are,' the nurse said.

She held the door open for me and the blood drained from my cheeks. It was like a scene from a movie. Jock was hooked up to drips and wires. A heart monitor bleeped and his face was as pale as the bed sheets. He was breathing heavily and grunting in his sleep.

'Shall I take those?' the nurse said, and I gave her the flowers. 'I'll put them in a vase.'

I sat there for a lot longer than five minutes and returned that evening at visiting time. Jock's eyes flickered open a couple of times, but he didn't know I was there. I wondered what had happened to Scratch, but I knew and pretended I didn't. Strays left behind by street people were taken to the vet and 'put to sleep'.

It was Thursday. I went straight from the hospital to Lowndes Square and put on my happy face. Summer was coming. Change was in the air and Claude varied the ritual. On the coffee table there was a dimpled decanter and a glass.

'Drink, drink. It's only water. I want you to drink it all.'

I hadn't eaten very much that day and it wasn't hard to chug it down; I was really thirsty and had the taste of chemicals from the hospital on my teeth. Claude left the room and returned in his dressing gown. We then went through to his bedroom, which I had never seen before. I thought he wanted sex – they usually do – but I was wrong. There was a hook on the ceiling that appeared to have just been installed and the paint around the fixture was still drying. He asked me to take off my clothes. He removed his dressing gown and dressed in his red judge's robe and wig. He spread a plastic sheet over the bed, then bound my hands in a silky length of white rope. I could just about loop the rope over the hook standing on the bed.

He stretched out between my legs. I used his tummy to lever myself up and swung back and forth on the hook. He didn't tell me what to do. I knew. I'd had it done to me enough times. When the urge came, I released a long stream of wee all over him and he opened his mouth to drink it.

He gave me £25 that night and the next day I went back to the hospital to see Jock. I sat alone in his room. The staff had grown used to me being there and didn't mind. I listened to the bleep and watched the green line on the heart monitor move along in waves. My palms were sticky and I could feel the throb of my pulse. I felt as if I were waiting for something to happen, but when it happened, it still seemed sudden and unexpected. The sound of the bleep became a continuous hum and the monitor flatlined.

It was a message, a warning. I had escaped Flash and the Maltese gangster. I had tried drugs and peed on a judge. I'd done it all. When Jock fell off the highwire, I should have gone home. I didn't.

CHAPTER 24

A Bird in a Cage

On my birthday, Donna, Debs and about five other girls had a 'surprise' party for me at Bar Italia. The waiter lit a candle and, when I blew it out, not a single wish sprang to my mind. We ate cake with strawberries and cream on top and I told them about the diplomat with a dessert fetish. They screamed with laughter and told their own tales of johns with kinky obsessions.

This was the best part of that life – being friends with other girls who had found their way onto the streets. We knew each other's stories. There were no judgements or feelings of superiority. Our bravado was all front, our air of self-assurance an act. We wanted to believe we were the masters of our own destiny when we were just corks bobbing on a tide of drug pushers, pimps and criminals, selling ourselves to dangerous men who thought of us as little more than the dirt on their shoes. They weren't all like that. But it only takes one.

You don't change from one day to the next, but sixteen seemed a lot older than fifteen. You can get married at sixteen. You can have sex at sixteen. I have never been able to work out why for men sex with a girl under sixteen is better than when they've turned sixteen, but it is. I studied myself in the mirror and wondered if I had lost the allure of being underage.

That night, during our weekly meeting, the police inspector pulled out a leather strap and I almost wet myself as he brought it down on his palm, the snap of flesh so loud in the silence a shiver ran up my spine. Could I have opened the door and walked out? No. Could I have begged him not to hit me? No. Once you are in that room in your short skirt, the deal is sealed. You smile. You strip. He has some mad vision in his mind and a terrible need to inflict pain on someone to balance something absent in himself. It was hard to believe that a policeman would contemplate such things, but I saw in his eyes that glazed look of mental illness I had seen on the faces of imprisoned patients at the asylum where they had given me EEGs.

I endured the misery and humiliation of being flogged, fucked and peed on by holding in my mind the worst scenes at the secure unit with the damp walls, the patter of rats, the forced medication and the feral males who came for us at any time. You get used to being raped. You don't even cry when it happens. You shut down. You close your eyes and pretend you're dead. This is how men are. This is what men do. I should say 'some men' but in my world it was more than some, it was like a virus, a sickness, the 'free love' of the Swinging Sixties by 1972 growing poisonous and debauched. Young girls were a commodity, a resource to be used and abused in what had become a throwaway society. Did I see it all then? No. Of course not. I had allowed myself to believe I was lucky. I wasn't being raped in an asylum. I was getting paid for it.

After limping home with my blood money, I found my room turned over and the word SLAG scrawled across the mirror in lipstick. I'd been robbed. Everything had gone, my clothes, make-up, shoes, the necklace with the gold cross the Bishop had given me after I had made him truly thankful. My tummy screwed up like a sheet of paper on a fire and I could hardly swallow my throat was so dry. There were pink stripes from the leather strap across my back and bottom. I was bruised and shaky. Being robbed is not like being raped, but it is like being hit, and I vowed never to see that sadistic copper again.

For a moment, I was paralysed. Then my heart began to race faster. I panted for breath as I went down on my hands and knees and peeled back the lino in the corner. Below, there was a loose floorboard and my heart only started to slow down when I saw the brown envelope with my savings still there.

It didn't take me long to work out who'd stolen my things. The next day Flash said he still had a room waiting for me. He wanted to look after me, make sure I was safe.

'From the thieves?' I asked him.

He said, 'You've got a lot of mouth for a little cunt, and let me tell you something . . . one of these days someone's going to cut your tongue out.'

What I did after the robbery was scrounge £200 and that was enough to pay a month down and a month's deposit on a bedsit in Covent Garden. The flat was one big room with a single bed, an electric stove, a table with two rickety chairs, an oak wardrobe and a chest of drawers with mismatched handles. I could see the Royal Opera House from the window and was two minutes from the fruit market in an area jammed with people and traffic. I loved it. The pink bruises on my bottom turned yellow and healed. Covent Garden was always noisy and you could vanish among the crowd. With my regular money from Claude, I just about had the rent covered, and would only need to pull a few johns each week to get by.

I sensed that Donna was jealous that I had my own place and she promised she wouldn't tell Flash where I was. She loaned me £20 to buy some things I needed and I spent £4 on an electric juicer. I bought bananas and summer berries that reminded me of going with Dad to the nurseries as a little girl and being given bags of strawberries.

It did occur to me that I could have taken that £200 and gone home. Inspector Yeoman had told me that at sixteen I had the right to take part in decisions made on my behalf, but there were several reasons why I didn't. Dad would have been mortified if he'd ever found out I'd been a prostitute. Not that I felt ashamed. When you've been physically and sexually abused as a little girl, sex with strangers holds no surprises. I had chosen the life over being locked up in a children's home where there was every possibility that I would suffer the irony of being raped without the compensations of the 'Square Mile of Vice' as the newspapers called Soho. I was in constant danger, I knew that, but felt an odd sort of loyalty to the streets, the only real home I'd had since I was twelve.

Aside from all that, I adored my flat and spent my money from tricks buying little things like cushions and posters to make it just right. It was July. The sun was hot and the city was buzzing. There were race riots, anti-Vietnam demos, hippies taking over squats, the constant whiff of cannabis. In the French Bar in Dean Street I met dirty old men who called themselves artists and young men with long hair working for the satirical magazines *IT* and *Oz*. I danced at the Flamingo like a normal girl and went with Donna to the Electric Cinema to see the John Boorman film *Deliverance* because she was still mad about Jon Voight, the star.

I also made a day trip with Debs to Margate. I thought I might run into Robbie Gillan on the beach, but I didn't. It was strange going back. Margate was where it had all started in a way. I remembered strolling along the sands with Bobby and the girls; the colours had been vibrant, the sea calm, the future as endless as the sky. Now it all seemed a bit tacky. The sea was grey and you couldn't see the beach for people. I bought a pair of heart-shaped sunglasses with red frames, another gush of nostalgia, but you can't recapture the past. When it's gone it's just dead, like Jock was dead, kicked into his grave by men in suits and skinny ties.

I had been living in the bedsit for about three weeks when Donna turned up one lunchtime wearing big sunglasses and carrying two carrier bags filled with clothes, shoes, undies and make-up. She was puffing away on a fag and heaped all the stuff on the bed.

'It's not junk, darling – some of these things I haven't even worn,' she said.

Donna moved about the room like a jumpy kitten. She was in jeans and it was the first time I'd seen her without high heels.

'Are you OK?'

'Never been better,' she replied. 'By the way, have you got that £20 you owe me.'

'It's about all I have got,' I said, and counted out what I had in my purse.

She shoved the money in her bag and pulled out a leather skirt from the pile. 'Try this on, it's great . . .'

I wasn't in the mood for 'playing boutiques', as we called it, but I was waiting for Donna to tell me what I already knew. I put on the skirt, a halter-top and white plastic knee-boots. This wasn't my style but it amused Donna to watch me model her clothes.

'Let me try on your sunglasses,' I said.

She looked back at me for several seconds before taking them off. She had two black eyes, a cut across the bridge of her nose and her blue eyes were brighter and more surreal than ever.

I sucked in a breath. 'The bastard,' I gasped.

'It won't happen again, don't worry.'

'Where are you going?' I asked.

She shrugged. 'I'm eighteen, Emmy. I can go anywhere I want.'

'You won't get far with twenty quid,' I told her, and she spread her arms with her palms out.

'Not a problem, you just put your hands out and it comes dropping in,' she said. She smiled for the first time, then looked sad again. 'I'm going to miss you, Emmy.'

We kissed cheeks and trotted down the stairs to the street. She got the Tube at Covent Garden to connect to the bus station at Victoria. The first time we'd met, I was in jeans and she was in a white dress and heels. Now Donna was leaving in denim and I was dressed for the street. We kissed once more and, as she vanished with the crowd, I knew I would never see her again.

Five minutes later I ran into Debs in Dean Street. She warned me that Flash was on the warpath and that's how I ended up in Play 2 Win, the amusement arcade in Old Compton Street, in Donna's fringed leather skirt and a halter-top talking to a man who called himself Bill and then found myself next morning naked and locked in a pink bedroom staring out from a fourth-floor window like a bird in a cage.

CHAPTER 25

Prisoner

The bolt clicks outside and the door opens.

'What about breakfast?'

I nod. 'Yes, please,' I say.

'Yes, please! You're a right little comedian.'

I follow him through to the kitchen. On the counter there's bacon wrapped in greaseproof paper, six eggs and a loaf of sliced white bread.

'Can I have my clothes, please?'

He stares at me. 'What?'

'I mean—'

'No,' he says. 'Get on with it.'

He points at the frying pan and toaster. I cook breakfast. We eat facing each other at the table in the living room. We drink tea and he rolls a fag.

'Let me tell you something. You might like living in a shit-hole, but I don't. You understand?'

I wash the dishes, put them away. I clean all the surfaces in the kitchen, then start vacuuming. He follows, watching, smoking. When I open the curtains to let in more light, he springs across the room, pulls the curtain to and slaps my bum as hard as he can.

'Did I tell you to open those fucking curtains?'

'I was just—'

'Don't fucking just anything. Who the fuck do you think you are?'

'I'm sorry.'

'You're just a little slag who doesn't know her place. Now get down on your fucking knees.'

He unzips his flies and I suck him off. He holds the back of my head and pumps his sperm into my mouth.

'Now, is that better?'

I nod. 'Yes,' I answer. 'Can I go home now?'

'Home? Home? What are you talking about? You are home. Where do you think you are?'

He is genuinely insane. I am naked in his flat and no one knows I am there. I shrug. I smile. I clean. He smokes. He turns on the TV and we sit on the sofa, his arm around me. He cups my breasts. He pinches my nipples and likes it when I squeal and wriggle. He runs his fingers between my legs then pushes them in my mouth to suck.

He goes out, locking the door, and returns with a carrier bag with food for me to cook and we do it all again, the cleaning, the smoking, the sex on the floor, the sofa, over the table, standing, on his lap, this way and that way like he's trying to invent a way to have sex that no one has ever thought of before. It is like taking part in a never-ending porno film. I am his toy, his cook, his child, his fantasy. I know by the bolt on the bedroom door that he has been planning this for a long time.

He locks me in. I look at the doll's house. The roof lifts up and the front opens. Inside, miniature people live among the miniature furniture and they all have smiles and old-fashioned clothes. I stand at the window, hoping that someone will see me, and one day a man in the flats opposite does. He raises his thumb in approval. He thinks I'm an exhibitionist and, every time I look out the window, he is there waiting to get an eyeful. I get used to being naked and being locked up at night away from the man is something I look forward to.

He introduces a new game. He brings home a dog collar and lead and I crawl around the floor. 'Come on, girl, come along. There's a good girl.' I balance on my haunches, paws up, mouth open. He feeds me biscuits and I lick the crumbs from his palm. He pats the back of my head and we do it doggy fashion. I cook the evening meal and he places my plate on the floor beside his chair. I have to eat the food without using my hands.

The man, Bill, whatever his name is, is more affectionate when I am on all fours like a dog. I bark. I sniff around the corners of the room. It makes him smile. He watches the television news. There are riots in Ireland, the Americans are bombing Cambodia. I curl up beside him on the torn sofa being stroked and begin to feel like a dog with a dog's sense of being comforted by my master.

I need to go to the lavatory. I go to speak but he puts his hand over my mouth.

'Come on, girl, what do you want?'

He stands holding the lead and I crawl along the corridor to the bathroom. His eyes light up. I have never seen him look so happy. He pulls on the lead and drags me back to the hall. 'Come on, girl, lift a leg. Be a good girl for daddy.'

I have been holding it for ages. I lift my leg, which is what male dogs do, but I'm only acting, and pee over the lino. He pats my head, then rubs my nose in it. 'Who's been a naughty girl, then?' I bark, I let my tongue loll from my mouth and he shoves his cock down my throat. 'Come on now, there's a good little bitch. Come on. Come on.'

He goes back to the TV and doesn't watch me go out of character when I clean up the pee, a game he makes me play many times in the coming days. He won't let me wash, and his only concession to decency is when I 'move my bowels', a phrase of my mother when she still believed there was a place for everything. It is her fault that I am locked in that flat being treated like an animal and abused four or five or six times a day in a way that you wouldn't abuse a dog. I act the wife cooking. I am the little girl playing at incest. Now it is bestiality that gives him the biggest kick of all.

It occurs to me that the man has thought this through carefully – bringing the dog lead home wasn't random. I had never been in his room, but I had seen from the door photographs of a woman and little girl. Had he abused the child and that's why his wife had left? Was I a replacement and he was punishing them by mistreating me? I wasn't a bird in a cage, I was a dog in a kennel.

I should have gone home when Jock was murdered. I should have gone home after I was lashed with a strap by the police inspector. I should have gone home when my room was robbed. Life is a list of 'shoulds' and is driven by cause and effect. My mother knew what Alan Briggs had done to me in his car. Mothers know and those mothers who let the men do what they do are equally guilty for not stopping them, for not reporting them.

Was there more I could have done to get away?

No. I was a girl of sixteen without my clothes locked in a flat with a forty-year-old madman seeking revenge on all the bad things in his life, his lack of success, recognition, purpose, money. His dreams, whatever they were, like the dreams of most men, most people, had not come true and my job was to make this one dream a reality. He had a toy, a child, a sex object that he could do anything with and there was nothing, absolutely nothing I could do to stop him.

After a man has sex with a child, he wants to violate another child, a different child. That's why there are paedophile rings, groomers, pimps; why girls are passed on, exchanged like second-hand cars. The addicts need a new fix, a fresh fix. I had lost count of the days, but about two weeks had gone by. The man had ravaged the depths of his own depraved imagination and done everything he could think of. I had complied and he was bored. I sensed it. There was a different look in his eyes.

He sat on the couch for a long time watching TV while I squatted between his legs in the dog collar. I sucked his cock, slow and steady, taking it all the way down my throat to my tonsils, the way he liked it. I sucked his balls. When he was ready to come, I sat back on my haunches with my mouth open panting like a dog while he sprayed his stuff over my face.

'Look at the state of you,' he said, and I smiled.

He slapped my backside with the dog lead. I peed on the lino and he watched, his face filled with revulsion. 'Open your fuck-ing mouth,' he ordered, and peed over my face.

He stormed off and came back with the kitchen knife.

'This is your lucky day, you know that? I'm going to make you famous.' He grabbed the dog collar and held the knife to my throat. 'I'm going to cut you into little pieces and leave them all over the fucking country.'

His teeth were bared like an animal. His eyes were black like holes. I was on my knees, trying to stay still, the tip of the knife touching my throat as I trembled.

'Please,' I said. 'Please. You'll get caught—'

'Then I can sell my story to the papers, can't I?' he said. 'Everyone's going to know who you are, what you do.'

'What you make me do—'

'Make you! No fucking decent girl would do the things you do. You're disgusting, you know that. You don't deserve to live.' He pulled closer and stared into my eyes. 'You're just scum. No one's going to miss you.'

Tears rolled down my cheeks. 'My dad will,' I said.

His expression changed and he shook the knife in front of me like I'd challenged him in some way. It had never occurred to him that I was a girl with a dad, a family, that I was a person.

'Listen, you little cunt, clean this fucking mess up.'

He stormed off. I did as I was told. He inspected the floor and locked me in my room with the smell of his piss and semen on me. I lay motionless on the narrow bed and watched the sky grow dark. Like they say about a drowning man, my whole life flashed before my eyes and I recalled being on a farm once with Dad when they slaughtered a pig. They hung it up by the back legs and made a slit down the belly to the throat. The blood pumped out like water from a tap.

That's what that man was going to do to me. I cried. Then I stopped crying. I had killed my baby. There's no worse crime than that. All the things I had done with those men didn't matter. I was nothing, a nonentity, a little slag. When the man slit my throat and cut me into pieces it would be all right. It was what I deserved.

A strange peace came over me. I didn't sleep. The hours went by and all I thought about was Tracy, my baby. I watched the sunrise light the pink room and lay there waiting for him to come.

The bolt on the door was pulled, the sound like an explosion, but he didn't come in to get me. I waited for a long time before I dared to peep out.

'Hello, shall I make breakfast?' I called.

There was no answer. He wasn't there. The door to his bedroom was open. I tested the main door. It was unlocked. I scavenged through his room for my clothes. The £10 was still in my white bag. I had been paid in the car and he had got his money's worth. I fled down the concrete steps to the street. I had no idea where I was. I asked the way to the nearest Underground. I was about ten minutes' walk from the Elephant and Castle.

I went back to my bedsit and everything was the way I'd left it, clothes on the bed, posters on the wall, my juicer. It was like time had stood still for two weeks. I was alive. I had survived. I dug out some jeans and a shirt from the pile and went to the West End Central police station. I asked for Inspector Yeoman and waited at the reception for her for two hours.

Could I describe the man who had imprisoned me and threatened to cut me into pieces? Yes. Could I find my way back to those flats in South London? Yes. Was there proof that I had been there? Surely, yes.

Did I tell the inspector?

No.

You just don't. You can't. There are no words to describe what has happened, not when you are sixteen years old and you've been kept naked, treated like a dog, abused in every orifice. You are ashamed. You blame yourself. You don't think anyone is going to believe you – when the things that have happened run through your head you can't believe it yourself. You reach the conclusion that it was in some way your own fault: the short skirt, bare legs, pink lipstick, uplift bra. You know what they say: she was asking for it. Alan Briggs had molested me the first time when I was twelve. Within weeks of arriving at the children's home when Mum put me into care, Harry, the gardener, had his hand down my knickers. When I was raped at thirteen and my baby was sucked out of my body, a little bit of me died. Everything that had happened since had been a prolonged punishment I believed was justified.

I had worn my sackcloth and ashes for a long, long time. I had paid the price. After getting so close to death with that madman who'd kept me locked up, I realised I didn't want to die. I wanted to live. I wanted a second chance. I wanted to be a normal girl again.

We drank tea and sat in a room where, last time I had been there, the inspector had sent out for a birthday cake. I was fifteen then. Now I was sixteen and more had happened in that last year than I could possibly remember. She lit a cigarette and stared at me with her piercing green eyes.

'I have intuitions sometimes, Emily,' she said. 'I knew I'd see you again.'

I shrugged. 'I should have taken your advice.'

'What advice is that?'

'You told me to keep my head down for a year and then, you know, I would be able to have a say in what happens to me.'

'It's seems as if you've done just that, although not exactly in the way I meant,' she continued. 'You've been on the Missing Persons list these last three months.'

'Oh my God, really?'

She stabbed out her cigarette and leaned across the desk. 'Now you tell me, where have you been?'

I admitted I'd been living on the streets as a prostitute since running away from the last home. She grilled me about drugs and gangsters, pimps and other young runaways. I was evasive, no names, nothing direct, no mention of the judge, the police inspector, the peer, the Italian diplomat. They were part of a world in which I had taken a part and, stupidly, insanely, it seemed at the time a betrayal to tell the authorities what really happens – that girls, mainly girls, often underage girls, are used, abused and broken, even killed, serving the rich and elite for sex that is often extreme and perverted.

People who have everything want to have a young girl and there are groomers and rapists who serve this insatiable market.

Girls are trained and exchanged, given as perks in business deals; they perform at orgies, they lose every last strand of self-respect and humanity. They are treated as products, like animals, and come to think of themselves as little more than animals. Rarely do girls speak out and, when they do, they are rarely believed. When they are believed, it takes years, decades, before investigations are complete and, by then, it is too late. There is no justice for the victims and the perpetrators slide back into their comfortable lives.

When it is known that important people, rich people, are involved in using underage girls for sex, is it covered up?

Yes.

Absolutely yes.

But I wasn't going to say anything. That life was normal for me; normal for the young girls out there in the Square Mile of Vice, and what's normal you don't talk about. The inspector smoked her way through most of the cigarettes in her packet of Rothmans and after a couple of hours she finally gave up trying to get more out of me than I had already revealed.

I was allowed to call my dad. He cried when I told him I was safe and at a police station in London. While we were talking, Inspector Yeoman must have called the probation service and I was taken into temporary care for a few nights. She kissed me on the cheeks.

'You're not going to run away any more, are you?'

'No.' I shook my head. 'I promise.'

She smiled. She was a good woman, good at her job, I'm sure. But I had a feeling, even then, as I looked back at her that she would never break through the glass ceiling and reach that place where the real power lies, where they make the decisions as to who is prosecuted for pimping and grooming and rape, and who is allowed to carry on untouched.

Dad came to London on the train and, together, we attended a multi-agency meeting where my future was discussed by 'experts'. I say 'experts' with an intake of air through my nose and a shake of my head. In my experience, the people who govern children's care never know what happens at the coal face, in the inky black shadows of night when poorly paid 'care' workers are left alone with little children, where untrained women abused by husbands and boyfriends abuse, as if through some causal coding in the human make-up, the abandoned children; where men bombarded by a sexualised society plastered with half-naked girls on every advertisement from toothpaste to refrigerators crave sex, normally with girls, the younger the better, sometimes boys, always leaving little bodies and minds damaged – forever. Forever. People who lose their legs with modern technology can lead full lives, same with the blind, the deaf. But the damage is still there. The same with abused children. You get on with your life, if you are lucky, but the deep-down scars of all that hurt never goes away and taints every relationship.

I was given the choice of four different units, two run by nuns, an open home and a notoriously strict all-girls' reform school, which I chose. I intended to work my way back to normality. Like my mum, that woman who had chosen me as a baby, I could turn on a performance and that's what I did, I acted the model inmate. I was polite, cheerful, willing; I cleaned and scrubbed. I volunteered. I said please and thank you, those magical little words damaged people forget.

Behind the scenes, Dad and his solicitor were negotiating with Mum, who still had the final say on my future. I would learn years later that it was my sister Amy who convinced her that I was 'good' now and I wouldn't cause any trouble if I were living with Dad. Mum always had to be placated, handled, manipulated, and only Amy, in her quiet way, was able to do this.

Three months later, I was released from the reform school. I received a hand-written letter from Alan Briggs, not my mother, who invited me to 'join his family', which I politely refused. I went home to live with my dad and Aunt Alice.

I never spoke to my mother again.

The Saturday after I arrived home from the reform school, Dad collected Amy and we went shopping before meeting Aunt Alice at the Conservative Club for lunch. Amy was thirteen, almost as tall as me, and was in what they called the Oxbridge band at grammar school. She was a maths wizard and finally went to the London School of Economics, gained a Masters and joined the Civil Service, working finally in social reform at the Treasury.

That day I bought a pale-blue dress with a white collar, white knee socks, a navy coat and flat shoes. I sat at a table set with starched linen and silver cutlery. My hair was tied back in a ponytail and my face was free of make-up. On the outside, I was the picture of convention, but beneath the blue dress I was wearing my favourite pink bra and knickers, a sign that I would always be a rebel.

Epilogue

After everything I had been through it took a long time to find my way. I didn't want to be confined in school – another mistake – and, thanks to Dad's many friends and contacts, I went through more jobs than I can recall – in a factory, a shop, a laundry, as a filing clerk, a trainee dental receptionist. I couldn't settle down and always felt as if, again, I was play-acting, that I was really a prostitute just pretending to be a normal sixteen-year-old girl making a career.

Getting fired from one job after another upset Dad, of course, but it made me feel as if I were hitting back at the system that had confined me, tortured me. Now that I was free to read what I wanted, to listen to the news, to mix with people my own age undamaged by 'care', I became more aware of the world around me with its chaos and inequality, the factory closures, strikes, food riots, anti-war demos. The IRA and the British army were shooting each other across the barricades in Northern Ireland,

and the Israeli team at the Munich Olympics were massacred by Palestinian terrorists. David Bowie was cross-dressing and his song 'Life on Mars?' was in the charts, a sign to me that life on earth had gone to pot.

From out of this cauldron of upheaval and change my own politics began to take shape. I finally returned to formal education. I got a degree in Women's Studies, followed by a post-graduate diploma in counselling and qualifications in community mental health, to which I have devoted a good part of my adult life, clawing my way back into the system to try to make things better, as opposed to staying on the outside hitting my head against the wall. Childcare and mental health services are vast bureaucracies, like liners at sea, hard to change course. There have been improvements in the last thirty years, but not as many as there should have been, and the system, in my experience, continues to be unfair to the poor and struggling, the working class, the underclass, the people who often need the most help.

Oddly, certainly against the odds, I was invited as an adult to join a government advisory council on child poverty and attended weekly meetings at the Houses of Parliament where I sometimes felt like a chicken in a cage of foxes. Amy was at the Treasury and we would meet for lunch, two adopted girls closer than any two sisters. I stood outside the South African Embassy in Trafalgar Square demonstrating against apartheid. I joined the battle against anti-union legislation, mental health and social welfare cuts, the hated policies of Thatcherism.

My adoptive mother had delighted in telling me my real mum was dead. It wasn't true. She was alive, and I had a brother,

Alex. It would be a long time before I met them. When I did, I learned about my real father. He had mental health problems. He had abused my mum, even in the days immediately after she gave birth to me. She had given me up for adoption, the same as Alex, for our safety, never imagining for a second that an adopting parent would become abusive. It took decades for us to find each other and, finally, we are a family.

It took a long time for me to realise that the abuse by my adoptive mother and her sadistic second husband were not my fault. My self-destructiveness was a direct result of that abuse, a constant cry for help. In care homes and remand homes I never got that help. On the contrary, I was raped, drugged, beaten and abused. It has been said before, I know, but it bears repeating.

Is it any better today – in the wake of the Jimmy Savile investigations, the revelations of abuse in council homes, hospitals, churches and the BBC? I don't think so. My story takes place in the early 1970s. The institutions are better now, a little better, but life for many children is not. As these words appear on the page, there are gangs of men in court accused of grooming and raping girls, some as young as eleven. Other men are serving sentences for the same offences, and still more men are prowling the streets in search of sad, neglected girls who just want to be loved. Neglect is usually the result of poverty and statistics released now, in 2013, at the time of writing, show that the numbers of children living in poverty has increased exponentially since the financial crisis and bank meltdown of 2007.

Girls are smuggled across borders to work as sex slaves and girls are pressured in Britain every day into arranged marriages and oppression. Girls as young as seven are dressed as sexual objects by parents mesmerised by corporate advertising and gluttony for profit. The greater the poverty, the greater the abuse. The boys abused by distressed, unemployed fathers will grow up to be abusers.

I would like to say once more, that those polite terms 'abuse' and 'sexual abuse' usually mean an adult man is inserting his penis inside the mouths, bottoms and vaginas of little girls. Abuse usually means fucking.

Figures from the NSPCC, the National Society for the Prevention of Cruelty to Children, state that 72 per cent of sexually abused children do not tell anyone about the abuse at the time; 27 per cent tell someone later. Police recorded over 23,000 sex offences against children in England and Wales between April 2010 and March 2011 – the tip of the iceberg, in my opinion. ChildLine counsellors in that same period dealt with nearly 670,000 contacts from children about bullying, sexual abuse, violence and mental health issues. On average, every week in England and Wales at least one child is killed at the hands of another person. Look into any classroom in any state school and three or four or five or six of those children are being abused in some way.

In a world where the boundaries of technology are constantly being broken in the fields of medicine, communication and travel, and access to information is available at ever-increasing speeds, we must not forget to pay attention to the fundamentals of human emotional well-being. Market forces seemingly dominate everything now but we ignore the emotional welfare of young people at our peril. Things have improved in material terms for many people since I was a teenager but, as I write, the gap between rich and poor is widening at an alarming rate, causing distress and hardship for disadvantaged people. It is only through education that people grow and develop, and learn right from wrong. It is the responsibility of those who hold the power to ensure that our children have a future, regardless of their parents' circumstances, regardless of their background. A compassionate society is one that doesn't tolerate exploitation of any kind – that works tirelessly to encourage a culture where children can discuss their feelings without recrimination; where we can be proud that the basic principles of kindness, respect and dignity are afforded to all citizens. We live in hope.

Emily MacKenzie & Clifford Thurlow